BLACKS ON THE BORDER

The Black Refugees
in British North America, 1815–1860

Harvey Amani Whitfield

UNIVERSITY OF VERMONT PRESS
Burlington, Vermont

PUBLISHED BY UNIVERSITY PRESS OF NEW ENGLAND
HANOVER AND LONDON

UNIVERSITY OF VERMONT PRESS
Published by University Press of New England,
One Court Street, Lebanon, NH 03766
www.upne.com
© 2006 by Harvey Amani Whitfield
Printed in the United States of America
5 4 3 2 1

Library of Congress Cataloging-in-Publication Data

Whitfield, Harvey Amani, 1974–
Blacks on the border : the Black refugees in British North America, 1815–1860 / Harvey Amani Whitfield.
    p.   cm.
Includes bibliographical references and index.
ISBN-13: 978–1–58465–605–0 (cloth : alk. paper)
ISBN-10: 1–58465–605–0 (cloth : alk paper)
ISBN-13: 978–1–58465–606–7 (pbk : alk. paper)
ISBN-10: 1–58465–606–9 (pbk : alk paper)
1. African Americans—Nova Scotia—History—19th century. 2. African Americans—Nova Scotia—Social conditions—19th century. 3. Freedman—Nova Scotia—History—19th century. 4. Refugees—Nova Scotia—History—19th century. 5. Slaves—United States—History—19th century. 6. African Americans—Migrations—History—19th century. 7. United States—History—War of 1812—African Americans. 8. United States—History—War of 1812—Refugees. 9. Nova Scotia—History—1763–1867. 10. Nova Scotia—Race relations—History—19th century. I. Title.
F1040.N3W47 2006
971.60496'073—dc22   2006016896

For David and Betty Sutherland of Halifax, Nova Scotia

Contents

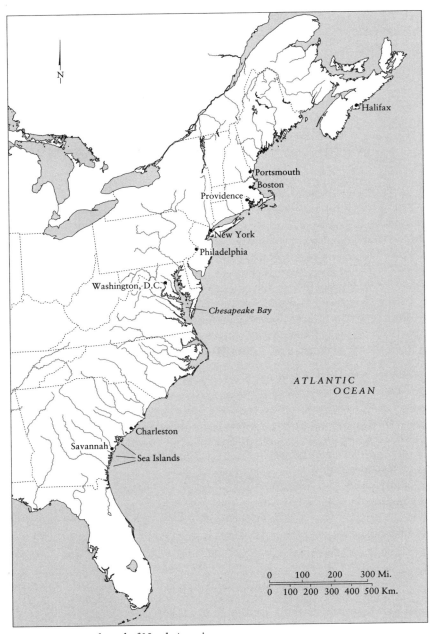

MAP 1. Eastern seaboard of North America

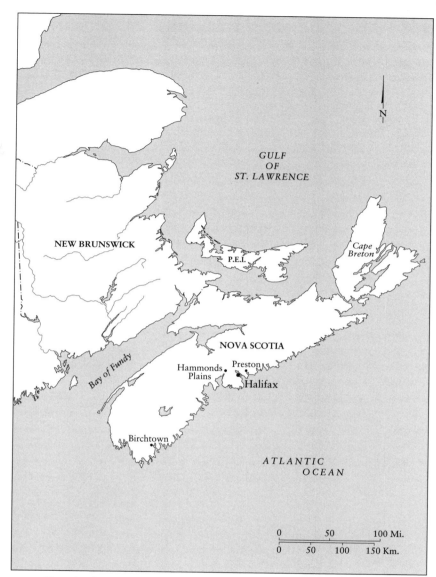

MAP 2. Nova Scotia

Preface

The migration of former American slaves from the southern United States to Nova Scotia after the War of 1812 included, as Paul Gilroy notes, "struggles towards emancipation, autonomy, and citizenship." The history of the Black Refugees allows historians "to reexamine the problems of nationality, location, identity, and historical memory."[1] The Refugee experience stands at the crossroads of several histories and historiographies including Canadian, British, American, African American, and African Canadian. This monograph highlights the contours of Black Refugee life by analyzing how former American slaves from disparate backgrounds became a distinct group of black people before the American Civil War.

This study builds on and extends a body of scholarship about African Nova Scotian history. In particular, the pioneering works of C. B. Fergusson, Robin Winks, Frank S. Boyd Jr., James Walker, John Grant, Barry Cahill, David Sutherland, Judith Fingard, and David States provide historians with an indispensable structure for understanding the contours of black life in Nova Scotia. This book represents my effort to understand the lives of black southerners in a new and challenging environment. The work encourages American and Canadian scholars to continue to investigate the history of black immigrants to Canada's Maritime Provinces. This study places the history of former American slaves in a transnational light in the hope of understanding how they formed a new community in the context of British North America. My own transnational experience as an African American living in Nova Scotia for seven years greatly influenced the ways in which I perceive the black experience in North America. Living among black people with historic connections to the United States, but who maintained a distinct culture, encouraged me to find out more about their history.

This book is the result of six years of research and writing. It relies on the research of Canadian and American scholars who have provided an essential base of secondary sources. For their part, the Refugees left very few written sources. The majority of Refugee voices come through newspapers, church petitions, land petitions, and poor people's petitions. With the notable exception of the African Baptist Association Minutes published after 1854, documents of black societies have not survived. Thus, insights into the community's organizations have been drawn from newspaper accounts and almanacs. Moreover, Nova Scotia censuses before 1871 are not nearly as detailed as those conducted in the United States. As a result, this book supplemented these sources with other documents including slave lists, shipping records, medical accounts, travel books, and government records and publications.

The research for this book has been carried out at the Nova Scotia Archives and Records Management, the Library of Congress, Dalhousie University Libraries, Florida State University Libraries, University of Massachusetts–Amherst Libraries, McGill University Libraries, Saint Mary's University Libraries, and the University of Vermont Libraries. I am grateful for the helpful guidance of the Nova Scotia Archives and Records Management staff. The University of Vermont generously provided me with financial support for research, writing, and travel.

Acknowledgments

This book would not have been possible without the advice and support of many scholars. First, I would like to thank those that read the manuscript in its entirety and offered many suggestions that made the book much better. Dona Brown (University of Vermont), Nora Faires (Western Michigan University), Barry Cahill (Independent Scholar, Halifax), David Sutherland (Dalhousie University), and the peer reviewers saved me from making many silly errors. My colleagues at the University of Vermont (Department of History) offered academic and emotional support, which helped me through the difficult process of writing a scholarly monograph.

Several other scholars read parts of the book or listened to conference papers and offered helpful suggestions including Bridgett Williams-Searle (College of Saint Rose), Kari Winter (SUNY–Buffalo), Bryan Rommel-Ruiz (Colorado College), Ira Berlin (University of Maryland), James Brewer Stewart (Macalester College), John Reid (Saint Mary's University), Stephen Vincent (University of Wisconsin-Whitewater), Denise Youngblood (University of Vermont), and Judith Fingard (Dalhousie University). John McNish Weiss (Independent Scholar, London) offered several helpful corrections that greatly aided my understanding of British involvement in the War of 1812. Matthew Carlson (University of Vermont) offered many important points about various historical methods. Also, Joseph Reidy (Howard University), Dennis F. Mahoney (University of Vermont), and John T. O' Brien (Dalhousie University) have provided me with encouragement and support as if I were a son. Lastly, I must thank my family for having faith in me.

H.A.W.

Abbreviations

AAS   African Abolition Society

ABA   African Baptist Association

ACS   American Colonization Society

AFS   African Friendly Society

CAS   Charitable African Society

Blacks on the Border

Introduction

DURING THE WAR OF 1812, thousands of Black Refugees from the United States rebelled against their owners and attempted to reach British military encampments. Among the runaways who escaped to the safety of the Royal Navy were the relatives of a Virginian slave named Richard. A tall, light-skinned man of imposing bearing with outstanding speaking abilities honed as a slave preacher, Richard obtained his freedom shortly after the war.[1] In hope of finding his mother, Richard traveled to British North America. He searched fruitlessly for her and almost gave up hope of finding her. Finally, after arriving in Nova Scotia, Richard found his mother at the largest settlement of Black Refugees in Preston, fifteen kilometers from Halifax. The reunification of mother and son encouraged the former Virginian slave preacher to adopt the township's name as his own.

Until his death in 1861, Preston attempted to create a distinct and cohesive identity among the Black Refugees in Nova Scotia by establishing a church and several political and social organizations. In 1846 he founded Halifax's African Abolition Society (AAS). This society dedicated itself to the eradication of an institution that had been illegal in the British Empire since 1834. Through the AAS, the Refugees held parades to celebrate British Emancipation, sponsored lectures about the American Fugitive Slave Law passed in 1850, and harbored runaway slaves from the United States. The American, Atlantic, and pan-African orientation of this movement can be gleaned from the society's promise to continue its activities "until the entire abolition of slavery has been secured." Preston's most significant contribution to black life revolved around the creation of the African Baptist Association (ABA) in 1854. This association, the result of his tireless travels throughout the colony, brought together people of African descent from various backgrounds under the umbrella of an independent black church. This association held annual meetings and retreats, and provided marriage and funeral services. For more than three decades, Preston presided over congregational duties and continued as the spokesperson for the local black community in a variety of affairs; he died in 1861. Despite his death, the African Baptist Association remained an integral part of the black community and still flourishes to this day.[2]

The life of Richard Preston has been enshrined by local folk tradition. In that tradition, Preston is remembered by recent generations of African Nova Scotians as a noble if mysterious figure, whose life is a story of black success and perseverance in the face of overwhelming obstacles. In the Refugees' mythology of Preston as a "great man" of his people, the timing of the leader's death—just as their brethren in the southern United States were on the cusp of freedom—is a tragic irony. As the folk tradition has it, the community was left leaderless at this crucial moment, the more so because Preston left no heirs.[3]

The story of Richard Preston raises the central question of this book: how did ex-slaves from vastly different backgrounds become a distinct group of African British North Americans after the War of 1812? This is a question that links United States and Canadian history. To answer it, I have examined the movement of people and their cultures, customs, work experiences, and traditions, from two points in the Black Atlantic—the Chesapeake and the Lowcountry—to Nova Scotia. The creation of a distinct black society in Nova Scotia can be examined as part of several historiographical contexts including the Afro–New England Diaspora, the Black Atlantic, Afro-America, black Canada, and British North America.[4]

I have investigated the creation and development of Black Refugee communities in Nova Scotia by studying their early settlement patterns, interactions with the colonial government, farming practices, struggles over wage labor, formation of families, and community development. These shared experiences, along with the quest for citizenship in Nova Scotia, transformed several slave identities into a cohesive and distinct African British North American community. Significantly, this process occurred along with an increasing identification with events and communities in Afro-America. In other words, the struggle to develop shared experience and community bonds in Nova Scotia remained significantly influenced by the Refugees' connections with black Americans. The Refugees used the border to distinguish themselves from African Americans, but the border also signified a more contested region, with which the Refugees engaged intellectually, emotionally, and psychologically by connecting their understanding of emancipation, migration, and memory with their former homeland. Although the Refugees were thoroughly intertwined with the local economy and society, they might be understood as part of the Afro–New England Diaspora, not because the black community in Nova Scotia originated from the migration of people of African descent from New England, but rather because of their similar work patterns, community life, external pressures, and demography.[5]

During the mid–nineteenth century slightly more than 4,900 people of African descent resided in Nova Scotia. In the Atlantic region of British North America and New England, Nova Scotia had the largest number of African American inhabitants after Massachusetts and Connecticut.[6] Given the number of scholarly studies about African Americans in Boston and Providence as compared with the lack of work on free people of color in the Halifax region during the early nineteenth century, it might be surprising to note that the black populations in these areas were comparable.[7] In 1850 nearly 2,000 African Americans resided in Boston, nearly 1,700 black people lived in the Halifax region, and approximately 1,500 African Americans inhabited Providence.[8] The numerical similarities between the black populations in Nova Scotia and New England underline the importance of rewriting the history of free people of color in New England to include the story of the Black Refugees. Incorporating the history of black people in Nova Scotia into studies about free people of color in the northern United States presents a broader picture not restricted by national borders and boundaries. In placing the Refugees in this context, I hope to encourage a conversation between scholars of blacks in the Maritime region and historians of African Americans in New England. This scholarly dialogue can bring out the relationships, in their complexities, contradictions, and contingencies, between people of African descent in each region.

The study of free black communities in Nova Scotia further expands our current definition of the term *African American.* As several studies have noted, African Americans also formed free communities in Haiti, Sierra Leone, Liberia, Trinidad, and British North America.[9] One of the most important components of the free black experience was the process of migration. As Elizabeth Rauh Bethel notes, many black Americans "believed it impossible, particularly after the enactment of the 1850 Fugitive Slave Law, to be both an American and a descendant of Africa, and an estimated 20 percent of the free black population left the United States to establish permanent residence in Canada, Hayti, or Africa between 1820 and 1860."[10] The difficulty of being an African and an American began after the American Revolution in 1783 as black people escaped to Nova Scotia,

England, Sierra Leone, and Trinidad in the years before the Missouri Compromise of 1820. In these areas, they did not shed their African American-ness or suddenly become African Nova Scotians, Black Britons, West Africans, or Afro-Trinidadians. Instead, they engaged with new forces, while retaining important aspects of their experience in the United States, which informed many of their actions and attitudes in these new locations. The new homes of African American expatriates did not erase older connections to the United States. As Bethel has pointed out: "[Black expatriates] maintained various kinds of connections to their American homeland, their persisting concern anchored in the politics surrounding U.S. slavery. As is the case with all diasporas, physical separation from families, neighborhoods, communities, and homeland did not eradicate the psychosocial ties of identity that bound people to each other and to place."[11]

The concept of migration is an essential tool for understanding the experience of the Black Refugees.[12] They typically experienced several migrations throughout their lifetimes. For example, during the War of 1812, the Refugees migrated from their farms and plantations to the safety of British encampments and the Royal Navy. Onboard the British naval vessels, they traveled up the eastern seaboard to Nova Scotia. Once in Nova Scotia, the Refugees continued to migrate, moving from one county to another and from rural settlements to the urban wage-labor market. Some migrations were regular and short distance; others spanned the Atlantic world. Refugee women engaged in regular travel from their rural homes to the local farmer's market in Halifax, while their husbands, brothers, and sons often found work on the high seas, just as free African Americans in Providence, Portsmouth, and Boston did. Other Refugees, dissatisfied with the economic and social conditions, left Nova Scotia for Trinidad, New Brunswick, or Upper Canada in search of better economic opportunities. The history of the Black Refugees consequently is tied to movement and migration whether in search of freedom, loved ones, or employment opportunities.

The movement of African Americans to new geographic regions resulted in a negotiation between older and newer forces that makes the story of black expatriates rich with insights about African American immigrant struggles. Although the Black Refugees had much in common with black communities in New England, Nova Scotia's geographic location in the North Atlantic as an important communications center between North America and Europe resulted in the Refugees maintaining linkages with both the United States and Great Britain. Indeed, while black communities in Boston and Providence were clearly lodged on the

American side of the Atlantic World, the Refugees were more central to two distinct portions of the Atlantic: the British and the American. Thus, their experience and history developed in a particular context that negotiated the contours of Afro-America, the United States, and the British world.

The Black Refugees' history developed on the border between the United States and British North America. Most studies of the contested nature of the border have focused on areas outside of the Maritime/New England area such as Florida, Mexico, Central America, and Latin America.[13] Although historians have discussed the development of the Canadian/United States border, most studies have focused on New France, the Great Lakes region, or the prairies.[14] However, scholars have not ignored the connections between New England and the Atlantic region of British North America. Several scholars have underlined the historic connections and complexities of New England settlement in Nova Scotia before the Revolutionary War. More recently, essays in John Reid and Stephen Hornsby's collection, *New England and the Maritime Provinces: Connections and Comparisons,* demonstrate the transition of this region from a borderland community with fluid boundaries to a region with a politically defined border. But, as this essay collection indicates, even after the demarcation of a firm political boundary line, the New England and Maritime borderland did not become absolute or sharply defined politically, socially, or culturally. Building on these important studies, this history of the Black Refugees provides another thread of inquiry into this contested and complicated borderland. Indeed, placing this group within a new geo-historical space of understanding, the Afro-New England Diaspora, that adds to our knowledge of the interactions between these two regions.[15]

Generally, the study of black people along the U.S./Canadian borderland has focused on the Great Lakes region and concentrated on the movement of blacks on the Underground Railroad. Historians including Nora Faires and Afua Cooper understand this region as a "fluid frontier" where blacks crossed and recrossed to maintain connections.[16] Calling for further study of these migrations, Faires notes there is evidence that indicates "a transnational black community in the Great Lakes region, knit together by formal institutions such as religious organizations; by networks of information such as newspapers, by regular participation in celebrations such as the festival of West Indian Emancipation held each August; and by less structured, more intimate ties of kin and friendship, reinforced by visits undertaken within this borderland."[17] The idea of a permeable border for blacks in Central Canada also played out for the Refugees in

Nova Scotia, but this border could also become a sharply drawn boundary for both groups. Perhaps any differences between the two groups, the Refugees and the Fugitives, can be accounted for in that the Refugees arrived much earlier in Nova Scotia than the vast majority of Fugitives who settled in Central Canada. Moreover (though outside of the scope of this book), some of the descendants of the Refugees would migrate to New England during the 1880s and 1890s as the Maritime Provinces struggled to adjust to the failure of John A. MacDonald's National Policy to benefit them.

The Black Refugees' unique position on the border opens up questions of how these migrants understood or constructed the American/British North American border. Though increasingly reified after the War of 1812, the border held contested meanings and understandings for Americans, indigenous groups, and British North Americans as they struggled to define the frontiers of North America. Some scholars of the North American borderlands have defined these areas as sites of struggles between competing nation-states and groups that reduced the abilities of indigenous peoples to resist domination.[18] Notably, in the case of the Black Refugees the transition from borderlands to border between British North America and the United States offered black expatriates opportunities not only to define themselves but also actively to construct the border between British North America and America, a border that eventually divided two separate nations.

For the Refugees, the border also represented the line between slavery and freedom. Yet, while it marked an important barrier between their old and new lives, the Refugees did not use it to cut themselves off from events in the United States. In 1818, after fighting with local whites at her farm, Refugee Maria Fuller defiantly informed her adversaries that "we are not now in the U. States, and we can do as we like here." Fuller regarded British North America as offering her greater opportunities for social protest than did the United States.[19] Despite this difference that the border provided some Refugees, in other cases the border became an area to be negotiated, as expatriate African Americans frequently discussed events that affected the lives of blacks within the borders of the United States. In short, the border served as a reified demarcation between slavery and freedom, but it was also a negotiated state of mind that connected the expatriates with events and persons in their former homeland.

PART I

Nova Scotian and American Background, 1605–1815

Chapter 1

Slavery and Freedom in Nova Scotia

FOR CENTURIES, NOVA SCOTIA's geographic location in North America has rendered it the site of interaction among various cultural groups, including Natives, French, British, and African.[1] This interaction has profoundly affected Nova Scotia's historical development. Nova Scotia was intimately tied to the development of both the French and British empires in the New World during the seventeenth and eighteenth centuries. As a result of commerce, politics, and culture Nova Scotia remained an important terminus and military depot for both France and Britain as they battled for control of North America. Although the British eventually gained control of Nova Scotia during the eighteenth century, elements of French culture remained and were joined by diverse elements of British American culture. The growth and development of the thirteen colonies influenced the so-called Neutral Yankees of Nova Scotia, but not to the point where the colony proved willing to leave the protection of the King's empire. As a result of the Loyalist influx after the American Revolution, Nova Scotia became more tied to the Union Jack, and during the War of 1812 Nova Scotia served as an important base for British armed forces.[2]

People of African descent played important roles in the development of Nova Scotia from the early seventeenth century to the War of 1812. English and American colonists brought a small number of slaves up the coast from the French and British West Indies to Ile Royale (present-day Cape Breton Island) and mainland Nova Scotia, slowly increasing Nova Scotia's black population. This settlement created a diverse population of people of African descent with roots ranging from West and Central Africa to British America. The pace of settlement increased in the decades between the American Revolution and the War of 1812, with thousands of people of African descent arriving in Nova Scotia, most as free people but some as slaves.[3]

Nova Scotia's encounter with people of African descent included interactions with both freedom and slavery. Yet the colony's ties to the Atlantic world's reliance on black slavery created conditions and attitudes that greatly influenced the local government's and the local population's attitudes toward the Black Loyalists and the Black Refugees.[4] The specter of the slave trade along with the continuation of the institution in Nova Scotia after every New England state had adopted emancipation or gradual emancipation reminds us that Nova Scotia offered freedom only to some African Americans in the late eighteenth and early nineteenth centuries.[5] Moreover, the presence of enslaved blacks profoundly shaped white attitudes toward all African-descended people in Nova Scotia, affording whites a convenient rationale for dismissing blacks' claims to equality.

In examining the experience of people of African descent in early Nova Scotian history, five periods emerge: early Africans to 1700; black people in Ile Royale, 1713–1758; blacks in pre-Loyalist Nova Scotia, 1749–1782; the Black Loyalists' and Slave Loyalists' influx, 1783–1793; and the Jamaican Maroon episode, 1796–1800.

Early Africans

The first Africans in Nova Scotia probably served as free interpreters or slaves during the seventeenth century. Europeans and Nova Scotia's dominant indigenous group, the Mi'kmaq, had traded with one another since early contact. Although this economic relationship could be troublesome, the Europeans displayed an insatiable desire for furs, while the Mi'kmaq found uses for copper kettles and other Western goods. Trading did not result in permanent European settlement until the French established themselves at Port-Royal in 1605, a small enclave on the western coast of Nova Scotia that survived only because the Mi'kmaq tolerated it. Led by Pierre Du Gua de Monts and Samuel de Champlain, the settlement hoped to take advantage of the monopoly granted by the French government if a viable community could be established. In order for Port-Royal to become sustainable, the settlers required interpreters to communicate with the Mi'kmaq.[6]

The first African in Nova Scotia, Mathieu Da Costa, may have served as an interpreter between the French and Mi'kmaq for more than a decade before 1619, the year about twenty Africans arrived in Jamestown. The meticulous research of John Johnston allows historians to piece together the few extant fragments of this early African's life. As it stands, historians do not know anything about Da Costa's physical appearance, family life, or when "he might have travelled to North America, how long he stayed, for whom he worked, and with whom he interpreted." Yet the few details available are fascinating.[7]

In 1607 Da Costa, a free "naigre," had been in Europe as a result of "enticement or kidnapping" by the Dutch. Pierre Du Gua de Monts' secretary traveled to Amsterdam partly to challenge Dutch interference in French trading. He also went to protest their dealings with Da Costa, who had been under contract to work for the French as an interpreter. One year later, Da Costa agreed to a contract that would have had him sail to Canada and "Cadie [Nova Scotia]." Under this three-year contract, de Monts agreed to pay Da Costa the substantial amount of 195 livres per year. Yet Da Costa did not leave Europe as planned in the winter of 1609. Instead, the authorities jailed him for the crime of "insolences." As Johnston notes, Da Costa's name comes up in subsequent court records over the following ten years in regard to the cost incurred by the French for retrieving Da Costa and other expenses related to him. However, this does not mean that Da Costa remained in Europe.[8]

Despite the paucity of information about Da Costa, it is possible to draw a few tentative conclusions. The fact that the French and the Dutch were willing to pay for his services as an interpreter in "Cadie" indicates that Da Costa must have been familiar with the language used by the French and the Mi'kmaq to conduct trade. It seems likely that he became fluent in this language through previous contact with the Mi'kmaq, presumably through earlier trade missions in the late sixteenth or early seventeenth centuries.

As Johnston notes, Da Costa should be understood in the wider context of the black experience in the early modern Atlantic world. His name suggests a connection to Portugal and the broader community of Atlantic Creoles who, as historian Ira Berlin argues, remained part of "three worlds that came together in the Atlantic littoral [Africa, the Americas, and Europe]. [These people were] familiar with the commerce of the Atlantic, fluent in its new languages, and intimate with its trade and cultures, they were cosmopolitan in the fullest sense."[9] Although historians do not know enough about the vibrant life of Da Costa, his role as an intermediary or interpreter between various cultures and communities demonstrates the possibly far-reaching experience of people of African descent in the early modern world even in the northern expanses of French settlement in North America.

Da Costa was not the only African in seventeenth-century Nova Scotia. An unnamed man had died on his way to Port-Royal in 1606 and another succumbed to scurvy at Port-Royal in 1608. During the 1680s, another African named La Liberte ended up at Sable Island off the eastern coast of Nova Scotia.[10] Throughout the early seventeenth century, Nova Scotia had only a small number of Africans, such as these three men whose histories are all but unknown. This changed with the founding and development of Ile Royale in the early eighteenth century.

The Ile Royale Slave Community, 1713–1758

Until very recently, scholars all but ignored slavery in French Nova Scotia. Kenneth Donovan's recent work has given historians much to reconsider. Donovan's research demonstrates that far from being an unimportant afterthought, slavery played an important role in the development of Ile Royale. His work reminds historians that slavery in the northern North American expanses of the French Empire was tied to developments throughout the Atlantic world.[11]

In 1685 the French government adopted the Code Noir for its growing slave population in the West Indies. The Black Code, and its revised version of 1724, formed the legal foundation for the regulation of slaves in the French Atlantic world. The code provided slaves with religious instruction, granted them Sundays and Catholic holy days off, set fines for owners who produced offspring with slave women, and offered the manumitted "the same rights, privileges and immunities that are enjoyed by freeborn persons." Yet the code also attempted to protect masters by forbidding slaves from "carrying any offensive weapons or large sticks." It also prohibited slaves from enjoying one another's company at weddings or other gatherings, because they might have included slaves from different owners. Moreover, slave owners could restrain and beat their property with rods or straps if masters "believe that their slaves so deserve."[12] Although officials in New France generally and Ile Royale in particular did not formally register the code, parts of it were observed in a customary fashion.[13] Perhaps this is significant for understanding that slavery in New France and Ile Royale, despite its connections to the systems of French slavery, still had local variations that made the slave experience in these colonies unique. The decision of the government in France to implement the Black Code paled in importance, however, compared with Louis XIV's support for the transportation of Africans to the empire's northern North American colonies.

In 1688 the governor of New France, the Marquis de Denonville, attempted to persuade Louis XIV to support the transport of African slaves to North America because of the colony's chronic shortage of labor. He believed that people of African descent along with Natives could perform a variety of tasks that would ensure the colony's success. One year later, Louis XIV agreed to the importation of black slaves to New France, but expressed doubt that they could survive in a climate so much different from that of their homeland. This decision did lead to an increase in the black population of New France, but in the colony as a whole during the eighteenth century the majority of slaves were Natives, not Africans. In Ile Royale, however, Donovan notes, over 90 percent of the slave population was black, a diverse group hailing from several different points of Africa and the African Diaspora and connecting the small settlement of Ile Royale with the Atlantic world.[14]

Founded in 1713, after the Treaty of Utrecht, Ile Royale became an important colony in the early eighteenth century because of its vibrant trade with the French Empire, especially in dried cod. Ile Royale also served as a market for products from the French West Indies, particularly sugar, which could be exported to mainland North America. Within this bustling trade, the sale of slaves also occurred between Ile Royale and the French West Indies. Although the slave population in Ile Royale did not exceed three hundred persons between 1713 and 1758, these people of African descent came from across the Atlantic world. According to Donovan, slaves in Ile Royale were "multilingual and came from the West Indies, Africa, India, France, Canada, and the British-American colonies."[15] Thus, the small slave population in Ile Royale came from some of the most important points of the Atlantic slave trade and tied the local version of the institution to the more developed slave societies in Africa, British America, and the West Indies.[16]

Although firmly embedded in the French Empire, the slave experience at Ile Royale shared many features with the various forms of the institution in New England and mainland Nova Scotia. In Connecticut and Massachusetts during the eighteenth century, for example, the slave presence accounted for a percentage of the population comparable to that in Louisbourg, the urban center of Ile Royale. Also, like most slaveholders in eighteenth-century New England, most Louisbourg slave owners possessed only a few slaves.[17] Not many slaves were employed in local fisheries, where they would have been part of large work groups; instead, the vast majority (over 90 percent) worked within a household. This type of labor encompassed a variety of tasks split along gender lines. For the most part, men "tended gardens, fed animals, cleaned stables, carried water, cut firewood, mowed hay, picked berries, gathered seaweed, shoveled snow, and ran errands." Women, on the other hand, "performed a wide range of household duties, from looking after children to cleaning clothes, scrubbing floors, preparing meals, and washing dishes."[18]

Hence, in a general sense Ile Royale was not a slave society, since it did not rely on the institution for economic sustainability, but the use of slavery for household labor resulted in blacks entering Nova Scotian society at the bottom of the social ladder. Thus, white Nova Scotians' first encounter with people of African descent was forged in a context of racial inequality. The emerging colony's position as a terminus of colonial wars between the British, the French, and the Mi'kmaq brought people of African descent from many parts of the African Diaspora to Nova Scotia. The trickle of slaves into Ile Royale during the early eighteenth century continued in mainland Nova Scotia as British colonists tightened their grip on the colony after 1713.

The British Presence in Nova Scotia

Mainland Nova Scotia became a British colony after the Treaty of Utrecht in 1713. Nevertheless, the French retained Ile Royale, while mainland Nova Scotia retained a significant Acadian population (a group of French settlers). Although the British had gained a foothold in Nova Scotia, the colony remained a marginal outpost with a small English-speaking population. In an effort to remedy this situation, in 1749 the imperial government supported an expedition under Edward Cornwallis to develop an English settlement to be named after Lord Halifax. Cornwallis established the town in 1749 with nearly two thousand settlers, possibly including black slaves. The settlement grew steadily, and in order to clear more land for the recruitment of even more English settlers, local officials displaced the Mi'kmaq and by 1755 had expelled and transported the Acadian population. During the Seven Years' War (1754–1763), Halifax served as a military base for the British effort to gain control of Ile Royale and New France. After repeated attacks against the French fortress at Louisbourg, the British defeated their French opponents at Ile Royale and Ile Saint-Jean (Prince Edward Island) in 1758. Despite these military victories, Nova Scotia's population remained small, and its economy struggled for development within the expanding British Empire.[19]

To increase the English-speaking population of Nova Scotia, in 1759

Governor Charles Lawrence offered substantial tracts of land recently stolen from the Acadians to New Englanders willing to move to the northern frontiers of the British Empire. As a result, between 1760 and 1774, at least eight thousand New Englanders migrated to various points in Nova Scotia including the Annapolis Valley and the south shore. These migrants came from Connecticut, Massachusetts, Rhode Island, and New Hampshire, states with small slave populations compared with the southern American colonies, but places where Anglo-American ideas of slaveholding were entrenched. These settlers brought these ideas with them, and Nova Scotia's government offered the New England planters more land if they brought slaves.[20] They arrived in a colony whose urban center, Halifax, was already a hub in the Atlantic trading system between Europe, North America, and the West Indies.[21] During the 1750s, Nova Scotians traded several different materials with Boston, England, and the West Indies. Generously supplied with natural resources in the fisheries and timber, Nova Scotia exported staves, shingles, boards, and fish to the West Indies in exchange for salt, sugar, and molasses.

Generally speaking, people of African descent made their way to Nova Scotia during these years through the business dealings of merchants or with families from New England. For example, in 1750, Captain Thomas Bloss of the Royal Navy brought sixteen black slaves who had been working on his ship into the emerging colony. Governor Edward Cornwallis commented that Bloss had purchased land outside Halifax where presumably his slaves would work as farmers and domestics.[22] But the use of African slaves by local merchants is most clearly illustrated through the business dealings of respectable smuggler Joshua Mauger. Mauger's interest in trading African slaves had its roots in his early years as a merchant in the French and British West Indies. He became one of the most important merchants in early Halifax. Although he traveled in the most elite circles in the growing town, Mauger also did everything in his power to maximize profits, while avoiding duties. After the founding of Halifax, Mauger saw the opportunity to trade fish, molasses, and slaves between Halifax, Boston, and the West Indies. He accomplished this in the cheapest manner possible: black slaves even operated some of his vessels.[23]

In 1752, after a successful trip to the West Indies, Mauger returned to Halifax and placed an advertisement in the local newspaper.

Just imported, and to be sold by Joshua Mauger, at Major Lockman's store in Halifax, several Negro slaves, viz. A very likely Negro Wench, of about thirty five years of Age, a Creole born, has been brought up in a Gentleman's family, and capable of doing all Sorts of Work belonging thereto . . . [such as] Washing, Ironing, Cookery, and every other Thing that can be expected from Such a Slave. Also, 2 Negro boys of about 12 or 13 Years old, likely, healthy . . . likewise 2 healthy Negro slaves of about 18 Years of Age, of agreeable tempers, and fit for any kind of business; and also a healthy Negro Man of about 30 Years of Age.[24]

Other merchants also attempted to sell black slaves at public auctions, alongside various items, such as brandy.[25] The sale of Africans at public auctions did not surprise the people of Halifax in the mid–eighteenth century. They took it as a matter of course, because the ties of Halifax to the Anglo-American world meant that the sale and enslavement of blacks simply continued a practice that many of the recent settlers had been familiar with at home in England, New England, New York, or during travels to the West Indies.[26]

Quite often, Africans or African Americans were brought into Nova Scotia to serve as domestics for a particular family. Well-to-do families had been bringing in black slaves to perform household labor throughout the colony before the New England planter influx. In 1752 Thomas Thomas, a New Yorker turned Halifaxian, arranged in a will for his "goods" and "negroes" to be disposed of properly, specifying in particular that "my negro servant Orange, that now lives with me at Halifax," be left to his son.[27] In 1759 Malachy Salter encouraged his wife to purchase a young "Negro" in Boston to be brought back to Halifax to help around the house because one of their domestic slaves had supposedly been nothing but trouble.[28] During the 1760s or early 1770s, Presbyterian minister James Lyon brought a young black slave to the rural township of Onslow from his original home in New Jersey. In Truro, another small town in the interior of the colony, local farmer Matthew Harris sold twelve-year-old Abram to Matthew Archibald. Harris had brought Abram and his mother to Nova Scotia from Maryland.[29]

As a result of the small slave trade into Nova Scotia and the influx of slaves brought by the New England planters, the small black population in Nova Scotia increased during the decades following the founding of Halifax in 1749. Yet according to the colonial census of 1767, the free black population in Nova Scotia barely exceeded one hundred persons.[30] This census certainly excluded the slave population. As scholar Barry Cahill notes, the "collection of quantifiable data is complicated by Black people not being enumerated in extant early census records. Blacks as a rule were slaves, slaves were chattels (movable property), and personality was not censual."[31] The precise number of black slaves in Nova Scotia before the

Loyalist influx thus remains difficult to calculate; nevertheless, we can examine the various tasks and labor that these blacks performed.

While most blacks were butlers, maids, or other household servants during the pre-Loyalist period, some engaged in other types of labor. The slaves of Captain Bloss and Joshua Mauger worked on the high seas and as farmers. As historian Bryan Rommel-Ruiz notes, historians can discover the work of slaves in Nova Scotia through an examination of slave advertisements.[32] In the autumn of 1751, skilled black slaves were exported to Boston. In September the *Evening Post* advertised recently "arrived from Halifax and to be sold, ten strong, hearty Negro men, mostly tradesmen, such as caulkers, carpenters, sailmakers and ropemakers."[33] As these skills indicate, in Halifax, some slaves probably worked in housing construction and the shipping business. They were tied to a profession that had included numerous people of African descent throughout the Atlantic world. Hardly immune from the role played by blacks throughout the New World on the high seas, people of African descent in Nova Scotia also participated in shipping industries and maritime life.[34]

The occupations of enslaved Africans in Nova Scotia emerge from a few local slave advertisements during the 1770s. For example, in 1776 a local man hoped to procure "a Negro woman, about 25 or 30 years of age, that understands country work and the management of a dairy."[35] The potential buyer expected that female slaves in Nova Scotia would be familiar with tasks associated with frontier farming in Nova Scotia. Three years later, the same paper offered for sale a young black woman who could not only perform a range of town duties but also had familiarity with country work in addition to being an "exceedingly good cook."[36] Town labor in Nova Scotia could involve an array of different tasks including shoveling snow, washing clothes, and trucking materials to market. On the other hand, country work could involve all sorts of arduous duties associated with frontier farming.

The nature of the relationships between slaves and masters in pre-Loyalist Nova Scotia remains elusive, but the story of Jeffrey Brace highlights the hostility that may have characterized some interactions. As traced by scholar Kari Winter, Brace traveled throughout the Black Atlantic during the last half of the eighteenth century, finally settling in Vermont, where he became a well-respected abolitionist. Born during the 1740s in Africa, Brace lived in relative peace until his teenage years, when slave traders captured him and sent him to the Caribbean. During the Seven Years' War, he fought for the British and traveled to Nova Scotia with his master, Captain Isaac Mills. One day his owner was in conversation with another white man when the man "came and took hold of my [Brace's] nose and chin, opened my mouth as a jockey would a horse's, in order to see my age or to insult me. While my mouth was open, he spit a cud of tobacco into it which made me sick."[37] Brace's encounter might have been exceptional, but it is indicative of attitudes about blacks as chattel that permeated the Atlantic world in the late eighteenth and early nineteenth centuries. Brace's short sojourn in Nova Scotia also underscores another connection of the emerging colony to the African Diaspora.

The Black Loyalists

The American Revolution brought dramatic change to the shores of Nova Scotia. In 1775, at the outbreak of hostilities, the Loyalist governor of Virginia, Lord Dunmore, offered freedom to the slaves of rebel owners if the slaves would be willing to help return the Old Dominion to "a proper sense" of its duty to the British Crown.[38] This form of limited emancipation resulted in American slaves seeking freedom under the British standard. Dunmore quickly armed some of these slaves, who formed the Ethiopian Regiment. The regiment subsequently fought against American forces and helped some slaves escape. In 1776 British commander in chief General William Howe followed up Dunmore's proclamation by offering similar conditions to the slaves of rebellious owners. The proclamation issued by Sir Henry Clinton went further: it offered "every Negro who shall desert the Rebel Standard, full security to follow within these Lines."[39] More important, he promised that they would receive land and provisions after the war in one of His Majesty's colonies.[40]

The idea of land and freedom held out a powerful allure for African Americans. As a result, thousands of slaves absconded from their owners and reached British lines. Still other African Americans escaped to pursue other opportunities for freedom, such as migrating to Florida (a Spanish possession), settling with Native groups, creating their own Maroon communities on the fringes of American society, living as free people in the north, or migrating after the war to other countries. Despite the displacements and confusion caused by the Revolutionary War, the Continental Army eventually prevailed over the British forces, who evacuated the Loyalists, black and white, from Savannah, Boston, Charleston, and New York.[41] As part of this exodus, approximately 3,500 Black Loyalists migrated to Nova Scotia along with hundreds of black slaves owned by Loyalist Americans.[42]

Eminent African American historian Benjamin Quarles has noted that slaves during the American Revolution were loyal to the ideal of freedom rather than to either of the combatants, but the Black Loyalists entertained ideas that may have set them apart from other African Americans who gained freedom through escaping to Florida or forming communities on the fringes of American society. According to historian James Walker, the "ideal of the black loyalist went beyond freedom: it was to become a small proprietor, self sufficient upon land of his own and secured by British justice in his rights as a subject of the crown."[43] However, these expectations of the recently liberated African Americans would be dashed, because the British did not fulfill their promises.

The Loyalist influx dramatically increased Nova Scotia's pre-Revolutionary population, and the addition of so many people of color shocked the host community. In the immediate aftermath of the rebellion, the government of Nova Scotia was unprepared for the influx of so many poor, possibly sick, and homeless immigrants. Although imperial policy had stated that all Loyalists should be given land in Nova Scotia, this stated goal favored those who had lost property or status as a result of the war. Generally, soldiers were supposed to receive one-hundred-acre grants of land along with fifty acres more per family member. Yet the mass influx of immigrants and the hierarchical nature of the colonial and imperial government meant that poor whites and the Black Loyalists were at the very bottom of the list of those to receive land. Some poor whites had to wait a few years to obtain their land, while, according to Walker, only a third of the Black Loyalists had received land by the late 1780s. Moreover, when the Black Loyalists acquired land, their grants were much smaller than those afforded to the white settlers. As would be the case with the Black Refugees after the War of 1812, the government also granted the Black Loyalists some of the worst land in the colony.[44]

Black Loyalists settled throughout the colony, from the south shore to Guysborough in the colony's northern fringes. Some also settled in the colony's political and commercial center of Halifax, but the largest contingent established themselves on the south shore at Birchtown, next to the larger town of Shelburne.[45] The local government's failure to give the Black Loyalists sufficient land forced many to seek livelihoods through wage labor or tenant farming. Predictably, the Black Loyalists provided Nova Scotia with a "free labor reserve that cleared the lands, laid the roads, and erected the public buildings."[46] The poor prospects in Nova Scotia led some Black Loyalists to sell their labor to merchants for periods of up to five years. Quite often, local businesses paid blacks much less than whites performing the same jobs. This discrepancy in wages caused an outbreak of violence in the Shelburne/Birchtown area in 1784 when local whites beat several blacks and destroyed their lodgings for agreeing to work for lowered wages. South Carolina native Boston King recalled the dreary employment conditions in Nova Scotia.

> [In the late 1780s], the country was visited with a dreadful famine, which not only prevailed at [Birchtown], but likewise at Chebucto, Annapolis, Digby, and other places. Many of the poor people were compelled to sell their best gowns for five pounds of flour, in order to support life. When they had parted with all their clothes, even their blankets, several of them fell dead in the streets, thro' hunger. Some killed and eat [*sic*] their dogs and cats, and poverty and distress prevailed on every side, so that to my great grief I was obliged to leave [Birchtown], because I could get no employment.[47]

The pervasiveness of white racism, discriminatory judicial proceedings, and the general attitude of Nova Scotians to the presence of free blacks curtailed the Black Loyalists' hopes for a meaningful freedom. One British observer simply could not find the words to describe the treatment meted out to free people of color in Nova Scotia. "It is not in my power to describe the scandalous and shameful conduct shewn to the free Blacks by many of the White people."[48] If they had set out from the United States with the hope for good land and fair treatment, the Black Loyalists were sorely disappointed with their situation in Nova Scotia. The problem of the Black Loyalists has been nicely summed up by one scholar who notes that most Nova Scotians were so "conditioned to thinking of blacks as slaves, the claims of the free black loyalists for equality were not always to be taken seriously."[49] The economic conditions and the failure of many Black Loyalists to achieve meaningful freedom convinced some that the best option might be emigration to Sierra Leone. In 1793, only ten years after their original settlement in Nova Scotia, nearly 1,200 Black Loyalists emigrated there, with the aid of British abolitionist John Clarkson.

Slaves of the Loyal Americans

For most scholars the story ends here or continues to Sierra Leone. Yet the story of blacks, including slaves, also continues in Nova Scotia. The Loyal Americans who brought slaves to Nova Scotia kept these blacks as their property. Indeed, slavery was legal in Nova Scotia after the American Revolution. In most treatments of the Black Loyalist experience, these black slaves usually merit nothing more than a few paragraphs. This scholarly omission arises because the historiography of Black Loyalists has largely fit into two related paradigms. The first paradigm contrasts the story of American bondage with the saga of Canadian freedom, and has been buttressed, perhaps unknowingly, by the more recent focus on the transition of blacks from slavery to freedom in the Atlantic world. The second historiographic thread focuses on the agency of those blacks who migrated to the African continent rather than submit to white hostility in Nova Scotia. Yet the complexities of transnational black migration to Nova Scotia cannot be entirely understood through either of these narratives. The story of these black slaves is a reminder that black migration in the Atlantic world also included the movement of African peoples from slavery in one area of the Black Atlantic to slavery in another area.[50]

Slavery existed in nearly every county in Loyalist Nova Scotia. In certain parts of Nova Scotia, such as the Annapolis Valley, some farms benefited from slave labor. Clearly, the growth of black freedom had been accompanied by the growth of black slavery. Slave owners tended to be respectable individuals who settled throughout Nova Scotia. In a study published over a century ago, T. W. Smith noted that several Loyalists arrived with large numbers of slaves. For example, Stephen Shakespeare arrived in Nova Scotia with twenty "servants," and Charles Oliver Breuff of New York settled at Liverpool with fifteen slaves and numerous indentured blacks. Captain Andrew Barclay's company of 104 people also arrived with fifty-seven slaves. James and Alexander Robertson, publishers in New York, later settled at Shelburne with twenty slaves.[51] Several other Loyalists brought only two or three slaves with them, but the numbers of bondspeople certainly lend credence to Barry Cahill's contention that in some fashion Loyalist Nova Scotia can be understood as a "colonial slave society."[52]

The most common occupation for slaves in Nova Scotia during the Loyalist period continued to be household labor. Some slaves brought to Nova Scotia also worked as tanners, carpenters, or at other trades.[53] One glimpse into the work experience of slaves from the United States who migrated to Nova Scotia derives from a letter written by the Loyalist governor of New Hampshire, John Wentworth. Wentworth, who became lieutenant governor of Nova Scotia in 1792, decided to transfer some of his "valuable" and "American born or well seasoned" slaves to Surinam to be used by his cousin Paul Wentworth.

> Isaac is a thorough good carpenter and master sawyer, perfectly capable of overseeing and conducting the rest and strictly honest. Lymas is a rough carpenter and sawyer; Quako is a field negro, has met an accident in his arm, which will require some indulgence. The other men are saw-

yers, and John also a good axe-man. Abraham has been used to cattle and to attend in the house, etc. All the men are expert in boats. The women are stout, able, and promise well to increase their numbers. Venus is useful in [the] hospital, poultry yard, gardens, etc.[54]

From their original homes in South Carolina, New York, and other states, Loyalist slave owners brought to Nova Scotia ideas about the exploitation of black labor. For the American exiles, the institution of slavery became an important link to their former home as they expanded the institution in Nova Scotia. Thus slavery, as much as freedom, influenced Loyalist culture and society.

The influx of Black Loyalists and the slaves of white Loyalists affected both local white and black populations. For many whites, the perceived failure of the Black Loyalists could be chalked up to African Americans' understanding of freedom: slaves were thought to believe that freedom meant exemption from labor. According to this conventional wisdom, black people needed slavery to protect them from the responsibilities of freedom. In this view, if people of African descent were not enslaved they would simply become a tax burden on the government and a drain on the resources of their white neighbors. These views became an essential part of the discrimination that the Refugees would face thirty years later. Although it would be too simplistic to argue that the blacks who remained in Nova Scotia represented a decapitated community, many of the leading Black Loyalists—Thomas Peters, Catherine Abernathy, David George, and Boston King—left the colony. Some black settlements, such as the one at Preston outside Halifax, suffered serious depopulation. Certainly, Nova Scotia's first encounter with a large black population had resulted in distrust, anger, and resentment among both people of African descent and the local white population. This level of distrust only increased with the arrival of the Jamaican Maroons in the mid-1790s.

Jamaican Maroons

In 1796 over five hundred Jamaican Maroons were exiled to Nova Scotia because of their guerrilla warfare against the British government. Unlike the majority of Black Loyalists who preceded them, the Maroons were not slaves and did not regard the British as liberators. The local government, under the direction of Lieutenant Governor John Wentworth, wanted to introduce them to Christianity and other aspects of Western civilization.[55] More specifically, Wentworth hoped the Maroons would give up their polygamous lifestyle, arguing that it was un-Christian. Meanwhile Wentworth's behavior, impregnating Maroon women, seemed hypocritical to those to whom he preached about the benefits of a Christian lifestyle. The Maroons refused to change their practices. As a result, there was a great deal of cultural conflict between the local government and the Jamaican Maroons. When they arrived in Nova Scotia, the Maroons became frustrated because the climate prevented the growing of familiar food crops such as bananas, yams, and cocoa.[56] Moreover, the Maroons resented the colony's attempt to use them as cheap labor. After vigorously protesting against the colonial government, nearly all the Maroons took advantage of the opportunity to resettle in Sierra Leone.[57]

Black Society after the Jamaican Maroons

Thus, by 1801 the fragmented black community in Nova Scotia consisted of former Loyalist slaves, Black Loyalists, and West Indians. The departure of the Maroons and Black Loyalists resulted in many people of African descent who had settled in the countryside migrating to Halifax in search of work, their rural settlements having suffered depopulation to the point that they were no longer viable. In Halifax, members of the black community had established themselves in two important occupations that provided steady income. One observer noted in 1812 that they were "good house servants, and make good common Hands on board vessels."[58] In addition to finding steady employment, according to James Walker, the free black population had started to break down the barriers of residential segregation.[59] These changes in black life before the War of 1812 can be attributed to the smaller population of people of color after so many left for Sierra Leone and the need for the cheap labor that the free blacks provided. Yet the smoldering embers of racial hostility would not lie dormant for long in early nineteenth-century Nova Scotia. As historian Robin Winks argues, the immigration of the Black Refugees during and after the War of 1812 would awaken dormant racial hostilities as some feared a repeat of the events of 1783.[60]

Nova Scotia's experience with black immigrants during the late eighteenth century left important legacies that would affect the War of 1812 Refugees. First, some local officials and many white inhabitants believed that people of African descent could never integrate into the colony's mainstream, both because of their race and because the Refugees were former slaves.[61] Nevertheless, the colonial government wanted to use the

Black Refugees as a semicaptive and cheap labor force, as they had attempted to do earlier with the Black Loyalists and Jamaican Maroons. Moreover, the Black Loyalists and Jamaican Maroon departures had convinced the local white population that black settlers did not deserve land grants, because they would abandon the colony, squandering any money the government spent on them. As a consequence, officials created land policies that ensured that black settlers would subsist, not as owners of land, but as squatters who could be used to satisfy local whites' need for manual laborers on their farms and in their communities. In 1815, one local resident encouraged the settlement of the Refugees in his neighborhood, for "[they would] afford assistance to us towards repairing the Roads, but likewise furnish us with Labourers of whom we stand in too much need to make any tolerable progress in our own improvements."[62]

Second, the perceived failure of previous black immigrants had led many to conclude that Africans were fit only for slavery, despite the fact that the colony began to phase out the institution in the early 1800s. According to this view, blacks did not and could not understand the "reward of labour."[63] The African Americans who migrated to Nova Scotia during and after the War of 1812, despite their wide variety of backgrounds and array of occupational talents, encountered a host population that considered free blacks to be inferior and dangerous to local society and the colonial treasury.

Chapter 2

Two Distinct Cultures of Slavery

THE BLACK REFUGEES who came to Nova Scotia during and after the War of 1812 brought several traditions and expectations from American slavery that influenced their struggles with freedom in the British Empire. The majority of these former slaves came from the Chesapeake, with a smaller contingent originating from the Georgia Sea Islands and coastal Georgia. The different cultures of slavery in these two distinct regions resulted in the Black Refugees entertaining different ideas about labor, language, and culture. Within these two systems of slavery, the Refugee experience also varied by plantation owner, gender, labor requirements, and location (urban or rural). Escape from slavery during the War of 1812 provided these African Americans with their first shared experience. The Black Refugees' common understanding was furthered by their declaration of loyalty to the British Crown and especially by their journey to freedom in Nova Scotia.

By the early nineteenth century, both the Chesapeake and the Lowcountry had self-reproducing slave populations. Possibly as a result, masters displayed more concern for slave families than had earlier generations of slave owners. However, this did not prevent them from breaking slave families apart in order to serve their economic needs. During the late eighteenth and early nineteenth centuries, the economies in both regions changed. Rice and cotton growing expanded in the Lowcountry, and mixed agricultural production intensified in the Chesapeake; both led to an increase in the labor of slaves. Slaves resisted changes to their work regime, winning some concessions from their masters in both regions. Generally, the social environment of slaves changed as many were moved from small or midsize plantations to larger ones. These similarities were exceptions in a broader picture of difference.[1]

In the Sea Islands, plantation managers employed task labor, a system of production notable for its lack of white supervision and for the time it offered slaves to pursue their own interests. This form of labor extraction required slaves to work intensively at a given assignment during the day. Completion of a task allowed slaves to use the rest of the day as they pleased. Most slaves spent this time cultivating their personal plots of land, hunting, fishing, socializing, or relaxing.[2]

Rice and cotton cultivation determined work culture in the Sea Islands. In terms of rice production, slaves had to plant or weed one-quarter of an acre per day, with the amount rising to three-quarters of an acre at harvesttime. A complicated process, the cultivation of rice included various tasks throughout the year. Before the planting season commenced, slaves constructed ditches and levees. In March slaves cleared swamplands and planted seed rice. This process was extraordinarily difficult and required "gangs of slave laborers."[3] After months of flooding and draining the fields, rice was harvested in late August or early September. All slaves on a given plantation were required to help with the harvest, but women were considered more adept at it. In the final months of the year, slaves threshed and prepared rice for market. In the Sea Islands, skilled slaves usually worked as ditchers or operated machinery in the production process.[4]

The production of Sea Island cotton, while perhaps not as difficult as rice cultivation, also required arduous field labor. During the growing season, slaves cleared weeds and grass while thinning out the cotton plants. In the fall, women gathered and sorted the cotton by quality. Observing cotton production on St. Simon's Island, British traveler Basil Hall stated that women performed "twice as much" cotton gathering as men.[5] After the cotton gin removed the seeds, slaves cleaned out seed fragments and packaged the cotton for shipment. Hall also noted that, on one Sea Island plantation, the majority of "taskable hands" were engaged in manual field labor, while the remainder were employed as cart drivers, nurses, cooks, carpenters, gardeners, and house servants.[6]

Perhaps the most striking feature of labor production in the Lowcountry was the autonomy of black drivers in crop production. Drivers were responsible for nearly every aspect of production, ranging from assigning a task to deciding if it had been adequately completed. They set the pace of labor and were responsible for slave conduct. For the most part, drivers also doled out food and punishments. Black autonomy and authority in the Sea Islands were contingent on the wishes of an owner or overseer. Although some slave owners gave their drivers considerable control over plantation life and labor, wealthy slave owner Pierce Butler's white plantation managers kept their drivers on a tight leash.

In the Chesapeake, plantation owners responded to the fall of tobacco prices during the European Wars (1792–1815) by turning increasingly to grain production, a type of farming requiring different methods of labor organization and production. Most planters who remained in the Tidewater region, as opposed to migrating to new slave regions farther south, reduced their labor force by selling surplus slaves to aspiring planters and planters in the West or hiring them out to smaller local farms or to employers in cities. Although planters did not completely stop tobacco production, they moved to a more diversified economy that included corn and wheat crops. As a result, slaves achieved specialization in a number of new and different tasks. For example, the new economy required a labor force able to mill, store, transport, ship, and market wheat. As historian Ira Berlin notes, this created new plantation specialists, such as plowmen and dairymaids. Instead of engaging in the process of hoeing tobacco, slaves sowed grains, pressed cider, plowed, lumbered, fished, and shucked corn.[7] In short, grain production entailed a switch from the hoe to the plow and an intensification of labor expectations.[8]

The development of this diversified agricultural economy led to new methods designed to extract as much work from slaves as possible. To rationalize production, planters and farmers instituted longer workdays and a more intensive work environment for slaves. These new demands changed slaves' work patterns. Before the switch from tobacco to grain, the winter months had been less labor intensive. Slaves were then responsible for only a few tasks such as clearing land and cutting firewood. In contrast, the new economy required slaves to spend the winter plowing ground, threshing and cleaning grains from the previous harvest, sowing crops, fixing fences, and cutting timber for the burgeoning town markets. During the growing season, March to November, slaves were under intense pressure to prepare ground, then plant, harvest, and seed. As historian Lorena Walsh states, this work regimen left "no season of leisure except in the worst winter weather."[9]

Female slaves suffered as a result of the switch from tobacco production to mixed agriculture. Tobacco cultivation had featured less variation in labor between the sexes, both male and female slaves using the hoe. The new emphasis on grain production did not open up many skilled positions for women. A few continued to spin, clean, wash, or perform other domestic duties for slave-owning households, but this labor remained largely the domain of poor white laboring women. For the most part, African American women were consigned to the most menial tasks in grain production. Female slaves "grubbed swamps and meadows, weeded corn and vegetables, hoed ground the plows could not adequately break up, erected fences, cleaned the stables, heaped the dung, spread the manure, harvested the corn, and at the end of the year, threshed and cleaned grain and husked the corn."[10] In addition to working in the fields, slave women were responsible for their own domestic duties (such as cooking and making clothes). As Lorena Walsh and Lois Carr note, female slaves suffered the double burden of gender and racial identity and came to be associated with the most "monotonous" and "inglorious" agricultural labor.[11]

Meanwhile some male slaves moved into semiskilled positions, such as plowing, carting, ditching, road construction, and brick making. The rise of cities required a supply of skilled craftsmen, such as carpenters and sawyers, to meet the housing demands of an emerging urban population. Urban slaves also worked in shipyards and factories. Skilled slaves enjoyed considerable autonomy and quite often set their own pace of work. In addition to urban labor, slaves also worked through the hiring system.[12]

Hiring was one of the most important elements of Chesapeake slavery during the late eighteenth and early nineteenth centuries. The switch from tobacco to mixed agricultural production left the region's wealthier planters with surplus laborers, primarily women and children. Planters hired out surplus slaves to poorer whites who could not afford to purchase their own chattel. This system made slavery more widespread, both geographically and in terms of the wealth of slave owners, as even tenant farmers on marginal lands could rent the services of a slave. Although hiring offered some slaves more autonomy and an opportunity to escape the isolation of plantations, it split up families and, as historian Jonathan Martin notes, was not necessarily a step toward freedom.[13]

There were other significant differences between slavery in the Sea Islands and the Chesapeake. More Chesapeake slaves adopted Christianity and had greater contact with the dominant Anglo-American culture than did their counterparts in the Sea Islands. In the Chesapeake, some slaves were brought into the Baptist or Methodist faith during the late eighteenth and early nineteenth centuries. Although Christianity had some influence in the Lowcountry, its impact on the Sea Islands is debatable. In later years, the Black Refugees recounted the nature of their religious services. The secretary of Nova Scotia's African Baptist Association recorded these stories.

The close of the American war brought scores of coloured people: men, women and children, from the United States, and among them many Baptists, whom when enquired where they got their religion, would frankly tell you, in the forests, behind the stone walls, in the cane brakes, in the cotton fields, and in the rice swamps . . . some would keep [watch for] the approach of the driver whilst a company of penitents would go up yonder and pray. They had to make a two-fold prayer: one for the conversion of their own souls, and the other to keep their hands from shedding the blood of the cruel monsters that were placed in charge over them.[14]

The African Baptist Association's secretary mentioned only Christian worship among the Black Refugees in Nova Scotia. However, Muslims had an important presence in the Sea Islands.[15] The Black Refugees who did not migrate to Nova Scotia, but preferred Trinidad after the War of 1812, included Muslims.[16] Some Refugees from the Sea Islands might well have been Muslims who found it difficult to sustain their faith in Nova Scotia. However, it is also possible that individual Muslim Refugees continued their faith but contemporaries neglected to record these people's religious beliefs and practices.[17]

The isolation of the Sea Islands from the main currents of Anglo-American culture and the continuing infusion of new Africans encouraged the slave population to retain important aspects of West African cultures. The role of "African" characteristics in Sea Island culture is evident in the Gullah language, naming patterns, religious ceremonies, burials, animal stories, and dances such as the Buzzard Lope and Ring Shout.[18] The slaves in this region "remained physically separated and psychologically estranged from the Anglo-American world and culturally closer to Africa than any other blacks on continental North America."[19]

The last major differences between the Sea Islands and the Tidewater region could be found in the Chesapeake's large free black population and slaves' greater opportunity for escape and rebellion in this region. On the eve of the War of 1812, there were over sixty thousand free blacks in the Chesapeake region.[20] African Americans maintained contact through familial relations, at black churches, and through the hiring of slaves to urban centers where they could establish or maintain contact with slaves and free blacks. Contact with free blacks might have encouraged slaves to abscond from their masters. Ideas of freedom and liberty were also imbibed through the circulation of knowledge of the American and Haitian Revolutions.[21] Taken together, these conditions created a volatile atmosphere. By the first decade of the nineteenth century, the Chesapeake had experienced two major slave conspiracies and numerous smaller ones, with Gabriel's planned rebellion perhaps including thousands of slaves and free blacks. Hence, the possibility of freedom was more immediate among slaves in the Chesapeake than for those in the Sea Islands.[22]

Slave owners in the Lowcountry feared the importation of Chesapeake slaves, as they were thought to encourage insurrection, insolence, and impudence. This is not to suggest that slaves in the Sea Islands were satisfied with their lot in life. They simply realized that their chances of escape or successful insurrection were minimal. Molly, an older slave on Pierce Butler's plantation in the late 1830s, explained the difficulties of escaping to Fanny Kemble. "[T]aint no use—what use nigger run?—de swamp all around; dey get in dar, an' dey starve to def, or de snakes eat 'em up— massa's nigger, dey don't neber run away."[23] As historian Philip Morgan argues, the white population's ability to "mobilize forces of repression" and the slave population's ability to create a "meaningful" social environment accounts for the lack of large-scale slave rebellions.[24]

Slavery in both the Chesapeake and the Lowcountry developed in a framework of contradictions. For example, as access to slaves extended throughout the Chesapeake to different class levels and new geographic areas, the free black population increased, and manumissions became common (before they were restricted in Virginia in 1806).[25] On the other hand, slavery became more entrenched in the Lowcountry with the expansion of rice production, while at the same time slaves gained more autonomy within the system. On the eve of the War of 1812, both systems of slavery had undergone serious changes that affected the work and family life of African Americans. These changes to slavery might have played a role in the Refugees' decisions to escape during the Anglo-American conflict.

Escape from Slavery

The War of 1812 developed primarily because of lingering feelings of discord between the United States and Britain that stemmed from the Revolutionary War era and the Royal Navy's search and seizure of American vessels, with young southern and western congressmen fanning the flames of conflict in order to annex parts of British North America to the new Republic. For its part, Britain hoped not to regain control over its former colonies but rather to teach the rambunctious Americans a lesson on the world stage, all the while remaining focused on its primary enemy, Napoleon. Consequently the British devoted few resources toward their war with the United States. For different reasons, the United States also had limited means to prosecute the conflict. The New England states and New York, centers of wealth and commerce in the new nation, offered little or no support for the war. Moreover, the United States' declaration of war notwithstanding, the country's armed forces remained unprepared. Despite both nations' limitations and the misgivings of many leaders on each side, the second Anglo-American war began only three decades after the Paris peace treaty of 1783.

For some black Americans, including slaves, the War of 1812 echoed the Revolutionary War in many respects, presenting similar opportunities and obstacles. During both the Revolutionary War and the War of 1812, the British offered freedom to American slaves willing to abandon their owners. These policies of expediency, whether Lord Dunmore's proclamation in 1775 or Vice Admiral Sir Alexander Cochrane's nearly forty years later, had little to do with abolitionist sentiments; they were tactics to defeat the United States. During the War of 1812, as a result of Cochrane's April 1814 proclamation offering freedom and subsequent settlement in the British colonies, thousands of African Americans made their way to British lines, and some served in the British armed forces. This military policy had been designed to create economic problems and a climate of fear in which white Americans would imagine blacks roaming throughout the countryside to murder them in their homes and churches. Despite the military nature of Cochrane's proclamation, antislavery motivations may also have played a role. Indeed, there had been a proliferation in antislavery sentiment in Britain during the early nineteenth century that only grew stronger after the war. However, Cochrane's proclamation was certainly based on military goals and necessity as opposed to antislavery sentiments.

Despite these overarching similarities, there were significant differences between each Anglo-American war. At the outset of the American Revolution in 1775, slavery still flourished in the British colonies, while British merchants participated in the transatlantic slave trade. This situation had changed by the War of 1812. For various reasons, economic and humanitarian, the Americans and British had ceased their participation in the slave trade, while the British had also attempted to establish a homeland for returned slaves and those captured from slaving vessels on the west coast of Africa. However progressive some of these endeavors might have been, they did not mean that the British government was committed to antislavery causes or in favor of black emancipation in the Caribbean or the southern United States. Indeed, the Treaty of Ghent was interpreted by the Americans to mean that the British would return the Black Refugees, and in lieu of this, after arbitration, His Majesty's government eventually compensated the Americans. Yet the situation on the ground remained more complicated than the political debates between British and American treaty officials. The letters of the British Admiralty and government during the second Anglo-American conflict indicate an unwillingness to return slaves to their owners particularly if they had helped the British and would be exposed to the anger of their owners upon return.[26] In other words, the British steadfastly denied Americans the right to retrieve slaves who had committed some act of bravery for His Majesty. Although this refusal can be seen in terms of humanitarianism, military necessity also played an essential role. If the British agreed to return slaves who had helped them back to their American owners, then no other slaves would have come over to the Union Jack.[27]

The Black Refugees' escape from the United States during the War of 1812 should be understood as a conscious rebellion against slavery. Although many African Americans absconded to British lines after Cochrane's proclamation, Refugees had helped to initiate this policy by escaping to the British as early as the spring of 1813, with the first African Americans arriving in Nova Scotia that fall.[28] The Refugees' exodus from American slavery marked an important foundation for the creation of their future culture and community in Nova Scotia. By the conclusion of the conflict, at least 3,500 slaves had escaped from their owners. Of that total, over 2,000 had arrived on the shores of Nova Scotia by the end of 1818, but about 400 went to New Brunswick.[29]

The development of British policy during the War of 1812 started well before Cochrane's proclamation.[30] African Americans knew that the sight of British ships in the Chesapeake Bay as early as the winter of 1813 might mean freedom, but from the British perspective no such plan had been adopted. His Majesty's officers in the Chesapeake realized that "the blacks of Virginia and Maryland would cheerfully take up arms and join us against the Americans."[31] Still the British hesitated. In lengthy instructions to his commanding army officers in the United States, Lord Bathurst strongly cautioned against any measures that might "encourage" the slaves to "rise upon their masters." However, he mentioned that "any individual Negroes" who offered assistance to the British could be freed and enlisted in the Black Corps or sent as free settlers to one of His Majesty's colonies including Nova Scotia or Trinidad. More specifically, Lord Bathurst hoped to send the Refugees from northern regions (Chesapeake) to Nova Scotia, while those from the southern regions (Georgia) were to go to Trinidad. But these intended destinations did not come to pass, and many Georgians ended up in Nova Scotia. Bathurst explicitly and firmly informed his commanders that they could not carry away American "slaves as slaves" but only as newly freed persons. His Majesty's government did not want to incite a slave rebellion, but it also prohibited its soldiers from taking American slaves and sending them to the West Indies.[32]

In some sense, the original British policy of the War of 1812 was even more limited than Lord Dunmore's proclamation during the Revolutionary conflict because it offered freedom only to "individual" African Americans who might help His Majesty's war effort instead of offering freedom to all slaves of American owners. This policy changed in 1814 when Admiral Cochrane received new government instructions and took command of the British fleet in the North Atlantic. Cochrane wanted to defeat the Americans thoroughly, regarding them as an inferior race of complaining babies. Cochrane likened Americans to spaniels and strongly believed that, similar to this boisterous dog, they needed to "be drubbed into good manners." He hoped to regain control of large tracts of the United States and encourage secession movements in New England. Given his grandiose war plans, it is not surprising that Cochrane saw African Americans as an important ally in the defeat of the United States. Cochrane strongly believed that the "cordial support" of African Americans would result in President Madison being "hurled from his throne."[33] Yet if he hoped to get the support of thousands of African Americans, Cochrane had to exceed the scope of his original orders from Lord Bathurst. On 2 April 1814, Cochrane issued his proclamation offering support to Americans willing to switch sides:

> Whereas it has been represented to me that many persons now resident in the United States have expressed a desire to withdraw therefrom, with a view to entering into His Majesty's Service, or of being received as Free Settlers in some of His Majesty's Colonies,
>
> This is therefore to give notice,
>
> That all those who may be disposed to emigrate from the United States will, with their families, be received on board His Majesty's Ships or Vessels of War, or at the Military Posts that may be established upon or near the Coast of the United States, when they will have their choice of either entering into His Majesty's Sea or Land forces, or of being sent as Free Settlers to the British possessions in North America or the West Indies, where they will meet with all due encouragement.[34]

The British government did not know about Cochrane's proclamation until after it had been issued. Upon finding out about it, the government was displeased but could not publicly disavow Cochrane. John Quincy Adams discovered on his trip to London in 1814 that Cochrane had not been authorized to issue the proclamation but that the British government supported his decision. Moreover, government officials informed Adams that the proclamation had not mentioned blacks specifically, but the future president commented in a letter to James Monroe that Cochrane's proclamation was "unquestionably intended for the Negroes."[35] Nevertheless, Rear Admiral George Cockburn, Cochrane's second in command, openly described the proclamation in a letter to his superior as designed to "encourage the Emigration of the Black Slaves from the United States."[36] Clearly, the Admiralty knew that the proclamation, though not addressed specifically to African American slaves, was intended for them.

In the Chesapeake, the ships of the Royal Navy represented the border between slavery in the United States and freedom in Britain and British North America. Many Refugees were willing to risk their lives to cross the fluid border between American troops and British military positions. According to Captain Barrie, the "senior officer in the Chesapeake," local slaves "were constantly escaping from the shore, and joining the British ships."[37] However, as the British did not occupy the region (that is, any land with the exception of Tangier Island), Refugee attempts to achieve freedom remained an arduous and life-threatening task. Quite often, they traveled several miles at night and sought out the nearest British naval vessel while threatened by slave patrols and the militia. Although they were valued as property, this legal status did not protect potential escapees from reprisals if caught fleeing to the British. The Richmond *Enquirer* reported that escaped slaves were often beaten or killed by local whites.[38] Nevertheless, thousands of African Americans risked their lives in order to achieve freedom. They realized that the opportunity to escape from slavery and possibly strike a retributive blow by fighting against the Americans might very well be a once-in-a-lifetime opportunity.

In other areas, slaves were more fortunate. The British navy invaded and occupied the relatively undefended Sea Islands and freed slaves as it went. Two large-scale slave owners in the Georgia Sea Islands, James Hamilton and Pierce Butler, lost their property in this manner. Other Sea Island slaves were not so fortunate. Some had to make trips of nearly fifteen miles to reach British positions and at times found Americans waiting to ambush them on their way. Moreover, after having made good their own escape, some Sea Islanders returned to plantations to encourage other slaves to abscond.[39]

Throughout the war, masters attempted to recover their slaves, but the

Royal Navy refused most requests. However, at the war's conclusion, the British did return some slaves who had escaped after the Treaty of Ghent's ratification. Still the Royal Navy did not return nearly the number of slaves Americans requested.[40] One historian has correctly referred to the War of 1812 as a conflict between the "Slaveholding Liberators."[41] Though not abolitionists, the British saw the emancipation of slaves as a desirable aspect of their military strategy. The British Admiralty remained concerned about the fate of escaped slaves and the performance of those who had helped form the Colonial Marines—a regiment composed of Black Refugees.[42] In one letter, Cockburn stated that it "would be very sad indeed if they [the Refugees] fell again accidentally into the Hands of their old Masters."[43] Cockburn and Cochrane both knew the risk that the Refugees were taking by fighting against the Americans when they could easily have found shelter and safety by remaining onboard Royal Navy vessels.[44]

The British had recruited black soldiers to serve in their armed forces because they were "more terrific to the Americans than any troops that could be brought forward."[45] Several hundred Refugees served in the Colonial Marines.[46] The Black Refugees participated in assaults on American positions in the Chesapeake and in Georgia. They also served as spies, messengers, and guides. The *Niles Weekly Register* reported that recently escaped slaves had served as messengers for a British raiding party in 1813.[47] On 25 June 1814, referring to an engagement fought in May, Cockburn reported that "the Colonial Marines, who were for the first time employed in Arms against their old Masters on this occasion . . . behaved to the admiration of every Body."[48] In another letter, Cockburn stated that the Colonial Marines were "indeed excellent men, and make the best skirmishers possible for the thick woods of this Country."[49] In 1815 the Colonial Marines participated in the invasion of Cumberland Island, the southernmost of the Georgia Sea Islands.[50]

Despite the Refugees' obvious hunger for freedom as demonstrated by their bravery in running away and performing military service, most slave owners refused to believe that their slaves wanted liberty, much less desired to take up arms against their former masters. The Refugees' escape predated the "positive good" justification for slavery, but slave owners' rationalization of the War of 1812 exodus presaged later claims that slaves were the happiest people on earth. Masters and plantation overseers claimed that the Refugees had been enticed away from their happy lives by promises of an easy postemancipation life complete with mansions and servants. As masters watched their supposedly happy slaves escape to the Royal Navy, they came up with rationalizations that painted the Refugees as pawns of the British. For example, plantation overseer Roswell King wrote wealthy slave owner Pierce Butler, "[d]o not think I shall be violent with your Negroes. They are more to be pittyed than blamed. It is the British Policy (that God suffers to be a scurge and Curse on all Nations that know them) that is to blame."[51] However, in another letter he blamed his "ungrateful Negroes," arguing that more "would have gone off if they had only a chance."[52] Some Chesapeake slave owners had these rationalizations dashed by their former slaves. Allowed to board British ships to appeal to those who had escaped, the slave owners encountered only defiance. In Georgia, where slave owners implored hundreds of former slaves to return, fewer than twenty did so.[53]

In escaping to the Royal Navy, the Black Refugees began their history of negotiating the border between the British and American worlds. In some sense, the escape from slavery to freedom reified the differences between the Refugees' American past and their British future. In the United States, they could not work for themselves, keep their families together without difficulty, or enjoy the right to come and go as they pleased. In contrast, once on the British ships, the Refugees had boundless hopes: for stable families, independent farming, and freedom of movement. The border between the United States and Britain protected the Black Refugees and promised them more opportunities in one of His Majesty's colonies. Yet the migration of the Refugees to the British naval vessels did not separate them from the relatives and friends that they left behind. As a state of mind, the differences between the British and American worlds became less clear. The Refugees constantly crossed this psychological border by paying close attention to the fate of their brethren in Virginia, Maryland, Georgia, or the rest of the United States. The physical separation engendered by the differences between American slavery and British freedom became less dichotomous as the border (and the differences it entailed politically and socially) did not destroy the psychosocial ties that bound the Refugees to those who remained on the farms and plantations of the American world.

When the Refugees escaped from the United States, they believed the British promise that they would enjoy meaningful liberty, reunify their families, receive land, and be accorded equal treatment. Several observers commented that the Refugees' main objectives revolved around hopes for land and freedom. Charles Ball, a slave who later achieved freedom, accompanied his owner on an unsuccessful attempt to recover the runaways. In his narrative Ball recalled the scene: "I was invited, and even urged to go with the others, who, I was told, were bound to the island of Trinidad, in the West Indies, where they would have lands given to them, and where they would be free."[54] G. R. Gleig, a British officer, also recalled the Refugees' emphasis on becoming free, as they were willing to serve in the British military if "we would but give them their liberty."[55] Despite the Refugees' attachment to the idea of owning land, legal freedom meant more to them. The main lure of the British offer of freedom for the Refugees was the opportunity to work for themselves and keep what they earned. As one male Refugee stated to an English visitor when asked about the differences between America and Nova Scotia, "what I works for here, I gets."[56]

Each individual escape probably involved the important hope of freedom. Yet there were other reasons that encouraged slaves to abscond, as the story of John Shaw illustrates. In the late 1880s, the elderly Shaw told the Halifax *Morning Chronicle* the details of his escape during the War of 1812. A young adult when the war broke out, Shaw had worked in the tobacco fields of Virginia. One day, with the British warships only a few miles away, Shaw's master "offered to give any of his slaves a pass of freedom if they wished to have their liberty."[57] Recognizing this offer as a trick, the slaves remained silent. In a few weeks their master died, and the estate passed to his son. "The young man was a hard master, with a sharp tempered wife, and the slave driver they employed was a cruel, merciless man."[58] Additionally, the slaves discovered they would be sold into the Deep South. These circumstances convinced Shaw and five others that the horrors of slavery in South Carolina or Georgia outweighed dangers of escape. They absconded under the cover of darkness and took a canoe to the nearest British vessel.[59]

Given the varied routes to freedom that the Refugees took, it is hardly surprising that they represented a diversity of American slaves. A breakdown of male and female runaways listed as "American Refugee Negroes" received in Halifax between April 1815 and October 1818 indicates that 892 runaways were men, 583 women, and 188 children. The majority of Chesapeake Refugees were from Westmoreland and Northumberland counties in Virginia.[60]

The high percentage of women and children among the Refugees indicates that some slaves fled from both the Sea Islands and the Chesapeake in some form of family unit or kinship group. In autumn 1815, the Nova Scotia government compiled a list of 375 recently arrived slaves from the Chesapeake. In this account, 215 men, women, and children arrived without families, while 160 men, women, and children were part of a family unit. In other words, approximately 43 percent of these people had arrived in Halifax with other family members.[61] Other existing records provide ample evidence that some Refugees were able to escape as family units. For example, Thomas Carter arrived in Nova Scotia with his wife, while Thomas Dines, his wife, and children fled as a family unit to Nova Scotia. Also Fielding and Gabriel Johnston escaped from slavery along with their wives before settling in Halifax.[62] The importance of family considerations in deciding to leave the United States can be gleaned from the comments of Sea Island plantation manager Roswell King. He angrily complained that while some Refugees left their wives and husbands (perhaps as a result of marital unhappiness), others "said they must follow their daughters and others their wives."[63] Interestingly, the majority of Pierce Butler's slaves on the list of Refugees received in Halifax were not married, but this does not mean that they were unrelated or necessarily from different families.[64] Although black families were torn apart by hiring and sales, some slave owners had encouraged marriage and family ties in order to stabilize their workforces. The result of this policy is reflected in the number of families among the Refugees.

The Black Refugees also possessed diverse skills and trades. In the Georgia Sea Islands most slaves labored in the rice or cotton fields. However, there were many artisans in this region, including blacksmiths, carpenters, and masons. In the Chesapeake, the majority listed by slaves' claimants' reports did not have an identified occupation and probably were field hands. Among those with an occupation listed, the most common for women were house servant, weaver, and spinner, while men held vocations including carpenter, sawyer, and servant.[65] The occupations of the Black Refugees are also found in records of ships entering Halifax in 1813. The vast majority of these Refugees were listed as farmers or laborers, while a smaller contingent held more specific vocations, such as blacksmith, servant, sawyer, hostler, washerwoman, or shoemaker.[66]

The Black Refugees brought many aspects of their work experience to Nova Scotia. Among the fortunate ones were Refugees trained in certain occupational skills, such as carpentry, that would help them to find work in Nova Scotia. Accustomed to living near water, many Refugees had experience working on boats and readily found employment in Nova Scotia's docks and shipping industry. In contrast, those Refugees who had been employed as rice and cotton workers in the Sea Islands could not use many of these skills on their lands in Nova Scotia (if these Refugees had been taken to Trinidad perhaps their work experiences would have been more helpful), where farming required breaking stones and cutting down trees in order to grow potatoes. Perhaps the most significant work experience brought to Nova Scotia was the transfer of market trading skills, which provided the Refugees with a significant source of income. Although the Refugees brought different work experiences to Nova Scotia, the British imperial government assumed that all had been farm laborers. As a result, imperial and local officials expected men and women, including some who had been domestic servants or skilled workers, to become subsistence frontier farmers.[67]

The Refugees also brought significant cultural aspects of their American background with them to Nova Scotia. The experience of separate black places of worship was continued in the woods of British North America. Indeed, forms of Afro-American Christianity prevalent in the Chesapeake generally, and Virginia in particular, were reproduced in Nova Scotia. Other aspects of slave life, such as extended family and kinship ties, took on added importance in Nova Scotia as many households contained several family members, ranging in age from newborn to elderly. During slavery, the Refugees had been mutually reliant on and supportive of one another. This trait continued in Nova Scotia as the more fortunate Refugees fed, housed, and cared for the poorer members of the emerging communities. The church, friends, and families would form the building blocks of the Refugee community in Nova Scotia.

In sum, the Refugees were a diverse group. They were old and young; skilled and unskilled; male and female; single and married; with family and without. For example, seventy-year-old Bob Cooper was not too old to enjoy the fruits of freedom. At the other end of the spectrum, Simon Massey was only five years of age.[68] One escapee, Sally, was blind and described by Nova Scotian officials as a true case of "charity."[69] In contrast, several Refugees brought special skills to Nova Scotia, such as July Hamilton, who possessed a "Knowledge of medicine."[70]

The Refugees' experience with different systems of American slavery, and their escape from the Peculiar Institution, left an indelible mark on their collective consciousness. Their movement up the Atlantic from slavery in the American world to freedom in the British world remained a point of comparison for the Refugees that they remembered in the creation of community institutions, public lectures, and the assertion of their rights as new British subjects. Their first shared experience had been forged in the fires of war, escape, and travel along the North American coast of the Atlantic world. The road to creating a distinct African British North American community in Nova Scotia had its roots in the plantations and farms of the southern United States and aboard the naval vessels of His Majesty.

Once in Nova Scotia, the Refugees drew on the enduring vitality of their broad range of vocational and labor skills. For the Black Refugees, Nova Scotia represented an unfamiliar ecological, economic, and vocational environment, to which these immigrants from the southern United States had to adjust quickly. The Refugees would rely on all the resources they had brought with them in an attempt to do what the grandchildren of those whom they left behind in slavery would also do once emancipated—that is, attempt to carve out as much economic independence as possible by applying traditional methods and knowledge in new ways. The Refugee story in Nova Scotia would be a constant struggle to become an independent people. Unfortunately, like black southerners after the Civil War, in key respects the Refugees obtained "nothing but freedom."[71]

PART II

*Opportunities and Obstacles
in Nova Scotia, 1815–1860*

Chapter 3

Settlement and Struggle

AFRICAN AMERICANS MIGRATED to several destinations outside the United States following the War of 1812. Colonization became an increasingly viable alternative as racial hostility increased in northern states and slavery continued to expand throughout the South. Although some African Americans remained suspicious of the motivations behind colonization, it offered opportunities for equal citizenship and economic improvement that barely existed in the United States.[1] Under the auspices of different organizations ranging from the racist American Colonization Society (ACS) to the Haitian government, black Americans migrated to different lands in hope of obtaining meaningful freedom. Between 1815 and 1860, tens of thousands of African Americans emigrated to Haiti, Liberia, and Canada. Like their brethren who migrated to Nova Scotia during and after the War of 1812, African American emigrants to Africa or the Caribbean hoped to find a "Promised Land." Yet in each setting, the Promised Land proved to be elusive. Black expatriates faced numerous challenges that partly defined their early settlement patterns and subsequent decisions to remain in their new locations or return to the United States. The experiences of African American migrants in Haiti, Liberia, and throughout Canada offer a broader context in which to understand the struggles and trials that the Black Refugees faced in Nova Scotia.[2]

During the 1820s, the Haitian government enticed thousands of African Americans to the Caribbean nation through offers of land and promises of equal citizenship. Armed with racial pride and the desire for economic improvement, the migrants attempted to settle on farms and contribute to the new country. In many ways, the possibilities seemed endless in Haiti, where the constitution, according to President Jean Pierre Boyer, ensured "a free country to Africans and their descendents."[3] Yet Haiti did not turn out to be a land of promise to the African American emigrants. They faced numerous economic and cultural barriers. Although they had been recruited to serve as independent farmers, some of the settlers hailed from urban areas and, once in Haiti, sold or rented their new lands to find work in towns. This set them at odds with the government. In an attempt to remedy the situation, Haitian authorities instituted laws that required rural people to stay on their farms, which angered many African American settlers, perhaps reminding them of slavery's denial of the freedom of movement. Some of the new settlers suffered from sicknesses, while others found it challenging to master a new language or accept Catholicism. These English-speaking, Protestant African Americans did not wish to adopt the culture and language of the host nation, causing tensions with the government and their Haitian neighbors. As a result, many of the emigrants returned to the United States, while some of those who remained "retained their American identity."[4]

Liberia presented another option for African Americans interested in leaving the United States. However, the African colony's connection with the ACS made it a less desirable destination than Haiti or Canada. The ACS wanted to resettle African Americans on the west coast of Africa supposedly to facilitate the Christian regeneration of the so-called Dark Continent, while ridding the United States of black people.[5] American Colonization Society goals were outlined during a sermon preached by the Reverend Calvin Yale to the society's Vermont Auxiliary in 1827: "The immediate object of the Colonization Society is, to relieve our nation from an onerous burden, the free coloured population, to redeem the same from degradation and crime, to place them on the shores of their mother country, in such circumstances, as favor their own improvement, and that of their kindred."[6] Managed by several wealthy slaveholders, the ACS appealed to different groups, including advocates of gradual emancipation, some southern slave owners, and black people who viewed Liberia as a place to establish an African American homeland away from the discrimination of the United States.

Despite the best efforts of the ACS, however, the vast majority of free people of color especially in the northern United States rejected the Liberian colonization scheme. Their southern brethren, including those who were offered freedom on the condition that they resettle there, provided the main source of emigrants to the West African coast. Many Liberian emigrants, both free and slave, hailed from southern states. They hoped to regain their African heritage, modernize West Africa, and help Liberia obtain redemption through Christianity. These hopes clashed with the realities the emigrants encountered in Liberia, including high mortality rates, small and scattered settlements, and hostility from indigenous people. As historian Claude Clegg demonstrates, "For many, dreams of a Pan-African utopia in Liberia were instantly shattered when they arrived in the country only to be confounded by their utter unfamiliarity with Africa and Africans. Their evolving political and material interests as Christian, 'civilized' settlers complicated their troubled relationship with the Africans whom they dispossessed of vast territories. Likewise, widespread penury, disease, and death made their adjustment to their new environment all the more difficult."[7]

Canada was the third major destination of African American migration. As a site for settlement, Canada garnered support from many sectors of the black population, ranging from slaves to the delegates at national conventions of African American leaders held between the early 1830s and the Civil War.[8] Between 1830 and 1860, African Americans settled in several different areas throughout Upper Canada including Wilberforce, Dawn, and Elgin.[9] The settlements at Wilberforce and Dawn, founded in 1830 and 1842 respectively, suffered from poor farmland, sporadic employment, and feuding leaderships, while Elgin, established in 1849, enjoyed some success. Farming on fertile soil, the Elgin settlers worked under the direction of the Reverend William King to produce various crops; the community thus avoided reliance on one foodstuff.[10] These settlements offered the black Fugitives a measure of safety from slavery, slave catchers, and the worst forms of racial violence and discrimination. Yet white Canadians' racial attitudes became increasingly hostile after 1850, as the numbers of African Americans in Canada increased following the passage of the Fugitive Slave Law in the United States. Abolitionist Samuel Gridley Howe captured the racism that stained relations between black migrants and their host country: "The truth of the matter seems to be that, as long as the colored people form a very small proportion of the population, and are dependent, they receive protection and favors; but when they increase, and compete with the laboring class for a living, and especially when they begin to aspire to social equality, they cease to be 'interesting negroes' and become 'niggers.'"[11] As a result of these attitudes, thousands of African Americans returned to the United States after the Civil War as Canada turned out to be far from a color-blind utopia.[12]

The Black Refugees of Nova Scotia

The story of the Black Refugees developed alongside the rich and complex interactions of African American expatriates in a variety of historical settings. In Nova Scotia, the Refugees faced several challenges and obstacles from the outset of their settlement in the British colonies. Yet they established families, farms, and new communities in ways that other expatriate African Americans accomplished in Haiti, Liberia, and Canada. The process of settlement for the Refugees meant defining the contours of freedom, but it also was marked by important steps in the transition of various American slaves into Black Refugees. The process of becoming a distinct group of African British North Americans continued after the Refugees landed in Nova Scotia. Despite their various backgrounds, once in Nova Scotia they experienced the initial struggle to overcome homelessness and the absence of familiar institutions and, for many, poverty and sickness as well. The struggle of settlement exploded any notions among the Refugees that Nova Scotia was a land of unqualified promise. Instead the shared experience of racial hostility, indecisive government policies, poor employment prospects, and arduous efforts to develop farming communities created the foundations for a new culture and community in British North America. There were three important aspects of the Black Refugees' early settlement: racial ideology and fears of ex-slave settlement in Nova Scotia preshaped government policy; these same policies were poorly planned; and an economic depression left the new settlers with few opportunities.

The first years of settlement in Nova Scotia (1815 to 1821) developed within a context of racial hostility, which emanated from the frustration of slavery's demise there after the War of 1812 being followed by another large influx of freed blacks. Not surprisingly, the government and population of Nova Scotia attempted to deny the Refugees the fruits of freedom and fair treatment under British laws and institutions. Many elements of the local white population resented the imperial government for having sent the Refugees to Nova Scotia. In an 1815 letter to the *Acadian Recorder,* a resident claimed that the decision to resettle the former slaves in Nova Scotia "was entered upon without being digested; without considering the difficulties and expence which would attend the prosecution. Thousands availed themselves of the invitation; we hope for the sake of the people of colour, they were the most worthless of that community."[13] These sentiments were not restricted to a few hostile voices in the community. The colonial government also shared this letter writer's views and unsuccessfully attempted to ban any further immigration of African Americans. In 1815 the House of Assembly stated that the number of blacks in Nova Scotia caused "many inconveniences," discouraged the immigration of white labor, and established a community that was "unfitted by nature to this climate, or an association with the rest of His Majesty's colonists."[14] Feelings of anger at the prospect of black resettlement in Nova Scotia continued for decades, and in 1834 the local government again unsuccessfully attempted to ban black immigration by passing "An Act to prevent the Clandestine Landing of Liberated Slaves."[15]

Nearly ten years after the Refugees' initial settlement, the editor of the *Free Press* decried the "impolitic conduct of the British government" in settling the Refugees in Nova Scotia.[16] Moreover, the erudite editor claimed that the Refugees' condition in Nova Scotia was worse than that of slaves in the Caribbean. Slavery, he argued, protected black people from the rigors of freedom and remained the preferable position for people of African descent throughout the British Empire. Popular notions that the Refugees had been happier as slaves also buttressed these opinions.

Although slavery had died out in Nova Scotia before the Refugees' arrival during and after the War of 1812, the institution still held an important place in the minds of local whites. Slavery withered away because judges in Nova Scotia made it next to impossible for slaveholders to reclaim black people in bondage who escaped and asserted their liberty in court. Moreover, slavery had not played an important role in the local economy. Nevertheless, slavery persisted in the shadows as some poor blacks turned to indentured servitude to survive.[17]

As historian Joanne Pope Melish notes in the case of New England, the end of slavery gave rise to ideas that ascribed racial difference to innate, unchangeable characteristics. In New England, the terms "free" and "of color" embodied "disorder and disruption that represented a threat to the stability of the republic."[18] In Nova Scotia, the Black Refugees represented this threat to colonial stability. The arrival of former slaves who suffered from sickness, poverty, and homelessness led some Nova Scotians to conclude that slavery should be maintained in the Americas to avoid the cost associated with black freedom. One government official commented that without the dread of the lash, the new immigrants would not work, because their "idea of freedom is idleness."[19] The government official was not alone in his opinion, as letters to local newspapers and the musings of local writers demonstrate. For example, "Z" declared that the "universal" opinion about the Refugees held that they would have been happier "had they continued in their previous condition."[20] Judge and historian Thomas Chandler Haliburton asserted in the late 1820s that the Black Refugees had "sighed for the roof of their master, and the pastimes and amusements they left behind."[21] These views denied the Refugees equal treatment in Nova Scotia by creating a racist environment that attempted to force the new settlers to the very fringes of colonial society.

The opinions expressed by different segments of Nova Scotia's population and government would have been familiar to African Americans in Massachusetts and black expatriates in other parts of British North America. Six years after the Nova Scotian Assembly attempted to ban black immigration in 1815, the Massachusetts state legislature considered a similar bill. The reasoning in Massachusetts mirrored that employed by the Nova Scotian government. Supposedly African American migrants to the Bay State increased the depravity of the underclass and threatened to take away jobs from whites.[22] Although the bill failed to become law, it demonstrates that many in both New England and Nova Scotia rejected political and social inclusion for African Americans, believing that such inclusion threatened hopes for a white state and colony. In British North America a similar situation occurred. Although black migrants in Nova Scotia and Upper Canada were considered subjects of the Crown and entitled to equal treatment under the law, racial discrimination in British North America sometimes mirrored attitudes of the nation to the south. For example, as many states in the Old Northwest attempted to ban the immigration of free blacks, so did Upper Canada's House of Assembly in 1830. The Assembly believed it had become necessary to introduce a bill to "prevent the introduction of Blacks and Mulattoes into this Province."[23] In 1850 local whites in Chatham, near the Elgin settlement, complained about the introduction of "indolent, vicious, and ungovernable" African Americans.[24] In Nova Scotia, such attitudes affected government policies.

Not only did the leaders of Nova Scotia's government harbor conservative political sentiments and racist ideas, but the arrival of over 1,600 African Americans caught the colonial government off guard. The consequence was policies inimical to the new settlers. The Nova Scotia government hoped that the Refugees would be temporary settlers like some of the Black Loyalists and nearly all of the Jamaican Maroons. Thus the government developed temporary solutions to serious problems rather than thoughtful policies based on long-term plans for incorporating the newcomers into the colony.

Again, ideology played a role. The lieutenant governors during the Refugees' first years in Nova Scotia, Sir John Sherbrooke and Lord Dal-

housie, strongly believed in Tory ideals as expressed by the British political establishment and government under Lord Liverpool. Recoiling from
the supposed excesses of the French and American revolutions, the political elite in Nova Scotia believed that British North America represented a
bulwark against the worst excesses of democracy and free-market capital-
ism. Along with British intellectuals, government officials in Nova Scotia
believed that distinctions between the laboring and ruling classes were desirable, necessary, and unchangeable. The idea of tinkering with what
many thought to be the natural place of men and women went against the
very dictates of God. The British and Nova Scotian political establish-
ments regarded this type of strict hierarchy as necessary for stability,
order, and reasonable government.[25]

Those who believed in the strict ordering of society placed black people
at the very bottom of the social, economic, and political ladder. The Refugees' status as former slaves convinced local officials that they should not
be independent landowning farmers but rather should work for the local
white population as servants or laborers for hire. These ideas should not
have been difficult to transfer into policy, but another element entered the
picture. After the War of 1812, Nova Scotia suffered a serious recession; at
the same time, European immigration increased. The result was intense
competition for very few laboring jobs.[26] A colonial government that
spent more time attempting to remove the Refugees from Nova Scotia
than developing a comprehensive and serious development program exacerbated these problems. From the outset of the Refugees' settlement in
Nova Scotia, the government wasted critical time fumbling around for a
solution to what its leaders perceived as a temporary problem.

The Black Refugees arrived on the shores of Nova Scotia in need of
medical attention, food, and shelter after their lengthy voyage up the Atlantic from the southern United States. Enduring the cold, damp weather
of Halifax harbor, the ex-slaves began their first shared experience in their
new homeland. They had no place to settle, and their paltry government
rations left them hungry. Lieutenant Governor Sir John Sherbrooke could
not have predicted the devastating postwar recession, which exacerbated
the situation confronting the Refugees. Still, his failure to institute the
British government's policy for dealing with liberated slaves helped turn
the already difficult task of settling and caring for the new homeless immigrants into a crisis.

In 1808 a British government circular had instructed Nova Scotian officials that the officer of customs must take "measures immediately" to provide ex-slaves with clothing, food, and shelter. Moreover, unemployed ex-

slaves were supposed to be enlisted in government service or apprenticed to learn trades.[27] Although Lieutenant Governor Sherbrooke believed that the Refugees provided "a large accession of useful labour to the agriculture of the Country," this situation did not last, as the end of the war resulted in severe cutbacks to the inflow of British capital, which had provided numerous jobs in the Halifax region.[28] As a result, local laboring jobs disappeared, and the work that the government had assumed would fall into the hands of the Refugees no longer existed. The sight of jobless blacks reinforced the views of some local whites that people of African descent "were too lazy to work" and stealing "was easier than to labour."[29] Other observers realized that the problem was structural: despite the Refugees' hopes for employment and their will to help themselves, they could not find work. Many Refugee women found employment washing clothes and some got steady work as domestic servants, but their meager wages barely provided enough food for their families. The situation for men was worse. In 1815 one government official recorded that, of the many families he had met, very few men had jobs. Instead, they spent their days at the temporary shelters provided by the government, tending children.[30]

Although the Refugees did not suffer the high rate of mortality that struck down black emigrants in Liberia, many did suffer severe sicknesses after arriving in Nova Scotia. In Liberia, black settlers "had to adjust to rainy and dry seasons, as opposed to the annual cycles of cool and warm climate that characterized North America."[31] The climate that the Refugees encountered in Nova Scotia also differed substantially from that of the southern United States. The Refugees had to adjust to significantly colder weather along with shorter growing seasons, differences in climate that made settlement trying. It must have been discomforting for the Refugees to witness ice flows in Halifax harbor during the first summers of their settlement. Most commonly the Refugees suffered from dysentery and malnutrition; some suffered from ulcers and others from frozen limbs that had to be amputated.[32] According to one observer, some of the new immigrants were in such bad health that they "could scarcely stand on their feet."[33]

More seriously, just as the numbers of Refugee arrivals in Nova Scotia increased, an epidemic of smallpox broke out in late 1814. This disease occurred because the Refugees were staying in various inadequate shelters ranging from the local poorhouse to temporary huts scattered throughout Halifax County. As a result of the unsanitary conditions, there had been several deaths, while hundreds of Refugees became ill and needed vaccination. Eventually, local officials contained the disease, but its outbreak illustrated the inability of the government to provide adequate shelter that might have prevented the outbreak of smallpox.[34] These problems associated with the Refugees' first months of settlement eventually convinced Lieutenant Governor Sherbrooke to use Melville Island, site of a prison during the War of 1812, as a quarantine center. Here the quarantined Refugees received a steady supply of food and the medical attention that had been absent at the outset of their settlement in Nova Scotia.

Resettlement on Farms

The Black Refugees' first months in Nova Scotia can be described as nothing short of dreary. The new settlers shared the problems of unemployment and scanty food provisions. Field slaves from Georgia and Chesapeake house servants suffered equally from the government's lack of direction and the racial hostility that confronted the new settlers at every corner. Gullah speakers and their more Anglicized brethren from Maryland shared the hardships of settlement in Nova Scotia, and this forced strangers with possibly very little in common to turn to each other for mutual support and understanding through the sharing of paltry foodstuffs and clothing. Differences among the African American expatriates remained, but the new environment of Nova Scotia facilitated the transition of American slaves from vastly different backgrounds to Black Refugees. This development continued when the government decided to permanently settle the Refugees outside Halifax.

The sight of Refugees wandering the streets of Halifax between Melville Island and the poorhouse, some begging for food, convinced local officials that something had to be done. With Nova Scotia's economy unable to furnish them laboring jobs, the imperial government decided to resettle the Refugees on partly deserted lands in the farming settlements of Preston and Hammonds Plains. In June 1815 the government in Britain, only starting to recover from a major European conflict, alarmed by the rising costs of caring for the homeless and hungry Refugees, hoped resettlement would make the Refugees self-sufficient. Colonial Secretary Lord Bathurst assumed that the vast majority of Refugees were "accustomed to agriculture" and as farmers would contribute to Nova Scotia's economy.[35] Although the British government proposed this policy, some evidence suggests that the Refugees played an important part in the decision to settle on farms. The Black Refugees wanted to become independent landowning farmers. After being presented with the plan to resettle on the farms, the Refugees responded that they were "desirous to become immediate Setlers [*sic*]" and very pleased with the opportunity to have their own land.[36]

Despite their interest in becoming landholding farmers, the Refugees faced an immensely difficult task that had forced many previous settlers to leave the colony. Immigrants to Nova Scotia and to British North America in the early nineteenth century, regardless of race, struggled to make a living if they had little or no capital. Much of the land given to new settlers, but particularly at Preston and Hammonds Plains, was relatively sterile. From Irish farmers in Cape Breton to soldier settlers in the western interior of Nova Scotia, new immigrants struggled to make the land productive and in many cases abandoned their farms with little or no improvements.[37] For example, in 1817 Lieutenant Governor Lord Dalhousie reported that a new settlement of disbanded soldiers was on the verge of total collapse. He complained that, without assistance, the soldiers "must quit" the land.[38] American Fugitives faced a similar situation of farming difficult frontier land in Canada West (formerly Upper Canada). The struggles of the Refugees in Nova Scotia and the Fugitives in Canada West were similar to those of their white brethren in that they endured "the challenges and vicissitudes of pioneer life just as others did in the Canadian frontier towns and villages." In other words, the experience of the Refugees did not develop in a vacuum, but rather alongside the struggles of many immigrants in British North America.[39] The Nova Scotia government had hoped that encouraging immigration to the colony would result in economic development. But for the most part the government found itself providing assistance for indigent settlers who could not make a go of it on the land.[40]

The poverty of the soil was only one hardship; another was the fact that demand for labor in Nova Scotia could be seasonal and sporadic even in times of economic stability. This situation hardly improved for the Refugees from their initial settlement to the early 1840s. Local observers stated that "no employment as labourers can be depended on" between November and April. Additionally, even white workers "spread themselves throughout the country and labour the whole winter for no other compensation than their food."[41] Unfortunately, the scarcity of employment was worse for the Refugees because "persons very generally prefer White laboring people to the Blacks." Thus the Black Refugees did not "have an equal chance of obtaining their share of even the little labor that is wanted."[42] By 1816, 924 Refugees had settled at Preston and 504 at Hammonds Plains, located approximately fifteen and twenty kilometers from Halifax respectively.

Despite the Refugees' happiness with the opportunity to become landowning farmers, the government's settlement policy had fundamenta flaws that limited its usefulness. Lord Bathurst, assuming that the Refugees had been field slaves of one type or another, ignored the vastly different skills that the immigrants brought to Nova Scotia. The experience gained in the rice swamps of Georgia or through farming mixed agricultural produce in the Chesapeake had hardly prepared the Refugees for frontier farming in Nova Scotia. More important, the lands given to the Refugees at Preston and Hammonds Plains were among the worst in the entire colony. Earlier settlements of white Loyalists and former soldiers on these lands had failed miserably, with each group abandoning their farms as unimproved after the Revolutionary War.[43] Rocky and barren, the land at Preston and Hammonds Plains was surrounded by thick forests. The poverty of the soil in these areas was well known, with topographical studies of the time describing the soil as "inferior and stony."[44]

The condition of the soil at Hammonds Plains and Preston was thus hardly a secret. Throughout several decades, newspapers periodically mentioned the problem facing the Refugees by noting the sterile nature of "the land they have been given to cultivate."[45] In reports to the government, local people noted the near impossibility of cultivating the soil at the Refugee communities. "[T]hese lands are sterile and unproductive in the extraim [*sic*]; insomuch that it would be impossible for any persons to support families on them."[46] In August 1818 a government inspection of Preston illustrated some of the problems that the Refugees found at this settlement. In Section A, the problems of the land seemed extreme on Lots 16 through 18. On Lot 16, John Coats had died, and there were no improvements to his farm, while Lot 17 was described as "Very Barren." According to the inspector, Lot 18 was barren and its occupant "Dead."[47] In a petition to the government in 1841, the Refugees mentioned that their lands were swampy and sterile.[48] In an article published during the early 1850s, the *Halifax Monthly Magazine* referred to the Black Refugees as the "worst accident that ever befell" Preston and Nova Scotia. But this same article admitted that the land given to the former slaves was "barren and rocky, and incapable of properly supporting them."[49] Nevertheless, several individuals and families attempted to develop the soil.

These conditions required the Refugees to expend immense effort to clear a very small plot, then face a tiny harvest. Expatriates in Liberia faced comparable conditions. The land selected by the ACS for these settlers in Africa constituted a "poor choice" because "stretches of intractable forest covered most of the hilly peninsula, and rocky terrain made any substantial agricultural activity impossible."[50] In addition to settling the Refugees on some of the worst land in the colony, the Nova Scotia government also gave the new settlers only ten acres per head of household regardless of family size or previous service to the British government. Land given to white settlers varied depending on family size and service to the Crown, but according to the *Free Press* the government guaranteed "each man on his arrival . . . if he wishes it . . . *one hundred acres of land.*"[51] Perhaps the government did not want to give comparable amounts of land to the Refugees, who might become temporary settlers like the Black Loyalists or Jamaican Maroons. Indeed, less than six months after agreeing to resettle the Refugees at Preston and Hammonds Plains, the government still harbored the hope of removing them to a warmer climate.[52] In addition to these problems, the colonial government gave the Refugees tickets of location (licenses of occupation) instead of freehold grants, which they regularly gave to white settlers. Tickets of location did not allow the Refugees to sell their lands and move to other parts of British North America. Instead, they were forced to remain on their farms whether the land was partly productive or sterile.[53]

These land settlement policies embodied the contradictory and indecisive nature of the colonial government's attitude toward the Refugees. On the one hand, the government expected the African American settlers to provide for their own subsistence by occupying small farms; on the other hand, the government placed them on land that had very limited potential for agricultural production. Moreover, the occupation of ten acres of land simply could not provide enough food for individual families. In Nova Scotia, immigrants that had any chance of survival as farmers needed at least one hundred acres because the majority of land, with the exception of the rich Annapolis Valley, was not fertile. Thus, the government's claim that it wanted the Refugees to provide for their own subsistence simply did not match the realities of placing the black settlers on these small, infertile farms. Some of the Refugees' neighbors recalled the pathetic situation in 1838: "it would be impossible for any persons to support families on [the Refugees' land]—And no class of settlers, let their habits be ever so industrious could possibly maintain their families on lots of the same size and quality."[54] In the early 1840s, aging Refugees and their children likewise explained their poverty and difficulties through the prism of the failed land settlement policy. The root of their problem, they stated, was in "being placed by Government upon ten acre lots, of poor land, many of them including swamps and likewise entirely barren & unproductive, and none of them sufficient to yield subsistence for a family however skillfull [*sic*]."[55]

It is very important to note that the land given to the Refugees was poor enough on its own to make one question the motives of the government. One explanation for the government's contradictory policy is that it hoped to use the Refugees as a captive labor force tied to uneconomical land, with their only option being to work on the larger farms of white neighbors or as domestic servants.

Refugee Struggle

Despite these substantial obstacles, the Refugees attempted to create farming settlements out of the frontier wilderness in Nova Scotia. Determined to bestow some modicum of familiarity on their new settlements, the Refugees reproduced aspects of their regional identities during their initial settlement at Preston and Hammonds Plains. Refugees from a particular farm in Virginia or plantation in the Georgia Sea Islands tended to settle near others from the same farm or plantation. Some of the former slaves of Sea Island magnates John Couper and James Hamilton settled at Hammonds Plains, and many black Virginians at Preston.[56] For example, Robert Hamilton, Richard Hamilton, Kitness Hamilton, Jacob Hamilton, and Anthony Hamilton settled on Lots 7 through 12 in Hammonds Plains.[57] Moreover, the vast majority of Pierce Butler's former slaves also settled at Hammonds Plains.[58] At Preston, several Refugees hailed from the Chesapeake, settling near friends and relatives. Originally from Northumberland County but owned by different individuals, Daniel Taylor and Peter Craney established farms in Section A at Preston. The two ex-slaves of Virginian William Woodhouse, John and Henry, both settled in Section D.[59]

In settling together at Preston or Hammonds Plains, the Refugees from different parts of the U.S. South attempted to re-create familiar institutions and customs, from cooking to familial arrangements. If slave communities had been grounded in family and fictive kinship ties, then these relationships were continued on the rocky and swampy shores of Nova Scotia.[60] The continuation of folk culture, family ties, and mutual understanding while emerging from slavery created commonality in the black settlements that would eventually be submerged, but not totally lost, after the Refugees had been settled for several years. In the original settlement of Hammonds Plains and Preston, two distinct stages defined the Refugee experience. First, the settlers reproduced relationships and communities that had existed in the United States. Second, the shared experience of attempting to settle in the woods of Nova Scotia set the stage for the Refugees' individual and communal attempts to become industrious and viable farmers.

The Black Refugees spent their first months of settlement cutting down trees and clearing rocks in an attempt to grow potatoes, cabbage, peas, and turnips. Most managed to clear about half an acre per household or more in these first few months.[61] On these tiny plots most succeeded in planting crops, but severe frosts in 1815 and 1816 destroyed their agricultural produce. Despite these setbacks, the Refugees did not give up husbandry. In 1817 observers reported that the Refugees had made substantial improvements and the weather also seemed to cooperate. Yet this time rodents destroyed the Refugees' crops.[62] As a result of these repeated agricultural failures, the Refugees could not feed themselves and risked becoming government wards. In addition, the Refugees turned to each other for support, some caring for the children of parents who continued to work in the fields or who found low-pay jobs building roads or washing clothes. Although the community's crops were not destroyed by weather or rodents between 1818 and 1821, the foodstuffs produced barely provided subsistence for families. The few Refugees who had good harvests supplied their less fortunate neighbors, but in the process these benefactors also ran out of food. The problems of inadequate food were exacerbated by poor housing and lack of clothing. Thus, the Refugees all felt the difficulties of frontier farming and subsequent poverty.[63]

Within the context of struggling to become viable farmers, the Refugees also attempted to build homes to give the new community material foundations. The government expected that while they cleared their farms, the Refugees also should build homes, but it provided them with only minimal materials to do so. The Refugees could not make lumber to build housing from the trees they cut down, because the wood was needed for fuel. Although a few of the new settlers were able to construct houses, the majority were only flimsy structures that provided little protection from the winter elements. One visitor to the Refugee settlements described the houses as "being made of green materials, & neither proof against the wet or cold, & having no cellars under them & some even no floors."[64] Refugees with training in carpentry might have constructed better homes than those with no background in sawing or woodworking, but even those with well-honed skills could not create homes without adequate building materials and enough time to devote to construction. The Refugees used this difficult experience to develop a system of mutual support, as they did with the similarly difficult struggles of farming, and as they had done earlier to resist the worst excesses of slavery. Many Refugees who did not have their own housing lived in the houses of their neighbors. These men could not have survived without the help of community members willing to attempt to provide for themselves, their families, and less fortunate neighbors.

In 1818 an inspection of the Preston community revealed that several Refugees still had "no House." Yet one observer reported to the government that at least some Refugees had built "comfortable houses."[65] Others were engaged in "House Building," while successful farmer Richard Smothers had erected a "Double House."[66] Thus there was some variation within the Refugee communities, but the majority lived in small huts that barely provided shelter from the inclement weather. In 1821, after several crop failures, the housing seemed to have deteriorated. The huts, Captain Scott noted during a visit, "are of poor contrivance generally without cellars or if they are provided with that convenience are so badly constructed as to occasion the loss of their Potatoes the first severe frost."[67] The Refugees' trouble with building adequate housing must be understood in the context of having to expend vast amounts of energy to plant, tend, and harvest even the smallest crop. They simply did not have enough capital or time to devote to the building of substantial houses.

The problem of housing was made worse because of a lack of clothing for many Refugees. Surveyor General Charles Morris reported that the Refugees' lack of clothing exposed them to the "severity of the Weather."[68] The results of poverty left some families with literally no clothing, and government reports commonly referred to the "almost naked" state of several individuals, even during the winter.[69] The Refugees with some clothing were described as having nothing more than a "covering of rags for their bodies."[70] Philanthropic groups attempted to help the Refugees by knitting socks and other clothes after visiting the black settlements at Preston and Hammonds Plains and seeing that "the Clothing of a whole Family [was] scarcely sufficient to protect one of its inmates from the inclemency of the Weather."[71] The lack of sufficient clothing would persist, but slowly former slaves who had been trained as weavers and spinners started to provide the community with clothing, although this did not completely offset the shortage of coats, pants, stockings, and mittens.

In addition to the shortage of clothing, many Refugees usually ran out of food. Successive crop failures and growing families resulted in the community consistently struggling to feed itself. The government continually provided the Refugees with scanty rations to help stave off starvation. In 1815, after only a few months of settlement, local store owner Seth Coleman reported that the Refugees subsisted on "literlly [*sic*] nothing."[72] In better times, they relied on potatoes as their main source of food, along with berries, turnips, beans, Indian meal, and salt fish.[73] Food supply continued to be a problem for many decades. In 1827 a visitor to Hammonds Plains was struck by the "scanty portion" of potatoes that provided the only source of food for many families.[74] During the early 1830s crop failures again enveloped the black settlements, and in 1833 Preston farmers had only several bushels of potatoes to feed hundreds of people.[75] After an epidemic of scarlet fever at Hammonds Plains from 1826 to 1827, following successive years of crop failures, the Refugees were near starvation, and they had become "indifferent to nearly everything" by 1834. An observer feared that these Refugees might "perish" unless given rations or moved to another part of the colony to find work.[76] The less fortunate farmers at Hammonds Plains were reduced to begging for food from their more prosperous neighbors and without their kindness would have perished.[77] In 1836 the community at Preston continued to struggle as the farmers who "every season make good Crops" were faced by a "number of distressed beings who surround them [and] are continually begging of their substance."[78]

The lack of adequate food and clothing at Hammonds Plains created a difficult situation in which the most basic comforts of life were denied to many Refugees. But they attempted to overcome these problems by redoubling their farming efforts and forming families. Emerging from slavery, the African American settlers attached great importance to family life. Despite the various troubles, the new settlements represented an opportunity to raise children and foster conjugal relationships that had been denied to many during slavery. The Refugees realized that the families they formed in Nova Scotia could not be sold apart or destroyed by the whims of an owner. Most Refugee households consisted of two adults and at least one child. In 1815 at the settlement in Preston, nearly all households with children consisted of two adults. Similarly, at Hammonds Plains over 90 percent of households had at least two adults (probably married) five years after the conclusion of the War of 1812.[79] The various family structures in Refugee society also included extended kinship networks that mitigated the difficulties of farming and settlement. According to an 1816 government report, nearly twenty Refugees were living in "houses with other Negroes," including older and sick men unable to help out on the farms.[80] Hope Maxwell and James Sanders resided together in Hammonds Plains with an adult woman, but the household also included two male children under the age of seven. At the same settlement, Josh Johnson and an adult woman (probably his wife) lived with Mary Parker and four young children. Such households fostered cooperative arrangements that helped the Refugees survive their first years in Nova Scotia.[81] These extended family units provided the first bulwark against racism, poverty, hunger, and illness. The formation of families and extended kinship networks thus forged new bonds between settlers, and these new relationships became the foundations of their new communities in Nova Scotia.[82]

The Black Refugees faced so many obstacles—including severe climate change, racial discrimination, indifferent government policies, sickness, and poverty—that, taken together, it is quite remarkable that the Refugees survived at all. But they did more than survive. The Refugees created families and the beginnings of communities that would serve and sustain Nova Scotia's black population. In addition to their struggles with farming, poverty, and poor housing, these African American expatriates developed shared experience and commonality that would be crucial to their developing identity as a distinct group of African British North Americans. Although the Refugees came from various backgrounds, they shared the hardships of frontier farming and poverty in a strange new land. These hardships encouraged the Refugees to rely on one another for support. Sharing food or housing among new friends resulted in the Refugees developing a tightly knit community that refused to separate, despite the best efforts of the colonial government to resettle them in Trinidad or Africa.

Trinidad

From the moment the Refugees arrived in Nova Scotia, the colonial government attempted to get rid of the new settlers. Local officials wanted to remove them because the permanent settlement of over 1,600 ex-slaves was perceived as an unbearable drain on the colonial treasury. The imperial government also wanted to resettle the Refugees in a "warmer climate" even before they had been permanently settled at Preston and Hammonds Plains.[83] The Nova Scotian government held attitudes toward free blacks that reflected prevalent beliefs among supporters of the American Colonization Society. Generally, black freedom in a society recently removed from slavery and still overtly hostile to people of African descent was an anomaly. This anomaly caused problems for politicians and intellectuals who believed that black people's inferiority made political inclusion and social equality unthinkable. Yet the idea of reenslaving blacks seemed inhumane; thus black freedom could be conceived of only in a context outside North America. Strongly supporting this view, Nova Scotia's government, under Lord Dalhousie, embarked on a systematic program to remove the Refugees from Nova Scotia between 1816 and 1820. Dedicated to the idea that the Refugees should leave Nova Scotia, Dalhousie had no firm view of where they should go, vacillating between sites in the West Indies as well as on the West African coast. Dalhousie even wanted to enter into a treaty with the United States, as "it would be most desirable to restore [the Refugees] to their masters in America."[84] Yet to the shock of his lordship, before this plan could be put into action, the Refugees mobilized to reject their planned reenslavement. Eventually, the government established an arrangement to resettle the Refugees in Trinidad, a place where some might be reunited with old friends and family members who had chosen to settle there after the War of 1812 instead of Nova Scotia.[85]

The plan to remove the Refugees to Trinidad developed slowly over a few years because the colonial government did not have enough money to transport what it assumed would be a large number of Refugees seeking resettlement in the West Indies. Finally, after securing the support of the Trinidad government and the lords commissioners of His Majesty's Treasury, the government had enough funds to send the Refugees to Trinidad. Although a few of the new settlers had expressed interest in removal to a warmer climate, the majority of Refugees rejected the government's plans.[86] They realized that people with ideas antithetical to the interests of their community had conceived of the colonization scheme. The recolonization of blacks to Trinidad had been calculated to appease hostile whites in the colonial government and in the local population. Despite the government's best efforts, fewer than one hundred Refugees migrated to the distant British colony, representing less than 6 percent of all Refugees.[87] Of those who left, the majority were from Hammonds Plains, with a smaller contingent from Preston.[88]

The Refugees who remained behind had several reasons for staying in Nova Scotia. Their rejection of the government's resettlement plan mirrored African American attitudes in New England toward the American Colonization Society. The ACS attempted to deny black people social, political, economic, and legal opportunities in the United States, while claiming to support black improvement by shipping African Americans across the Atlantic Ocean to Africa. This denial of black political and social inclusion under the guise of humanitarianism defined racial attitudes in New England and Nova Scotia. The thought of black and white integration struck many as politically unthinkable and socially repugnant. Although Nova Scotia did not have organizations dedicated to the removal of the Black Refugees, the ACS found support among the white population in Halifax. In New England, the movement for the removal of free blacks found supporters in nearly every state, but ironically one of the most vigorous local auxiliaries was in Vermont, which had a very small black population. During an address to the Vermont Colonization Society in 1826, John Hough asserted that if allowed to remain in the United States, free blacks would continue being "the same degraded, unenlightened, unprincipled, and abandoned race . . . equally worthless and noxious in themselves and equally a nuisance to the public."[89] As a result, the removal of blacks promised the "prospect of signal benefits" to the United States.[90] The editor of Nova Scotia's *Free Press*, while questioning the practicality of removing blacks to Africa, also considered it undeniable that "getting rid of a large and increasing portion of people of colour" would greatly benefit the colony.[91]

The proposals for removing blacks from New England and Nova Scotia were resisted by the black populations in both areas for similar reasons. Most black New Englanders found the American Colonization Society's plans to be an offensive scheme cooked up to separate free blacks from their enslaved brethren. Moreover, they believed that the ACS wanted to strip free blacks of citizenship rights that they had earned by fighting in the War of 1812. Iconoclastic author David Walker summed up the position of many free blacks by stating in 1829 that the United States "is as much ours as it is the whites."[92] Afro-Yankees had established several communities with deep roots as illustrated by the vibrant black populations ranging from Portsmouth to Boston to Providence. These African Americans were not willing to risk the destruction of their communities to resettle in a new country. Most significantly, the majority of free blacks simply believed that the ACS and other colonization advocates in the white community had little interest in doing any favors for people of color. In Nova Scotia, the Black Refugees also refused to believe that the government had their best interests in mind. In fact, they held that the colonial government wanted to "sell them to their former Masters in the United States."[93]

Also, the Refugees did not want to give up on the communities that they had started to build at Hammonds Plains and Preston. They realized that removal to Trinidad would mean the destruction of new friendships and families that had been established under the difficult conditions of emigration and settlement in Nova Scotia. The Refugees refused to realign and reform their identity by moving again to a new location, as the Jamaican Maroons and some of the Black Loyalists had done several years earlier. The Refugees' struggle for settlement and citizenship in Nova Scotia had provided shared experience and mutual support systems that would make removal to Trinidad or anywhere else nothing more than an attempt to destroy the newly forged bonds of community.

The decision of the majority of Refugees to remain in Nova Scotia demonstrates that in this sense they used the border to sharply demarcate the prospect of American reenslavement from their current freedom in British North America. Despite the struggles associated with settlement, the formation of families and communities free from slavery had drawn a strict line between their lives as slaves in the southern states and as nominally free persons in Nova Scotia. Yet the small number of blacks who migrated to Trinidad indicates that the Refugees did not entertain a unified or simple understanding of the border or perhaps that they saw the whole Atlantic as a place of settlement for blacks. The Trinidad migrants saw the border in more fluid terms than their brethren and risked leaving British North America for another British colony despite the fact that an unscrupulous ship's captain could have sold them into slavery in the Caribbean or the southern United States before they reached their final destination. The border was slightly more fluid for the Trinidad migrants who saw shifting meanings of freedom between the Caribbean colony and British North America. In contrast, the majority of Refugees viewed the border, at least in this one example, in hard and fast terms that if crossed could result in reenslavement.

The Black Refugees' decision to remain in Nova Scotia was a crucial moment in their development as a distinct group of African British North Americans. By rejecting the government's offer to move them to Trinidad, they differentiated themselves from previous groups of black immigrants to Nova Scotia. The Refugees refused to bow to the racism of the general population and government, while claiming the right to remain in Nova Scotia. Once the decision to stay in Nova Scotia had been made, the Refugees redoubled their efforts to improve their economic situation and build community institutions in the shadow of persistent racial discrimination.

Chapter 4

Working Folks

IN NEW ENGLAND, the problems of severely limited job opportunities, along with increasing competition from European immigrants, resulted in many free blacks working in unstable and low-paying forms of employment. In Nova Scotia, a similar process occurred, but the work patterns of the Black Refugees were unique because the urban center of Halifax had nearby black hinterlands where many Refugees combined urban labor with farming. The rural component of the Refugees' working life offers many suggestions as to how black southerners adjusted to the economy of a new environment. This chapter outlines the contours of poverty and economic struggle that partly defined the Refugees' experience in Nova Scotia, while highlighting the former slaves' various responses to these problems.

Several scholars have studied the work patterns of free African Americans. Free black employment in the northern United States was defined by few opportunities, sporadic employment, increasing competition from white immigrants, a fluid line between the economically stable and those less fortunate, and a significant percentage of light-skinned blacks in skilled or entrepreneurial positions. Work was, first of all, restricted to the lowest levels of pay and status. According to historians Lois Horton and James Oliver Horton, many African Americans in the northern United States suffered from "the racially restricted system of employment [which] practically guaranteed that many free blacks would become poor, dependent, and, perhaps, criminal."[1] The majority of black people in New England worked in unskilled or semiskilled occupations, but these categories do not capture the complexity and plurality of tasks that African Americans undertook to feed their families.

In *Making a Living: The Work Experience of African-Americans in New England,* Robert Hall and Michael Harvey note that in "New England cities black male workers often pieced together a living by plying several trades."[2] These various trades ranged from domestic service to dock work to skilled occupations. Black women also pieced together several occupations but found steadier employment as domestic servants. Similar to seaboard towns and cities such as Portland and Boston, Halifax was a coastal urban environment that offered several forms of wage labor and access to work in the maritime industry, on the docks or at sea. In Boston, Providence, and Portsmouth, free people of color engaged in several forms of employment that the Black Refugees also performed in Nova Scotia.

In Boston, unskilled African Americans worked at a variety of occupations to make ends meet. During the 1830s and 1840s, black people working at unskilled or semiskilled occupations might have comprised between 70 and 80 percent of the black workforce; in 1850, 72 percent of blacks worked unskilled or semiskilled jobs.[3] The unskilled work they performed was irregular, poorly compensated, and physically demanding. These forms of employment included day laboring, seafaring, or domestic service. Again, however, the high percentage of African Americans in the unskilled category hides some important differences. James Oliver Horton and Lois Horton highlight these differences in their study *Black Bostonians.*

> Although the vast majority of Boston's black workers were unskilled, there were important distinctions between those who worked on a temporary daily basis and those employed more regularly. Traditional class divisions are inadequate for understanding the occupational structure of black society. The occupations of porter and laborer, for example, were generally considered of equal worth in white society—both lower-class jobs. Yet, for blacks, the job of porter was more desirable because most black laborers were employed on the docks where the work was more sporadic and seasonal than that available in the downtown commercial areas for black porters.[4]

During the same period, 26.7 percent of Boston's African Americans held skilled or entrepreneurial positions. Those in the middling ranks worked at artisans' trades, including hairdresser or blacksmith, while others enjoyed their own small businesses. At the very top of Black Boston's occupational ladder (1.3 percent) was a small cadre of lawyers, doctors, ministers, and educators.[5]

In Providence, as in Boston, the familiar structure of racially restricted menial occupations dominated the work patterns of many African Americans. These occupations included seafaring, domestic service, day laboring, and cooking.[6] In 1850, 67.3 percent of blacks worked in unskilled occupations. Like their counterparts in Boston, many of Providence's black workers "went from menial task to menial task, unable to count on regular employment, eking out a living from day to day."[7] Nevertheless, a few families accumulated property, and other individuals held positions as small businessmen. As of 1850 Providence's black professional class included ministers, teachers, and clerks. Ten years later the black community in Providence included a few doctors and an engineer.[8]

Portsmouth, New Hampshire, has recently had its African American heritage examined through the work of Mark Sammons and Valerie Cunningham. In this northern New England city, as slavery ended, blacks found that their occupational "options were limited to tasks so menial and subservient that virtually no whites would do them."[9] One of the most important forms of employment for blacks in Portsmouth was work as mariners. Although this type of employment could be dangerous, mariners could earn decent pay, had occupational mobility, and could enjoy "special esteem among family and friends."[10]

In terms of employment, Nova Scotia and other British North American colonies did not represent a promised land compared with Boston, Providence, or Portsmouth. But economic prospects were much better in Upper Canada than in Nova Scotia. In comparison with the later-arriving American Fugitives in Canada West (after 1841), the Refugees seem to have had much less opportunity for economic improvement. Although the Fugitives had access to better land than the Refugees, many still migrated to towns and urban areas such as Windsor, Chatham, or Amherstburg. Here black people found employment on "nearby road, rail, and canal projects." It is true that the number of blacks in Upper Canada and later Canada West dwarfed the smaller population in Nova Scotia during the mid–nineteenth century. Yet this should not obscure the facts that American Fugitives opened shops and nearly one-half of "Chatham's black workers were skilled or semiskilled; many of those were shoemakers, carpenters, and blacksmiths." The black community also included an emerging professional class that published newspapers—something else that was absent from the ranks of the Black Refugees.[11]

The Refugees' work patterns shared several similarities with those of their counterparts in New England. But one of the unique elements in the development of the Black Refugee community was the economic struggle the Refugees endured as farmers in Preston and Hammonds Plains. The difficulties of building settlements, clearing land, harvesting crops on the sterile soil of Preston and Hammonds Plains, and finding seasonal employment had a leveling effect on the community. The trying conditions of frontier farming in Nova Scotia resulted in a poverty-stricken economic structure that dominated nearly every Refugee household. As a result, the Refugees relied on one another for help with food and labor, which according to one government official left the new settlers in an "equality in wretchedness."[12] What this observer called wretched was simply part of the story of a distinct community that had developed through shared experience and mutual support. Within the contours of this type of poverty another story emerged as the Refugees responded in several different ways to carve out as much independence as possible in an economy that often left them dependent on government rations. The Refugee work experiences were much more than the simple struggle against white racism and indifference. Racism curtailed opportunities for the Refugees, but the responses to this were not unified, homogeneous, or simple.

The Refugees did not passively accept the overwhelmingly difficult challenges associated with frontier farming and sporadic urban employment. In attempting to achieve a measure of autonomy and meaningful freedom, they pursued two options. First, some Refugees continued farming and petitioned the government for more land or occupied abandoned lots in an effort to wrest a living from the sterile soil. Most important, these farmers increasingly sold their produce and other items at the Halifax public market. At this place of commerce, the Refugees became fixtures and were noted for their entrepreneurial spirit.[13] Slowly, at Hammonds Plains and Preston, a few Refugees acquired more acreage, land grants, and livestock. This did not solve their farming difficulties, but it would be a mistake to simply view the experience of the Black Refugees in bleak and static terms.

Second, many Refugees abandoned cultivating those lands. Successive crop failures, rocky and swampy farms, and small returns on long hours of agricultural work led some Refugees to Halifax for better economic prospects. Those former slaves who had been trained in a specialized occupation saw the urban market of Halifax as an opportunity to use their special skills, an opportunity that frontier farming in Preston or Hammonds Plains did not offer. In Halifax, the Refugees engaged in wage labor or sporadic day-to-day employment, such as breaking stones for roads. A few left the colony and found work on the high seas. However, the work experience of the Black Refugees should not be understood as a linear progression from rural farming to urban labor. Although Preston and

Hammonds Plains suffered from out-migration during the 1820s and 1830s, a core of farmers and families remained at these settlements. The complex and multilayered patterns of work performed by the Refugees defy simple explanation, but their employment patterns might best be described as a combination of persistent farming and innovative urban laboring.

It is worth asking why some of the Refugees decided to remain on sterile and difficult farms when they could have migrated to Halifax or left the colony for another part of British North America. Several scholars have stressed the importance of land to ex-slaves or free blacks.[14] In *Southern Seed, Northern Soil*, historian Stephen Vincent highlights the significance of landownership among black migrants who developed Beech and Roberts, settlements on the Indiana frontier.[15] Possession of land deflected some of the worst aspects of racial discrimination and brutal wage labor. Moreover, landownership offered African Americans some modicum of autonomy. The history of southern slaves owning property carried over to Nova Scotia, where the Refugees sought the recognition of their brethren regarding land and also from the colonial government. By obtaining freedom in Nova Scotia the Refugees, while struggling to obtain ownership of their farms, were in the process of developing a legal consciousness that led them to challenge the government's policy of providing black settlers with tickets of location as opposed to freehold grants.

The importance of land to defining freedom and minimizing discrimination is certainly part of the Refugees' story. Yet they were not as fortunate as the migrants who founded the Beech and Roberts settlements in Indiana. Having access to farmland offered the Refugees some protection from a hostile and difficult urban labor market, but it also left many of them partly dependent on either government rations or the support of their neighbors. Thus the linkage between possessing land and its connection to autonomy was problematic for the Refugees. Although they lived on farms, the distress of being stuck with sterile soil was compounded by the fact that the Refugees did not own their farms outright. Within the larger context of the significance of landownership for black people in North America, the Refugees wanted not only to work the land but also to own the farms, even if successful agricultural production remained elusive.

During the difficult early years of settlement, the Refugees' petitions to the government evinced a deep commitment to agriculture. From these documents, it is clear that they tied the possession of land to economic prospects, self-confidence, and autonomy. In 1822 Jacob Allen informed the government that after years of struggling with the soil he wanted more land to follow "the calling of husbandry" because it was his only "prospect" for survival in Nova Scotia.[16] One year later a single mother of several children petitioned the government for increased acreage as she had no other way to maintain "herself or family but by the calling of husbandry."[17] In 1836 a local official attempted to explain to the government why the Refugees wanted to stay on such barren lands. "They seem to have some attachment to the soil they have cultivated, poor and barren as it is." This official, E. H. Lowe, believed that some Refugees seemed "willing to remove to any other part of this province, where the land is more fertile and a larger portion can be given to them."[18] But any such move had to include the possibility of landownership.

Farming

The hope of controlling their own land resulted in the Refugees remaining at Preston and Hammonds Plains long after their farms had been exhausted. In the beginning, the Black Refugees simply attempted to make their small farms productive. But, for the reasons already discussed, those determined to remain as farmers had to change their techniques. As Vincent notes, "black farm families' overall success or failure normally hinged upon their access to farm land, the demand for farm labor, and their abilities as farmers."[19] Unfortunately, the Refugees' access to land was extremely limited, but some were able to obtain more acreage. By 1818 an important shift had taken place among a select group of black farmers at Preston and Hammonds Plains. It had become clear that the ten-acre farms simply could not produce sufficient food or supplies for the growing families of the Refugees. The small farms were supposed to provide enough food for the Refugees to stay off government assistance, but this rarely occurred, because their lots also needed to furnish a supply of firewood, fuel, and enough wood to build ladders or other products for market. As their original acreage became exhausted of productive woodlots and decent soil, some Refugees petitioned the government for more land.[20] Between 1819 and 1830, a number of Refugee household heads demanded larger farms from the government because, as nearly every petitioner contended, the new settlers could not feed their families, owing to the "size and Sterile quality" of the plots.[21] Refugee petitions ranged from those made by single families to ones from several families applying together, possibly hoping to farm their land communally. In a few cases, over thirty families applied for land together. Although the petitions are very valuable in demonstrating the Refugees' attempts to increase their land-holdings, they are not necessarily an accurate guide to the amount of land actually granted even if the council approved a certain amount of acreage. Nevertheless, they are the best source for understanding the Refugees' farming practices.

Described by government officials as an "able and industrious man," one of the earliest petitioners from Preston was Richard Smothers, who had cleared two acres of land by May 1816.[22] In 1819 Smothers petitioned for over one hundred acres. He realized that to be a viable farmer in Nova Scotia it was necessary to obtain enough land not only for fuel but also to compensate for the possibility that much of the new acreage might be sterile.[23] The same year another farmer at Preston, Septimus Clark, petitioned the government. Clark had diversified his food production by growing other vegetables in addition to potatoes, but he had exhausted the land and would be "destitute of wood for fuel." As a result, the married father of five children asked for over two hundred acres to continue his progress. The surveyor general offered Clark only an additional fifty acres.[24] In 1820 Suther Blair, "one of the oldest of the Preston Settlers," wrote that he had by "hard labour got as much as six acres under cultivation . . . [and possessed] one cow and expects to make fodder sufficient for two." Yet Blair was quickly running out of land for "fuel and pasture." He applied for the lot next to him, which had been abandoned by a neighbor who had "given up the hope of making a living" in Preston. The government approved transfer of the small lot to Blair.[25] The younger generation of Refugees also petitioned for land. For example, in 1824 Gabriel Hall noted that he had been "too young at the time of the formation of the settlement in Preston to have lands allotted to him." Like most other petitioners, Hall maintained that he had "no means of making a living but by husbandry, and intends immediately to settle on and improve the lands he is now about asking your Honour for." The government preliminarily approved Hall for twenty-five acres.[26]

Throughout the 1820s, individual Refugees petitioned the government for larger farms. In a few cases these petitioners were willing to leave the black settlements and, as one of them stated, "go any distance into the woods" to obtain land.[27] This petitioner, David Page, had escaped from Virginia and was listed as a sawyer. In Nova Scotia, he attempted to maintain himself through farming combined with woodworking.[28] Yet the vast majority of petitioners wanted to remain close to the community, while increasing their landholdings. In 1820 Bray Cooper petitioned the government for a larger farm. In May 1816 Cooper had cleared three-quarters of an acre and built a small hut for his family. Over the next four years Cooper improved his holding. As his sons matured, Cooper realized that the "small lot" could not keep "himself and his sons employed." In addition to his two sons, ages seventeen and twenty, he also had to take care of two small children. Dedicated to farming, Cooper maintained that his only hope for subsistence and income was through "the calling of husbandman." Cooper asked the government for one hundred acres for himself and fifty acres for each son. Unfortunately, the surveyor concluded that Cooper "cannot expect to be placed on a better footing than the whole population of Blacks in Preston." Cooper's initiative was not rewarded: the government approved only fifty acres for him. His children could "once of lawful age . . . petition for themselves."[29]

Similarly, in 1823, after nearly a decade in Nova Scotia, Basil Crowd petitioned the government for additional land. He had experienced difficulty during his early settlement at Preston and by May 1816 had cleared only a quarter of an acre.[30] Nevertheless, by the early 1820s he had exhausted his land; the small, barren lot could not support him, his wife, and six children. Crowd claimed that "there are not three Acres capable of cultivation out of the whole location, so that he finds it impossible to earn even the common necessaries of Life." He asked for one hundred acres, but government approved only twenty-five for him.[31] His neighbor, Solomon Crawley, had also settled at Preston early on and by May 1816 had cleared more land than Crowd. He stated that the government had settled him "on one of the Smallest Lotts." Crawley was married and had five children who simply could not be sustained on ten acres of sterile land. He was bereft of fuel, and his family had been "suffering." The government approved Crawley for fifty acres.[32] These grants brought the Crowd and Crawley households only to a bare minimum of acreage to support subsistence farming. Indeed, in 1841 the government admitted that "in this severe climate at least 100 acres would be required for each family in order to afford a proper supply of fuel." Despite this admission, the government still blamed the Refugees for having "wasted their fuel by burning the wood into charcoal."[33]

Some Refugees engaged in communal petitioning for land, although this did not mean that they necessarily farmed the land as a group once the government granted it. They could have broken the new grant into separate segments and farmed individually. On the other hand, group petitioning did sometimes result in families sharing food, clothing, cooking, farming, and child care, which seemed to promise more success. The former slaves realized that creating and expanding kinship networks might alleviate the problems of farming. The slow mixing of American slaves from different backgrounds through communal land petitioning also marked an important opportunity for expanding kinship connections and reinforcing the bonds of the emerging communities at Preston and Hammonds Plains. New connections and family alliances could also allow for greater access to land and eventual property ownership.

At Preston a few families petitioned early on for land they would jointly farm. In 1820, for example, William Bunday, Winslow Sparkes, Henry Lee, and his son applied for larger farms, as the land they held in Preston was swampy and sterile. Incredibly, their tickets of location accounted for about twenty acres among the four men and their families. They hoped that by applying jointly for thirty acres they would induce the government to offer them enough land so that they could continue as farmers. The government approved the petitioners for thirty acres to be parceled out equally, but this would still hardly be enough to provide subsistence.[34] In 1822 Naith Johnson and James Downing hoped to settle their families together. They had suffered through the crop failures of the early 1820s, and the prospect of obtaining more land and sharing farming duties presented a better option than remaining on their small lots in Preston. Their original farms were both "short of ten acres." Downing and Johnson were "willing to go any where into the woods" to obtain more land. They asked for one hundred acres, but the government thought twenty-five acres a more reasonable amount.[35] At Hammonds Plains in 1819 a group of thirty-six Refugees applied for land that had been abandoned. This group had already built houses and improved the abandoned land.[36] This type of large-scale petitioning was rare, but it points to the willingness of the Refugees to change their tactics in order to compensate for the soil's poor quality by putting more of it into production. Fifteen years later at the same settlement, thirty households paid "Sixty" pounds of Nova Scotia currency for nearly six hundred acres. These families were granted the land.[37]

Four men—William Dear (also spelled Deer, Dare, and Dair), John Collins, Nace or Naith Leach, and Henry Broad—initiated an especially intriguing group petition at Preston in 1824. After several years of attempting to create viable farms, the petitioners concluded "that owing to the limited size of their lots, they cannot make anything like a comfortable living for themselves and their families." Dear and Leach were both married with three children, while Collins and Broad were also married with one and two children respectively. The government apparently still expected these families to support a total of seventeen people on their original settlements totaling less than fifty acres of land. As a result they were willing to move to "the back woods of Musquodobit," where they might be granted larger farms and "have some better prospect of obtaining a living." Like other farmers at Preston, these men maintained that they were "all husbandmen and depend on that calling for a livelihood." The petitioners hoped for 150 acres each, but the government offered preliminary approval for only 100 acres each.[38]

At least two of the petitioners, William Dear and John Collins, continued to farm, the government granting each man additional farms in 1842—nearly two decades after the joint request. In the meantime, Dear had emerged as one of the most successful among the small group of Refugee entrepreneurs. In addition to his farming, Dear and his wife established the Stag Hotel near Preston, a popular spot for travelers and other visitors that remained well regarded throughout the nineteenth century.[39] Dear advertised that at the Stag Hotel visitors would find "the best Cheer, Brandy, Whisky, Hop, Spruce, and Ginger Beer." Moreover, he promised clean beds and provisions for horses, while promising to "suit the Public taste, 'tis clear, Bill Dear will Labour, so will his dearest dear."[40] Dear's success as an innkeeper is unique, but the story of his occupational plurality and his attempt to acquire more land fits into a wider Refugee pattern.

Petitioning for land was not the only route that the Refugees pursued in order to continue farming. As several Refugee households abandoned lands at Preston and Hammonds Plains, their brethren who wanted to continue farming acquired increased access to land. It is true that some of this land might have been of poor quality, but the opportunity to increase landholdings remained an important goal for a core group of Refugees. At Hammonds Plains, several individuals occupied the abandoned lots of their neighbors. For example, Joseph Pence had originally settled at Lot 2, but by the mid-1830s William Leigh lived at that small farm. Phoebe Lee decided to continue farming on the land vacated by Alexander Cooper. Kindness Hamilton originally settled at Lot 29, but by 1835 Rose Hamilton occupied that farm. From an inspection of the settlement at Hammonds Plains completed in the summer of 1835, it is clear that despite some of the problems with the soil, several Refugees were willing to use formerly abandoned lots for their own farm production.[41] According to the inspection, "24 Families has settled themselves on lots [for] which they have no card."[42] In Preston, eager farmers applied for abandoned land if there was any hope that it might be made productive. In 1818 the death of Richard Gross resulted in "several applicants for this Lot No. 19."[43] In 1842 the government granted several Refugees lots that they had not been originally assigned. For example, William Dear, Marada Stanley, and John Collins obtained extra land. And although Armiston Currie had not originally settled in Section A, the government granted him four farms in this section.[44] Seemingly, Currie had taken time to improve these farms to the point that the government willingly granted him the land.

Perhaps realizing that petitioning for more land usually met with disappointment, few Refugees made such requests. Instead many continued to farm their small lots at Preston and Hammonds Plains. When this did not provide them with subsistence, these Refugees relied on a combination of help from their neighbors, government assistance, and extra work in the country or in Halifax. Many Black Refugees supplemented their meager farming income with an array of jobs ranging from domestic service to wage labor in Halifax. In the late 1820s and again in 1836, Preston weaver William McLaughlin attempted to employ several Refugee women at Preston because "the black women are generally good spinners." He hoped that the government would provide wool so that the women could "procure a livelihood," but the colonial government did not support this endeavor.[45]

The most important source of income for the Refugees was selling goods—including vegetables, fruits, fish, and wooden items such as brooms or barrels—at the Halifax public market. Many Refugees, especially women, had been familiar with selling items at local markets in Georgia and the Chesapeake during slavery. After settling in Nova Scotia, they applied familiar techniques and tactics in a new environment.[46] The Refugees' settlements at Preston and Hammonds Plains were fifteen and twenty kilometers from the Halifax public market respectively. The Preston Refugees had to walk along poorly constructed roads barely passable in the winter before taking a ferry across Halifax harbor to the town.[47] At times, the Preston Refugees walked around Bedford Basin if they did not wish to use the ferry. The Hammonds Plains Refugees endured an even longer walk to the public market. One visitor to Nova Scotia witnessed Refugees traveling to the market in the late 1820s and described the scene in his *Letters from Nova Scotia:* "In summer, large parties of negroes [*sic*] may be seen entering the town by seven in the morning, having walked all that distance, to sell the wild fruits they gather in the woods, and to procure their supplies. In winter too, they are seen bringing in a few shingles or brooms, and, with the exception of some of the young women, always clothed in rags, exhibiting the picture of wretchedness."[48] Selling produce at the market seemed to be a communitywide activity. According to one newspaper in 1832, "a line" of Refugees going to the market extended "for half a mile."[49] In accessing the public market, the Refugees joined other

Nova Scotian farmers who relied on the sale of produce in Halifax for subsistence.

The countryside near Preston and Hammonds Plains offered the Refugees various berries and flowers to sell at the market. In particular, strawberries, raspberries, and blueberries garnered the Refugees a decent income. The Refugees dominated the trade in berries, supplying Halifax with hundreds of bushels of various berries that locals used for "preserving purposes."[50] One observer believed that the Refugees had no other way to make a living but through the sale of "wild berries."[51] Joseph Howe, a newspaper editor and proprietor, described Refugee women as "pouring strawberries down the throats" of the local population.[52] In 1850 the *British Colonist* reported that Hammonds Plains blacks had asked for assistance in delivering blueberries to Halifax.[53] By the 1850s and 1860s, several travelers noted the Refugees' control over the colony's trade in berries. During the 1860s, Elizabeth Frame saw several black people with "birch barks resting on their heads, filled with strawberries," which they offered for sale.[54]

In addition to berries, the Refugees sold a variety of other items at the market. Although it might have sounded overly optimistic when Surveyor General Charles Morris claimed in 1815 that the Refugees could make a living from selling berries, these fruits did become their main source of income. Moreover, his suggestion that they provide the market at Halifax with "laths, shingles, hoop poles, Brooms, axehelves, oar rafters, Scantling, Clapboards" was also followed by the Refugees.[55] Some Refugee males had worked as sawyers or woodworkers in the Chesapeake and applied these skills to supplement their farming income. The *Novascotian* described the Refugees as bringing "brooms, charcoal, tabs, and trout" to Halifax.[56] As forest surrounded their settlements, the Refugees used this to supply Halifax with various products made from timber including hoops, brooms, baskets, and tool handles.[57] The Halifax public market allowed many Refugees to continue as farmers because it provided one of the few outlets to sell goods for cash. The market provided sustenance and stability, which remained elusive for most of the Refugees' economic endeavors.

The goal of land ownership kept many Refugees at Hammonds Plains and Preston. By the early 1840s, the government had finally changed their tickets of location to grants. The change occurred because of years of persistent protest by the Refugees; it also signaled the transition in Nova Scotia's political culture from Tory-style paternalism to Reformism.[58] For many emerging Reformers, the colony's land policy contradicted their ideas of fair play. They believed that converting the Refugees' tickets of location to freehold grants would give the local black population an opportunity to compete on equal terms. Yet the granting of land was not simply a blessing. With greater integration into the capitalist economy, Refugee farmers risked new forms of debt and possible dispossession.

Despite the problems with the land at Hammonds Plains, various Refugees owned every lot as of the summer of 1835. Interestingly, many of these very same lots were unoccupied. Indeed, thirty-six of the eighty-two farms were not being used. Yet the importance of landownership, even when the land was not occupied, emerges from the inspection of the lots performed in 1835.[59] The unoccupied farms could have been seen as providing a means of escape, if necessary, from the nearly all-white settlements in Halifax County or the harshness of the wage labor market. Perhaps the unused farms would be rented or sold at a later time. For the Refugees at Preston, the process of gaining grants for their farms was also a long struggle that involved much protest; their plight was similar to that of black southerners in the United States during the early Reconstruction period.

For many black American southerners, freedom was tied to the possession of land but, more importantly, to the legal ownership of farms. After the American Civil War, black southerners faced hostile northern officials who refused at first to recognize their claims to property. Eventually the Southern Claims Commission started to respect the former slaves' claims to property.[60] In Nova Scotia, the Preston Refugees fought a long struggle to get the colonial government to recognize their claims to ownership of the settled land. In petitioning the government, the Refugees demonstrated an understanding of the colonial legal structure and the importance of property holding to the ideal of freedom or liberty. Despite receiving several petitions from Preston Refugees about the sterility of the soil, government officials continually refused to change the tickets of location to freehold grants. From the Refugees' struggle to obtain land grants, two important themes emerge. First, the Refugees were not willing to see their community destroyed by breaking into smaller groups and moving to various regions throughout Nova Scotia. Second, landownership remained an important community ideal that the Refugees fought for, insisting that the government acknowledge it. The poor conditions of Preston had led some Refugees to consider moving in smaller groups to other parts of the colony, but in the end they rejected this idea.[61] The Preston Refugees were "determined to remain: nor will they consent as I [Lieutenant Governor Colin Campbell] have proposed to be distributed in detachments, in different parts of the Province."[62]

Eventually, the lieutenant governor realized that the only way to reduce the amount of government support needed by the Refugees was to grant them land. A letter Campbell wrote to the imperial government reveals the Refugees' land problems by highlighting their farms' "small dimensions" and the fact that they were "miserably sterile."[63] Campbell hoped that the imperial government would be willing to incur the expense of moving the community to "more fruitful Soil" in Nova Scotia. Not surprisingly the British government refused because, as far as Colonial Secretary Lord Glenelg was concerned, Campbell entertained a "mistaken & mischievous notion" that if the Refugees "were to subsist at all, it must be as proprietors of Land and not as Laborers for hire."[64]

This predictable reply only made issues worse between the colonial government and the Black Refugees. During the late 1830s and early 1840s, the Preston Refugees petitioned the government to turn their tickets of location into freehold grants. After twenty years of farming land that they did not own, the Refugees were angry. They had "repeatedly applied for their Grant" but without any success. As a result the Refugees asked that the government "take such measures that Memorialists [the petitioners] may receive a grant for the land which they have been so long improving, to include all the land which they occupy in Preston."[65] This petition did not result in enough action, and in 1841 the Refugees again protested against their treatment by the government. In this document, they outlined their history, memories of slavery, and difficulties in Nova Scotia.

> Petitioners are Refugees, brought from the Plantations of the southern States, during the American war or their decendants [sic], being placed by Government upon ten acre lots, of poor land, many of them including swamps and likewise entirely barren & unproductive, and none of them sufficient to yield subsistence for a family however skillfull [sic] and industrious, they have dragged on a miserable existence but few, if any of them, rising above the level of hopeless poverty. But few white men in this country seldom make a living upon ten acres of good land, and Petitioners believe that any number of them similarly placed . . . in a strange country, and beneath a rigorous climate, after being recently relieved from the associations and pressures of slavery and the heat of a southern sun, would have for many years presented the same spectacle that the coloured people of Preston have exhibited.[66]

After years of protest and struggle, the government granted the Preston Refugees their farms. The Refugees focused their continued efforts to stay on the land they had settled, but on terms that would make their families and communities viable. To do so, they continued to farm this marginal land; take up abandoned plots; pursue additional, nonagricultural work;

and repeatedly petition for larger allotments that they would own as free-holders.

Despite this achievement, hardship continued for the Refugees after 1842.[67] During the 1840s and 1850s the Refugees continued to face food shortages, and periodically the government provided them with seed potatoes for planting and Indian meal to improve their diets.[68] At Preston the early 1840s seem to have been promising, as the Refugees later reported that they had attempted to maintain themselves by their "industry."[69] The Refugees enjoyed some success until the mid-1840s. Then the economy contracted sharply. As commerce in the North Atlantic sagged, the British imposed free trade on their colonies. At the same time, most rural Nova Scotians suffered crop disease and lost traditional markets for their goods.

In 1846 and 1847 Preston residents petitioned the government for relief. According to the 1846 petition, the Refugees' chief food source was potatoes, but the community had been reduced to poverty because of crop failure.[70] One year later they suffered another crop failure as a result of potato blight and poor weather. Even those Refugees with larger farms, such as Basil Crowd, William Dear, and Armiston Currie, had been reduced to asking for rations.[71] In 1848 one of the original land petitioners from Preston, James Barron, again petitioned the government on behalf of several black families who had settled in the "wilderness" of Guysborough Road outside Preston. He and others had been reduced to starvation, and "some have sold their only cow and all their disposable articles in order to procure the means of subsistence." This difficult situation was worsened by the fact that several households included as many as six children. The petitioners offered to build roads or engage in any public works in exchange for desperately needed provisions.[72] That same year the Preston residents also found themselves in a state of poverty. One government official observed that the Refugees were in their "usual state of want" and still supported themselves by selling items made out of wood.[73] Again in 1849, 1850, and 1852 the Refugees suffered from crop failures. The failure of 1850 was particularly devastating because the community had attempted to produce hay. But this farming innovation was cut short by another crop failure.[74]

Despite these difficulties it would be a mistake to conclude that hardly anything had changed since 1820. By the 1840s the Refugees still relied on potatoes for consumption and to sell at the market, but some crop diversification had taken place. In 1841, for example, a Refugee reported to a local newspaper that he planted cabbage, beans, turnips, and peas.[75] Moreover, an 1847 petition on behalf of blacks in Halifax County demonstrates changes and improvements in the Refugees' farming experience.

The petition was written in the midst of two years of crop failures at Preston, and the negative tone of the document must be understood in the context of potato blight and poor weather. According to this petition, many Preston Refugees had "no store of provisions," and several households were in a state of poverty. The majority of Refugees depended on what they could "procure day to day" for survival. But there was variation within the community. Over time certain families had been able to obtain farm animals, with the petition stating that the Preston Refugees, comprising 136 households, had sixteen horses, twenty-six cows, seventeen oxen, three young horned cattle, and one colt. While these numbers of domestic animals may seem paltry, they represent a considerable gain for a settlement that had begun only with poor land and no livestock.[76] The families at Preston with horses were able to "make a living by bringing charcoal, hoop-poles, and other articles to market." Nevertheless, because of the Refugees' "little farms of ten acres each, they can make but little in this way." The petition concluded that most Preston Refugees were "poor," except for the twenty families with farm animals.[77]

In Hammonds Plains, the situation seemed slightly better during the late 1840s. By 1847 seventy-three families had increased their livestock holdings, which included eighteen horses, thirty-nine cows, twelve oxen, eighteen young horned cattle, two pigs, and six colts. More significantly, some young men were coopers and "have profited from the high price of fish-barrels." These men and families with horses had a "present supply of provisions." Yet of these seventy-three households at least forty-one families needed relief during this period of the colony's economic distress.[78] Two years later the Hammonds Plains Refugees experienced further difficulties, with the failure of the potato crop resulting in destitution for many families. The Refugees had sowed oats and wheat for the first time, but this crop also failed.[79]

Urban Labor

Despite these hard times, the Hammonds Plains farmers persevered, and the population at this small settlement increased during the 1840s, while Preston's experienced a small decrease.[80] Husbandry did not come easily to the Refugees, but the dream of independent farming, while never a reality for some families, continued as a community ideal for many. The ideal of rural farming, however, did not attract every Refugee. In fact, many searched for day labor in Halifax or Dartmouth (Halifax's twin town across the harbor) as a means of survival. After the Refugees obtained free-hold grants, this allowed some to move to Halifax, after selling their land to those who wished to remain farmers. In Halifax, the Refugees integrated with indigenous African Nova Scotians in the black district of Dutchtown in the near northern suburbs. This community, with roots in the eighteenth century, benefited from the influx of Refugees to the urban area.

Nova Scotia's 1838 census gives historians a small window into the work experience of black society in Halifax.[81] However, the census omits crucial occupational information. First, black female household heads were listed either as widows, having no occupation, or as spinsters. Unfortunately, this does not shed light on the various forms of employment that black women pursued in nineteenth-century Halifax. They pursued a variety of tasks including domestic service, laboring, and washing. In 1838 the black population had at least one minister from the African Baptist Church who happened to be mulatto. Moreover, a few blacks served as constables during the 1830s, but the census does not include them.[82] Another occupation left out of the Nova Scotia census was that of servant. Despite these short-comings, it is possible to create a general profile of work patterns for black people in Halifax.

The occupational structure of black people can be divided into un-skilled (laborer) and semi-skilled or skilled, which includes more specific forms of employment.[83] In some ways, there seems to have been even fewer opportunities for employment or occupational mobility in Halifax than in Boston or Providence. Most notably, there were very few professionals in Black Halifax. The professional class was limited to one clergyman from the African Baptist Church. The first indigenous black lawyer in Halifax did not finish his degree until 1898. The vast majority of black households, near 80 percent, were listed as being headed by laborers or widows. The remaining households were headed by men who worked in a range of occupations including glazier, trader, seaman, sailor, truckman, mason, dyer, carpenter, blacksmith, sawyer, barber, hairdresser, shoemaker, cooper, and sweep. Although only a few household heads were listed as seamen or sailors, this occupation probably included several people listed as "labourers." It is possible that the hairdresser or barber owned a small business. Occupational mobility was limited, but William Barrett, listed as a laborer in the late 1830s, had become a hairdresser by 1856; he worked with Charles Roan, who had been a barber as early as 1838.[84] Also, the truckmen were entrepreneurs, and at least one of them, Scipio Cooper, made a good living. The wealthiest black person in Nova Scotia, Mr. Campbell, owned a livery stable and was described as "no mean personage" by a British traveler. Campbell's coach was sought after by the Halifax elite to take them to various engagements.[85] The more fortunate segment of urban black society in Nova Scotia consisted of carpenters, truckmen, blacksmiths, and perhaps a glazier.[86]

The 1838 census offers an effective way to create a general profile of black people in Halifax, but to analyze the various forms of employment pursued by this segment of the population, this source must be supplemented by government documents, newspapers, and travel books. The term "labourer" as employed by the census was a generic way to describe a wide range of occupations that helped the Black Refugees and other people of African descent make ends meet. In 1829 a local writer described the Refugees as generally "improvident and indolent" but grudgingly admitted that "many are good labourers and domestic servants . . . who find employment at a good rate of wages."[87] E. T. Coke, a visitor to Nova Scotia during the early 1830s, commented that the Hammonds Plains Refugees were "good servants."[88] In 1842 the African school, an institution that provided basic schooling for local blacks, claimed that many of its adult learners were servants.[89] Moreover, the African Abolition Society sometimes placed advertisements in local newspapers asking white employers to give their black servants Emancipation Day off.[90]

From the outset of their settlement in Nova Scotia, the Black Refugees had migrated to Halifax or Dartmouth to find work. In some cases this migration was permanent, with some Refugees completely abandoning their farms at Preston and Hammonds Plains. As early as 1816, the local government had attempted to restrict the movement of Refugee males because too often they "go themselves to Halifax in search of employment or pleasure."[91] This migration continued for several decades. In 1837 the government commented that Refugees visited Halifax twice a week in search of employment during the summer but as "often as they can in winter," when there was less work to be done on the farms.[92] As late as 1849 one observer reported that "several families have removed to town" who formerly resided at the rural settlements.[93] The level of desertion from Hammonds Plains and Preston remained relatively high during the 1820s and 1830s. Between 1816 and 1838, the number of Black Refugees at Preston dropped from 924 to 525, while the population of Hammonds Plains dropped from over 500 to a low of 196.[94] Perhaps neighbors abandoned their farms in groups. For example, Peter Peer, Squash Hamilton, Richard Hamilton, and Brass Hamilton lived near one another during the initial settlement at Hammonds Plains. By 1835 they had left this rural area. Several Refugees occupying lots 59 through 65 at Hammonds Plains had also abandoned farming by 1835.[95] At Preston a similar pattern developed, with neighbors leaving farming for other types of employment.[96]

The urban work environment, though harsh in many respects, did offer the Refugees various opportunities that were hard to come by in Preston or Hammonds Plains. The movement from farmer to urban laborer offered an opportunity for advancement for a few Refugees, though many worked either as servants or laborers. Originally from the Chesapeake, Jeremiah Page settled at Preston and labored as a farmer for several years. But he eventually moved to Dartmouth and worked as a sawyer.[97] Jacob Ford also attempted to settle at Preston and cultivate the soil, but he possessed a skill that opened up many possibilities for him in Halifax. As of 1838, Ford had migrated to the urban area and worked as a mason.[98] Scipio Cooper had originally pursued husbandry in Hammonds Plains, but he moved to Halifax and became a successful truckman.[99] Yet he also retained ownership of a few farms in Hammonds Plains.

More typical of the Refugee experience were Isaac Kellum, John Floyd, Nim Carter, and Samuel Turner. These men had attempted to become farmers in Preston, but after years of crop failures they opted to find steadier employment in Dartmouth or Halifax. According to an 1816 report about agricultural production in Preston, the government listed Nim Carter as "Idle," with no hut built. Carter was not necessarily lazy but preferred the urban wage labor market to farming. Carter, Kellum, Floyd, and Turner migrated to Halifax or Dartmouth and worked as laborers or servants.[100] Sometimes the route to urban employment could be a last resort. George Winder had been a relatively successful farmer during his initial settlement at Preston. After only a short period of farming he had cleared an acre of land and built a hut.[101] Yet several farming difficulties encouraged Winder to turn his dwelling into a small lodge. In 1829 he petitioned the colonial government and asked for financial assistance to "enlarge his house and build a small stable" for his visitors to use. Unfortunately this endeavor did not work out, and by the late 1830s Winder had moved to Halifax to pursue wage labor.[102]

In the urban areas the Refugees engaged in various tasks that highlight the diverse meanings of the word "labourer." Several Refugees found employment as domestic servants, including Benjamin Roberts of Maryland, who worked for Nova Scotia's chief justice.[103] Other Refugees such as Dean Atkins served as apprentices.[104] Quite often, government relief to the black settlements came with strings attached, and many young men were expected to work on roads in Halifax and other areas.[105] In 1843 the government wanted to regulate or at least determine the number of chimney sweeps in Halifax, including the number of black people involved in this type of employment.[106] One example of the type of sporadic day-to-day labor that many black people endured in Halifax is seen in the story of a man named Williams who worked for a white butcher. This man earned a livelihood by carrying trays of meat to customers throughout the Halifax area. Unfortunately, the only reason why this small piece of work history made the newspapers is because on his way to deliver meat in 1844 Williams died of a broken blood vessel.[107] Others, such as an older man named Miller, made a living by carrying water to families in Dartmouth and running errands.[108] Philliman Hawkins supplemented his farming income with a fascinating occupation in Halifax. Hawkins's job included accompanying prisoners to the Office of Examination. He also worked at the city workhouse and whipped inmates who misbehaved.[109]

Halifax's location on the Atlantic Ocean allowed some Refugees to find work in various maritime industries and as sailors. On the docks, the Refugees and other black seamen sang work songs while "hoisting out the bales, and boxes, and hogsheads."[110] As some Refugee families made barrels, they also spent time on the waterfront selling this product for people to store fish. The sea presented opportunities for travel, income, and advancement. It seems that the Black Refugees turned to seafaring quite soon after their settlement in Nova Scotia. In his history of Nova Scotia published in 1829, Thomas Chandler Haliburton claimed that some Refugees, "charmed with the privilege of locomotion, have become sailors, in order to indulge their propensity to ramble."[111] In his article "Black West Indian Seamen in the British Merchant Marine in the Midnineteenth Century," Alan Cobley notes that between 1845 and 1854, sixty black seamen were recorded as having been born in Halifax, Nova Scotia, while 174 originated from the neighboring colony of New Brunswick.[112] While benefiting personally from their work opportunities, the black seamen from Nova Scotia could also benefit the Refugee community by bringing back information about relatives left behind in the United States or other areas.

A few Refugees who attempted to farm at Preston or Hammonds Plains either left their rural farms altogether or supplemented their farm income with work on the high seas. For example, John Carter worked as a ship's cook in the late 1810s.[113] Another Refugee, Brister Webb, abandoned his lot at Hammonds Plains and found employment as a seaman because of his previous experience with the occupation.[114] William Hall, a son of Refugees, won the Victoria Cross for his actions during the Sepoy Rebellion in India. In addition to serving in the British navy, Hall also spent time in the U.S. Navy during the late 1840s. Hall's story is significant not only because he won an award for gallantry but because it connects the story of the Refugees to that of colonized people throughout the British Empire.[115]

Local schools attempted, among their other endeavors, to prepare blacks for careers as seafarers. For example, the African school taught young black men navigation and sought to increase "the qualifications of the people of colour as seaman." By 1840 Halifax's mercantile community had recognized the local black seafarers' "aptitude" as "merchant sailors."[116] Black people in Halifax continued their work at sea and on the docks. In 1871 the government conducted the most accurate census to that date. According to historian Judith Fingard, of the enumerated black workers, "27 per cent engaged in marine-related work as seamen, coopers, riggers, and stevedores."[117] Despite the dangers of seafaring, as Jeffrey Bolster notes in his book about African American seamen, such work became an important source of income for black people in Nova Scotia.[118] Black Refugee seamen migrated around the world and in many cases redefined the borders around Nova Scotia for themselves. The ships they traveled on were sites of interracial cooperation and conflict, but black seamen from Nova Scotia exhibited a willingness to push the limits of the local economy and secure their own livelihoods through seafaring.

The years between the War of 1812 and the American Civil War were crucial in the development of a Black Refugee identity as a distinct group of African British North Americans through the shared experience of adjusting to the economic conditions of Nova Scotia. The struggles of farming and wage labor were familiar problems for the Refugees and their descendants. Former slaves from Maryland, Virginia, Georgia, and other areas mixed together and attempted to make a living on the land or through the urban workplace. The urban wage labor market in Halifax offered sporadic employment for some but also crucial income for families to survive. The Black Refugees endured an economic system that would have been familiar to African Americans in New England. In both regions, the vast majority of men found seasonal and sporadic work in different forms of menial labor ranging from the jobs in the maritime industry to trucking materials throughout towns. Women provided a steadier and essential portion of family income through domestic service. In both regions, a small percentage of black people found employment in semiskilled or skilled positions or owned small businesses. Most important, the experience of the Black Refugees in Halifax was unique because of their continuing connection to the farming communities at Preston and Hammonds Plains. The ownership of farms allowed the Refugees to move back and forth between the urban and rural economies in an effort to feed their families and friends.

Chapter 5

Community and Identity

IN AN 1838 LETTER to Queen Victoria, Nova Scotia's African Friendly Society (AFS) thanked the new monarch "for the blessings of civil and religious liberty we have enjoyed under your illustrious house." Moreover, the society promised to "teach our children to remember that your Majesty and your immediate ancestors liberated our people from bondage, and restored to them equal rights."[1] The identity of the Black Refugees—that is, their consciousness of shared experience and group understanding of their social position—revolved around assertions of loyalty to Britain and British institutions.[2] The pillars of this identity were two distinct community institutions: churches and societies. The African Baptist and Methodist churches, along with associations such as the African Friendly Society, not only encouraged the development and sustenance of a shared identity, but also engaged in several battles to define the contours of black life in Nova Scotia.

These battles would have been familiar to African Americans in New England. In both regions, free black communities formed churches, established various organizations, celebrated their own freedom, fought for political inclusion, and promoted abolitionism. Black people in New England cities also named many of their community institutions "African" to memorialize an important part of their identity. Despite these similarities, there were local variations between Providence, Boston, Portsmouth, and Halifax. Among the differences were the absence in Halifax of "Negro" Election Days, which were holdovers from eighteenth-century slavery in New England and the fact that a chapter of the African Masons did not develop until the mid-1850s.[3] But the importance of the black church and community organizations can be found in each of these historic venues.

In Halifax, community institutions built on the shared experience of former American slaves and slowly resulted in the creation of a distinct African British North American community and identity.

The Refugees intertwined their abolitionist beliefs with Britain because of their original liberation from slavery. Moreover, public displays of loyalty to the Crown helped them define themselves as a distinct group. This loyalty also signified one of the ways in which the Refugees sharply drew the border between freedom in Nova Scotia and the British world in opposition to the slaveholding Republic. Yet the Refugees also crossed this border by encouraging runaway American slaves and holding meetings that discussed political events in the United States. They did not use the border to simply detach themselves from friends and relatives left behind in the southern states. In other words, the community held several different views of the border. The development of Black Refugee communities in Nova Scotia was informed by the wider context of racial attitudes and race relations in Nova Scotia, which presented obstacles and opportunities that the Refugees used to their advantage. This chapter examines several important aspects of the Black Refugees' community development including churches, organizations, public displays of loyalty to Great Britain, and abolitionism.

The Racial Context

As John Wood Sweet and Joanne Pope Melish note for the case of New England, black freedom resulted in a hardening of racial attitudes in the late eighteenth and early nineteenth centuries. Certainly tensions existed as "Bobalition" broadsides, a genre of racist depictions of African American celebrations of the end of slavery and the slave trade, inhabited the same space as the abolitionist work of William Lloyd Garrison. In New England, as Melish highlights, many whites did not know how to perceive free blacks who lived in the region. Eventually, many New Englanders came to view African Americans as the opposite of white Americans and hoped that they would simply disappear. On a wide variety of fronts, white New Englanders denigrated and harassed black people in an effort to reinforce notions that black inferiority could not be changed. Similar developments can be found in the treatment of the Black Refugees in Nova Scotia.[4]

The local press in Nova Scotia engaged in a consistent campaign to depict the Refugees as fit only for slavery, unendingly stupid, and depraved beyond redemption. The presence in Nova Scotia of free blacks who resisted the government's offer to remove them to Trinidad offended many elements of the white population. As it slowly became clear that the black settlers would not leave, racial rhetoric appeared periodically in newspapers, which claimed that the Refugees "regret their delivery from the house of bondage."[5] In 1843 a local paper interviewed an "old negro [*sic*]" who said he wished he had stayed in the United States instead of migrating to Nova Scotia, which led the editor to ask "whether the Slavery of the Southern States was not in truth and practicality, a more suitable lifestyle for the negro [*sic*] than the miserable state they live in at Preston."[6] The Black Refugees were supposedly better off as slaves because they could not understand the rudimentary elements of Anglo-American civilization. Moreover, any attempts at moving into the colony's mainstream were lampooned in the press as pathetic imitations. In the early 1840s, the *Morning Herald* printed a satirical piece about the fictitious Royal African Society. The editorial made fun of black organizations and portrayed the membership speaking in some sort of white-manufactured black dialect and using the word "nigger."[7] In using this dialect to discuss black speech and thought patterns, the editor was making the less than subtle point that people of African descent generally, and the Black Refugees in particular, were incapable of even conversing in the English language. Other papers, such as the *Morning Chronicle,* printed various stories that highlighted black people's alleged stupidity. For example, one short piece recounted the tale of a black man who removed his hat during a rainstorm. When it was pointed out that he should have kept the hat on, the man replied "hat belong to me—head belong to massa."[8]

Given the perception that the Refugees were quite stupid, some newspapers took great offense at the fact that certain blacks were eligible to vote in local elections. In 1847 one letter writer to the *Novascotian* claimed that the Refugees were a "constant tax on the man who pays all taxes" and should not be allowed to vote.[9] Four years later, the *Sun* asked why "illiterate, negro beggars, hundreds of them hardly raised in intellectual capacity above the inferior order of the animal creation continue to be invested with the Elective Franchise."[10] The movement of black people into sacred spaces of white supremacy such as jury service also upset several local newspapers. In 1845 the *Sun* ambivalently denounced black jury participation. The paper carefully noted that, in contrast to the United States, local black people supposedly had "equal rights with their white brethren." Moreover, in "this free country [Nova Scotia], thank God, there is no proscription of colour, but it is a little too democratic, to place the man who to-day stands behind [a] gentleman's chair to change his plate, to-morrow vis-à-vis with him . . . to discuss the public business."[11] Another newspaper claimed that new grand jury lists associated "negroes and scoundrels with honest and reputable men in the discharge of the most important duties of citizenship."[12] Clearly, in the opinion of the paper, honesty and respectability were traits that the local black population simply did not possess.

In addition to various assaults on an imagined black character, newspapers also verbally attacked Refugee females. As early as 1815 black women were singled out in letters to local newspapers and accused of "depravity" because of their clothing. Black women were portrayed in the press as being the opposite of the ideal of dignified white womanhood in that they were not gentle, delicate, or quiet.[13] In response to a letter that claimed black women misbehaved in public, the *Morning Herald* encouraged "every decent person to administer a dose of club law to those dark harpies."[14] In addition to verbal attacks, local whites also resorted to violence in an effort to push the black community to the margins of society. For example, in 1833 local thugs broke the windows in the newly constructed African Baptist church.[15] In 1853 white youths broke into the African Methodist church and disturbed New Year's Eve services.[16] Several months after the conclusion of the American Civil War arsonists also "set fire to the African church in Dartmouth."[17]

Perhaps one of the more revealing incidents of racism was the meeting between American abolitionist Samuel Ringgold Ward and famous Nova Scotian author and judge Thomas Chandler Haliburton during the early 1850s. As poet and scholar George Elliot Clarke argues, Haliburton was deeply devoted to conservative ideals, which assumed that poor people should remain in their God-ordained place for life.[18] Moreover, Haliburton had very negative views toward people of African descent and believed that they should remain as slaves. Perhaps he held this opinion because his grandparents had owned slaves. During his meeting with several "gentlemen," Haliburton made comments that infuriated Ward. First, he rejected the idea of a college for people of color in the British colonies, because higher education should be reserved for the education of gentlemen and "a gentleman, among that race [blacks], was entirely out of the question."[19] Haliburton also stated that he "shared in the prejudices generally entertained by Americans in regard to Negroes; and could not regard such feelings as unnatural or unjustifiable, but as inevitable." According to the learned author and jurist, "mixing with Negroes was naturally" disgusting and revolting. Haliburton also complained about the emancipation of slaves in the West Indies, which convinced Ward that this Nova Scotian "was entirely with and for slavery, and that it was next to impossible to find a more malignant enemy to the Negro."[20] After listening to Halibur-ton rant about black inferiority, the abolitionist concluded that "judging from his own words, and from the likeness of feeling to himself on the part of his fellow citizens, I do not at all wonder that the blacks of Nova Scotia are deprived of many of their rights by them."[21]

These racist images certainly summed up the attitude of some white Nova Scotians toward the Black Refugees. However, from the outset of the Refugees' settlement, there were a few white voices that defended them in the press and to the government.[22] But these voices were lost in a wider tide of hostile racist rhetoric during the Refugees' first fifteen years in Nova Scotia. Yet two emerging themes created room for the Refugees to assert themselves politically and socially during the mid–nineteenth century. The first involved the development of liberal thought in the person of Joseph Howe, the most important political figure in nineteenth-century Nova Scotia. He found all-encompassing racial views distasteful and anti-thetical to the philosophy that each person should rise in society accord-ing to his or her talent. He defended the Refugees from their detractors on several occasions and in an 1832 editorial made several surprising sugges-tions. Howe argued that black people had both intellect and ambition and questioned if any harm could come from "a gentle infusion of black blood into those dignified orders [law, medicine, business, and government] of the state?"[23] Second, and possibly more important, was the rising senti-ment in some quarters of Nova Scotia to define the colony in opposition to the United States. In part, this meant tying the small colony even more tightly to other British colonies and highlighting differences between Brit-ish North America and the Republic.

Several editorials in Nova Scotia's press attempted to outline the differ-ences between the United States and the British Empire. Allegedly, Nova Scotia was the home of rational and orderly government that did not en-slave a significant portion of its population. Yet anti-Americanism in Nova Scotia involved more than hostility to slavery. For the Tories, American support for the rebels in Upper and Lower Canada during the late 1830s was simply an example of the Republic's frenzy for territorial expansion, especially with the calls for "Manifest Destiny" in the 1840s. This expansion threatened to turn British North America into an American colony. For most British North Americans, with the notable exception of the Annexa-tionist movement of 1849, union with the United States remained distaste-ful for various reasons. The Republic seemed to be home to unrestrained democracy, hypocrisy, and the ultimate sin of slavery. Moreover, despite anger over the loss of imperial preference in terms of trade, feelings of loyalty to the Crown struck a chord with many in British North America. Lastly, important political and religious figures worried that a union with the Americans might undermine their own positions in society and government. Indeed, Tories, some French Canadians who feared that union would be the end of their culture and homeland, and the Church of England saw union with the United States as dangerous and undesirable.[24]

As the sectional crisis in the United States intensified in the 1840s and 1850s, local newspapers went on the attack against the Republic. In 1844 the *Morning Chronicle* called attention to the number of runaway slave advertisements in southern newspapers and stated that "we never look at one of them without wishing him [a runaway] God-speed" and hoping that he had "found a resting place beneath the sheltering protection of British Institutions." The paper also sarcastically remarked that "the 'Great Republic' is . . . [a place] where human rights alone are perfectly enjoyed."[25] At times one newspaper could claim that slaves in the United States were happy with their lot, then several months later change its tune by stating that in "physical force and courage, the Negro, as a race, is not inferior to the blonde" and the Fugitive Slave Law should be condemned.[26] In 1854, after the return of Anthony Burns to slavery from New England, one local paper sarcastically noted that the "land of liberty was not what it is cracked up to be . . . [since] slaves spread over the land gives one a sorry idea of freedom," while Nova Scotia enjoyed the "blessings of rational liberty."[27] Other newspapers attacked the Peculiar Institution by asking why a slave should be denied freedom especially "when not merely one-half, but three-fourths, seven-eighths, or more of his blood came to him through the Randolphs, the Taylors, the Calverts, or Jeffersons."[28]

The Black Refugees represented a tangible example of the difference between Nova Scotia and the United States. Indeed, in an 1867 letter to the British government against Canadian Confederation, Joseph Howe argued that, unlike the United States, Nova Scotia had settled its racial problems within the framework of the British Empire and should be allowed to continue as a self-governing colony.[29] The tension arising from Nova Scotia's being part of both the British and the American worlds encouraged the Refugees to use their place on the border to strategically define themselves as British subjects vigorously opposed to American slavery and any type of political affiliation with the United States. More important, in doing this, they carved out a niche that used Nova Scotia's ambivalence toward the United States to their advantage.

Community Differences

Although the majority of black people in Halifax County during the mid–nineteenth century were Refugees, some people of African descent had roots in the Caribbean, Europe, or were descendants of the Black Loyalists. Thus, in some ways black societies and churches not only served as sites of adaptation for the Refugees but also brought together a local black population that came from different backgrounds. For example, in Halifax, free black sailors from the Caribbean could mix with the indigenous black population, some of whom had been slaves and others always free. In the same sense, the Black Refugees might interact with descendants of the Black Loyalists who had never been slaves. Former slaves from the Loyalist influx could also trade stories of bondage with the more recently arrived Black Refugees. In this small town, Halifax, black people from a multiplicity of backgrounds interacted and formed a diverse community. In these ways, the black people in Nova Scotia got to know one another and became familiar with people of African descent, with whom they may have had little in common except for the color of their skin.

The creation of churches and societies strengthened the bonds of community among the Refugees and other elements of the black population. Certainly, these institutions provided support for the black community and helped to define an identity in the new environment of British North America as former American slaves forged an entirely new community in a foreign land. However, shared experience and mutually supportive community institutions should not be seen in simple terms. Although the community remained relatively supportive of its members, this did not translate into a society without conflict. Alongside the development of community institutions were inevitable disagreements among different personalities. The Refugees' various ideas and attitudes also might have been informed by their different points of origin in the United States, various experiences of migration to Nova Scotia, and different residential communities in Preston, Hammonds Plains, and Halifax. The creation of a distinct African British North American community and identity did not mean that the Refugees or other black people held similar opinions and focused solely on presenting a common front against white racism.

Local newspapers highlighted some of the tensions among the Refugees. For example, in the early 1840s disputes developed at the African Baptist Church among members who disagreed over church protocol and possession of the chapel.[30] Occasionally disagreements became violent. In

1843 the *Morning Herald* reported that a mob of nearly fifteen black men and women pounced on the local "coloured" constable, Septimus Clark, because he had intervened in a "pugilistic" dispute between two black women.[31] In another incident, George Ginnian assaulted Hector Johnson with an axe because Johnson caught Ginnian taking a pole from his fence.[32] In 1849 "humane and benevolent" citizens distributed food to several households in Preston. But, for reasons that remain unclear, some Refugees used degrading language toward their benefactors. This incident upset several respectable leaders of the Preston community. As a result, they placed a notice in the *British Colonist,* stating that they "regret that any coloured person should use any insulting language" to people distributing food. Moreover, these types of "conduct the coloured people deprecate in the highest terms."[33]

More significantly, the black community did not agree about religion or politics. Although the majority of Black Refugees would eventually become Baptists, the African Methodist Church also enjoyed a substantial congregation during the 1840s and 1850s. In addition, some black people attended the Anglican Church, which might have been a tactic to establish connections with some members of Nova Scotia's political elite. In terms of politics, the Refugees split their votes between Tories and Reformers in proportions depending on the election year or what either party had done or failed to do for local blacks.[34] The community developed by the Black Refugees represented a specific example of a much larger trend that scholars have identified of "creative tension between social solidarity and difference among African Americans."[35]

Given the existence of community disputes and disagreements, it is important to ask how the community governed itself or constructed ways of conflict resolution. The Refugees solved disagreements, violent or verbal, either through individual community leaders or through Nova Scotia's legal system. At times, the Black Refugees brought their disputes, which ranged from assault to theft, before local courts.[36] At times, important community leaders were not black. For example, the head of the Baptist Church, John Burton, who welcomed the Black Refugees into his church, played an important role in resolving disagreements among them before the establishment of the African Baptist Church in 1832. According to the *Christian Visitor,* Burton "was a king among them, and they rendered unto Caesar the things which are Caesar's. He reigned with undisputed sway amongst them . . . the justices and even the Governor of the Province acquiesced in Mr. Burton's decisions." The secretary of the African Baptist Association recalled that Burton "proved himself so wise an administrator of justice that civil authorities gave him entire control of these [colored] people whilst he remained their pastor."[37] Perhaps these sources give too much credit to Burton, but his position as a preacher to the Black Refugees during their early years of settlement allowed him to deal with problems within the framework of the emerging black society. Black community leaders, such as Joseph Smith, also attempted to settle disputes between neighbors. A deacon of the African Baptist Church at Preston, during "his life he was the ruling spirit in the settlement. Disputes of any sort whatever, when brought to his notice, were always amicably arranged."[38] That comment reminds us that the presence of disagreements should not blind us to the mutual support and shared experience that defined the development of the Refugee community.

Churches and Religion

For most free black communities in the United States the church remained the most significant institution before the Civil War. Many African Americans found in churches solace and sanctuary from an otherwise harsh and difficult world. Black churches provided spiritual guidance, community services, and social and political action. Black religious worship united secular and religious life, while emphasizing spirit possession and experiencing God.[39] In Nova Scotia, former slaves brought several traditions from the United States and reestablished them in the form of the African Baptist and African Methodist churches in various parts of the colony.

Before the development of the African Baptist and Methodist churches, one observer reported in the late 1820s that the Preston Refugees listened to a "Reverend" who was "in the habit of holding forth to a weekly congregation." At these meetings, the congregation listened and responded to a distinct style that seemed "to be complete 'Greek' to a white man."[40] The Black Refugees placed tremendous emphasis on experiencing God. Several years later, Rev. Richard Preston summed up this religious orientation by stating that only the "Holy Fire and the Grace of God" could inspire preaching.[41] Local Anglican missionaries found the Refugees' religious beliefs astonishing and revolting, especially blood visions, which meant a strong and close relationship with Christ.[42] In the beginning, the Black Refugees worshipped God through informal gatherings and at John Burton's integrated Baptist Church. According to the first history of the African Baptist Church, the Refugees "were spiritually cared for by this servant of God."[43] Eventually, following the leadership of Richard Preston, the black community preferred to create, maintain, and worship at their own church away from the eyes of the local white population.

The development of separate and organized churches did not occur until the late 1820s and early 1830s. The Hammonds Plains Refugees had applied for a grant to build their own church in the 1820s, but it was Richard Preston and his followers who wanted to build a separate and independent African church.[44] After reuniting with his family in Nova Scotia, former Virginian slave Richard Preston hoped to pursue a religious career and became an apprentice of John Burton. In the early 1820s, Preston became the first black delegate to the Nova Scotia Baptist Association.[45] Although John Burton continued to offer spiritual guidance to some people of color, Preston's popularity among the recent immigrants increased during the 1820s as he traveled to each black enclave in and around Halifax. Preston's speaking abilities, his personal familiarity with the Peculiar Institution, and (as historian Frank Boyd notes) his "vision of [black people's] collective future" allowed his sermons to serve as an important vehicle in the black population's transition from American slaves to Black Refugees to a distinct group of African British North Americans.[46] Preston had been "accustomed to preach among many of the colored persons residing at Halifax, Preston, and Hammonds Plains [in favor of building a separate place of worship and was] anxious to carry the object of the people into effect."[47] The process of the black Baptist population's developing collective aspirations resulted in their decision to establish their own church.

The Refugees wanted an ordained minister who could conduct baptisms, marriages, and funerals away from the watchful and hostile eyes of the local white population. In a petition to the colonial government, Preston and a few others claimed that "circumstances of an unpleasant nature having existed between the white and colored members of the Baptist Church in Halifax, [it has been] rendered necessary that the latter should disconnect themselves altogether from the Church."[48] As a result, Preston raised enough funds to travel and study in Britain under the supervision of the West London Baptist Association. In addition to becoming ordained, he also hoped to collect enough money to build a chapel for people of African descent to hear the Gospel.[49]

After arriving in Britain during the winter of 1831, Preston immediately began his studies. The gathering storm against slavery and the advance of the abolitionist movement made Preston an attractive figure to many people. As an African American intimately familiar with slavery, he became a popular speaker at numerous churches as he discussed slavery, postemancipation societies, the problem of racism in the Anglo-American world, and the black population in Nova Scotia. The secretary of the African Baptist Association recalled that Preston "had the pleasure of hearing the Invincibles of Freedom argue the matter [slavery], which fired his soul with zeal that lasted him his whole lifetime—such men as Wilberforce, Clarkson, Buxton, O'Connel [*sic*], and Brougham—with these gentlemen he became a familiar figure. Coming as he did not long from the furnace of slavery himself, he was a good measure to put in their scales for their lecture platforms."[50] Indeed, congregations received Preston's addresses well, and the *Brighton Herald* reported that "[h]is manner of delivery is exceedingly pleasing and in his dissertation he evinces clearness and perspicuity."[51]

As Preston's experience shows, blacks in the Halifax region exchanged ideas and participated in events within the wider context of the Black Atlantic world. Moreover, their geographic separation from black America did not result in an insulated and static community of ex–African Americans trapped in the cold weather of British North America. Like Frederick Douglass several years later, Preston brought his ideas about slavery and the black North American experience to a wider audience.

Upon his return from England, Rev. Preston and his followers established the African Baptist Church in Halifax in 1832 and helped spread its influence to other black settlements in the surrounding area. In addition to the main church in Halifax, several branches were established at Preston, Hammonds Plains, Dartmouth, and Beech Hill. Yet the major service was held in Halifax. It is interesting to note that Preston built the mother church in this location. Certainly, the vast majority of blacks lived on the fringes of Halifax during the 1830s. Preston seemed determined to increase the black population in the city, perhaps intending it to be drawn out of its disparate elements in the nearby rural settlements with the new church as the center of the community. The African Baptist Church also created several church offices that allowed ordinary people to obtain positions of leadership within the community. For example, Jacob Ford and Prince William Sport, a mason and barber respectively, served as deacons at the Halifax church. At Preston, two farmers, Meredith Stanley and John Collins, served as the deacon and the elder.[52] The African Baptist Church conducted various services for the community ranging from marriages and funerals to social and political activities throughout the 1830s and 1840s.

Preston's major contribution to black life in Nova Scotia revolved around the creation of the African Baptist Association in 1854.[53] This association, the result of his tireless travels throughout the colony, brought together people of African descent from various backgrounds under the umbrella of an independent black church. Despite his increasing age, Preston regularly presided over congregational duties and continued as the spokesperson for the local black community on a variety of issues. The African Baptist Association is significant because it published minutes of its yearly meetings after 1854, which provide historians with a rare glimpse into the religious, social, and political life of the Black Refugees.

At the first meeting, the membership recalled the initial establishment of the African Baptist Church in Halifax, which had been possible because of donations collected in Britain. The Black Refugees and their descendants referred to "Old England, God Bless her, forever." The association also made an important resolution that highlighted the labors of the church in attempting to unite black people throughout the colony, while using the memory of Africa to describe the racial designation of black people in Nova Scotia: "That the abundant success which attended the labours of our missionaries during the year, together with the increased demand for the continuation of their labours, in watering and strengthening the churches in connection with our body scattered over so large a portion of the African race in Nova Scotia; also the new and extensive fields opening on every hand, call upon us, as with a voice from heaven, to increase our exertions in sowing the seed of truth, and thus increasing the Redeemer's Kingdom."[54]

During the late 1850s and early 1860s, the majority of the association minutes focused on the numbers of new and deceased members and on church happenings during a given year. The minutes also reveal the Refugees' religious orientation and memories of slavery, particularly at the memorial services for important community members such as Richard Preston or the popular preacher at Hammonds Plains, John Hamilton. Many sermons emphasized that earthly poverty would be replaced by spiritual fulfillment and happiness in Heaven. In 1858 the association listened to a sermon that emphasized that "[t]he poor have the gospel preached to them." The economic difficulties of the Refugees and other people of African descent were said to be outweighed by the wealth of religious understanding harnessed at the ABA's annual meetings. "Although the [sic] most of our churches are poor, as it regards this world's goods, yet Jesus is very rich in Grace: and by Grace he has saved a great number of souls from the thraldom of sin and woe, the past year."[55]

In 1861, as fighting raged throughout the United States, the association reminded its membership in words that would have been familiar in many black churches throughout North America, "Princes shall come out of

Egypt and Ethiopia shall stretch forth her hands unto God. Finally brethren dwell together in love, and stand fast in the liberty where-with Christ has made you free;—be not entangled again in the yoke of bondage."[56] The year after the Emancipation Proclamation, the ABA made several biblical references to black freedom and understood this act as the work of God as ordained through the story of Israel.

> The first source of happiness to Israel in the wilderness, was their deliverance out of the land of Egypt, and out of the house of bondage; in allusion to which, it is said, 'O! people, saved by the Lord!' And all the people of God are now happy in salvation from the guilt and tyranny of sin. They were in captivity and bondage, but Jesus has proclaimed liberty to the captives, and they are now free from the law of sin and death . . . Israel wandered in the wilderness, but they were happy in a prospect of Canaan. Their enemies, who depended on the strength of their high places, set them at defiance; but the Lord said, 'They shall be found liars unto thee, and thou shalt tread upon their high places.' The true Israel have the Promised Land in their view, the heavenly Canaan, where their present happiness will be perfected for ever.[57]

The African Baptist Association also gave sermons in memory of recently deceased members of significance to the local community. These sermons highlight several aspects of the community's consciousness such as the memory of slavery. In 1861 the association recalled the life and labors of the recently deceased Richard Preston. In the "Circular Letter," the border between British North America and the United States played an important part in describing Rev. Preston's early life. "I feel, says he [Preston], doubly free, free from sin and free from slavery;—thanks be to my God, and thanks be to Old England for thy good laws. The slave that gets his foot upon thy shore, his chains fall, and binds him no more . . . at times he would say I must go and show [to American slaves] the way to heaven and to England." That same year, the Refugee community suffered from the loss of "beloved brother" John Hamilton. In memorializing this important community preacher, the association highlighted its understanding of slavery and the slave trade: "[o]ur brother was an African man, stolen from Africa, sold in America, as you would sell a horse, for the harness, or an ox for the yoke . . . and at the time of the American war, he was one amongst the many, that was brought to a free soil."[58] The African Baptist Association served the community spiritually and socially, but it also maintained and preserved the community's history through sermons.

Although the black community in the Halifax region did not exceed two thousand people during the mid–nineteenth century, the African Baptist

Church was not the only religious house of worship for people of color. In August 1846 the African Methodist Episcopal Zion Chapel was established.[59] The African Methodist Church retained connections with the United States, since black Methodists in Halifax participated in the New England Conference of the African Methodist Church.[60] According to the church history, missionaries found "considerable work in Nova Scotia, New Brunswick, Canada, and one or two in the West India Islands."[61] Unlike the African Baptist Church, the Methodist congregation went through several ministers during the late 1840s and the 1850s. In other words, it did not enjoy the stable leadership that defined the first thirty years of the African Baptist Church. Between 1848 and 1859, the Reverends Ross, Kennedy, Posey, and Mars conducted services, marriages, and funerals.[62] Yet this turnover could have been by design more than internal disunity, as the African Methodists sometimes rotated ministers rather than establishing them in congregations for any great length of time. The congregation also ran into financial difficulties in early 1847 and was forced to leave its unfinished building "in a rude state."[63] But in 1848 the *Novascotian* reported that the chapel could hold 200 people and Sunday services regularly attracted this number. In contrast, the paper claimed, only about 150 persons attended services at the African Baptist Church.[64]

The African Methodist congregation in Halifax has received far less attention from historians than the Baptist church, but the membership of the Methodist church was active in sponsoring communitywide activities. For example, in 1849 several female members of the African Methodist Church held a bazaar to collect funds to complete the interior of their house of worship.[65] One year later, the "Females of the Coloured Methodist Society" organized a soiree and another bazaar to "assist the Trustees in finishing the Church."[66] In 1852 the church continued to hold respectable "tea meetings."[67] Like the African Baptist Church, the Methodist congregation also sent one of its members to England in an effort to obtain funds. In 1853 Royal Navy veteran Henry Jackson hoped to solicit money for the construction of a meetinghouse for the members of the African Methodist Church. But the British authorities arrested him for allegedly begging under false pretenses. After receiving several assurances from Halifax that he was a "most respectable man" and had been charged by the church with collecting funds, the authorities released Jackson.[68] Like Preston, Jackson had traveled to Britain not only to solicit money but also to discuss the black community and slavery to an audience outside the confines of North America. Despite denominational differences, the African Baptist and African Methodist congregations actively supported abolition. Both Rev. Posey and Rev. Preston shared the stage at antislavery events and lectured on the evils of the Peculiar Institution.[69] The African churches, in particular the African Baptist Church, were intimately connected with various societies that advocated social and political causes that remained important to many black people in the Halifax region.

Community Organizations

The African Baptist and African Methodist churches formed the foundation for community organizations. For example, Prince William Sport and Septimus Clark served as president and secretary of the African Friendly Society during the 1850s, and they also held the positions of deacon and secretary in the African Baptist Association.[70] Richard Preston headed the African Baptist Association and also remained active in the African Abolition Society (AAS). These organizations embarked on several campaigns that carved out a place for the Black Refugees in Nova Scotia's political culture and helped forge various aspects of the former American slaves' identity in British North America. It is possible to divide the goals of black societies into two distinct but overlapping groups.

First, some organizations fought for equal liberty in Nova Scotia. It must be noted that legally all Nova Scotians were subjects, but I use the terms citizen or citizenship to include certain rights—voting, jury service, and equal treatment before legal and social institutions—that eluded the Refugees and other people of African descent in early nineteenth-century Nova Scotia. The Black Refugees suffered from de facto discrimination. There were no explicit racial legal barriers to voting, membership in juries, serving as witnesses at trial, or holding public office. But, customarily, it was rare for black people to serve on juries or have their testimony taken very seriously. As late as 1841, the Refugees complained to the government that they were harassed when trying to vote.[71] The Refugees faced strong sociolegal discrimination but not the type of formal legal discrimination that existed in many U.S. states. Thus, the struggle for equal liberty entailed a fight against social barriers that prevented the exercise of rights that the law formally granted all loyal subjects of the Crown.

In fighting for equal citizenship and meaningful freedom, the Black Refugees challenged formerly all-white spaces of politics and respectable activities such as festivals and parades in honor of various British royalty and local government officials.[72] Additionally, Refugee women held teas and soirees to raise money for the African Baptist and African Methodist churches.[73] In holding these events, black women, so disparaged in the local press, claimed an understanding of middle-class female activities that they supposedly could not comprehend. Contesting public space also occurred within the context of increasing political activity that provided a practical outlet for the Refugees' continuing attempts to claim equal citizenship. Taken together, the fight for citizenship through various black organizations provided an important thread of the Refugees' identity.

Other black societies in Nova Scotia focused on the abolition of slavery. The Black Refugees' push for abolition forged a connection with the United States and the British West Indies. The African Abolition Society sponsored lectures, discussed various events and laws in the United States, aided American Fugitives, and celebrated Emancipation Day, which challenged and claimed public space throughout Halifax. In the case of the United States, these festivals of freedom were sites of public memory, the pursuit of citizenship, and the development of identity.[74] In Nova Scotia, the African Abolition Society provided another aspect of the Refugee identity, which was the connection and engagement with the United States. Black societies represented the claim of former American slaves to civic, social, and political rights. They accomplished this by challenging sacred spaces of whiteness, by claiming the right to British institutions and British justice.

Before discussing in depth the Refugees' fight for equal citizenship, it is important to highlight the important place Africa held in the memory of the Black Refugees, as demonstrated by the names of their various societies. The Refugees named many of their societies "African." For example, several groups with various focuses ranging from relief to political inclusion memorialized Africa, such as the African Baptist and Methodist churches, the African Friendly Society, the African Society, the African Union Society, the African Constitution Society, and the African Penny Society.[75] These societies were founded after 1830, mostly during the 1840s and the 1850s, well after many black American societies had gone over to using the term "colored." It is interesting to ask why expatriate African Americans continued to use "African." Although there were a few Black Refugees from Africa in the 1840s, their presence alone cannot explain the use of "African" in societies' titles.

It seems that community members held onto a deeply felt cultural connection with Africa, which many Refugees considered their long-lost home. The Refugees did not fear expressing cultural affinities with Africa in the mid–nineteenth century as did some of their counterparts in the northern United States. Some members of the African American elite believed that too much identification with Africa among free communities of color would give ammunition to the American Colonization Society, which hoped to deport blacks to Africa. Also, they feared that identification with Africa made an implicit argument that blacks were not really Americans but rather Africans residing in America.[76] An example of the change from African to colored is provided by Boston's African church, first named in 1806, which became the First Independent Church of the People of Color during the 1830s. The name change came about because "the name African is ill applied to a church composed of American citizens."[77]

Halifax's black societies did not believe that alignment with Africa inhibited their claim to British or Nova Scotian citizenship. Indeed, the African Baptist Church kept its name throughout the nineteenth century. Although the title of the African Methodist Church used the word "African," in an 1847 petition the trustees referred to themselves as "Citizens of Color" and their congregation as the "Colored Methodist Episcopal Zion Church."[78] The African Baptist Church and the community's societies also used "African" in their titles, and in an 1833 petition Richard Preston and his followers referred to their house of worship as the "Baptist African Chapel."[79] But Refugee petitions to the government commonly used the phrase "people of color." The terms "African" and "Colored" coexisted, as they did in some cases in New England, and the image of Africa remained an important part of the black community's public persona. Also, the use of the term "African" suggests the importance of memory for the local black community and the need to include an image of their distant homeland as part of their emerging identity in the 1840s and 1850s. More importantly, the titles of various organizations represented one aspect of Black Refugee consciousness that would be buttressed by a battle for equal citizenship and access to public space.

Political Involvement

Between 1838 and the American Civil War, the Black Refugees and their descendants waged several campaigns to claim contested public space and make a push for equal citizenship through political involvement. Historian David Sutherland has noted the importance of the Black Refugees' participation in Queen Victoria's 1838 coronation day parade.[80] During that event several dignitaries and various community organizations came together for a procession through the streets of Halifax. The African Friendly Society joined the festivities and wore beautiful outfits and carried signs, which claimed that Britain and the new Queen offered and se-cured black freedom.[81] In celebrating the coronation of Queen Victoria, the Refugees tied themselves closely to Britain and in the process sharply demarcated the border between free Nova Scotia and the slaveholding United States. Moreover, they carved out not only a place for their own identity but also one for the general population in Nova Scotia and British North America, because the Refugees were living examples of the differ-ence between the Republic and the Queen's Empire in North America. The Black Refugees' participation in this coronation celebration was an important foundation for several other events in which the Refugees chal-lenged formerly all-white public spaces and became politically active.

The Refugees obtained freehold grants of land at Hammonds Plains and Preston, which allowed them to participate in local elections. Before obtaining these grants the Refugees were, as one local politician put it, nothing more than "tenants of the Crown."[82] The Refugees were also painfully aware of their position. As they argued in an 1841 petition, "hold-ing under Tickets of location, we cannot sell to advantage, we are tied to the land without being able to live upon it, or even vote upon it, without being at every Election questioned, browbeaten and sworn."[83] Securing freehold grants allowed the Refugees to become more than tenants of the Crown. Instead, they were able to exercise the rights and responsibilities given to landholding property owners in the 1840s.[84] These grants resulted in a flurry of activity by several groups of Black Refugees interested in ex-ercising the franchise or participating in electoral politics.[85] The 1830s and 1840s were an exciting and troubling time in Nova Scotian politics. Like much of the Western world, British North America and the United States had experienced several social and economic upheavals that changed the face of politics. In the United States, the extension of the franchise and the development of a market economy changed American politics. Uprisings in Upper and Lower Canada during the late 1830s underlined the need for change in British North America, which had been ruled by small cliques of men who acquired their position through a combination of nepotism and political connections. Although the uprisings failed, they forced the British to reconsider the role of the entrenched elite in both colonies.

In Nova Scotia, a vocal group of small businessmen, journalists, and others argued for an increased role in governing the colony. They believed that positions of importance in the local government should be decided solely on the basis of merit and rejected Edmund Burke's conservative ideal of classes, with everyone remaining in the positions to which they had been born. These challenges were significant in that Nova Scotia particularly before 1830 had been a bastion of conservative Tory ideology. Several lieutenant governors who were devoted to maintaining order and good government in the wake of the French and American revolutions had ruled Nova Scotia in the early nineteenth century. The Tories believed that paternalism, order, and class privileges remained necessary aspects of good government. The Reformers, however, were not anti-British in any sense but rather desired constitutional reform within the imperial system. Thus the 1840s were defined by a widening and increasingly hostile struggle between the Reformers and Tories. The Reformers wanted Nova Scotia to become a self-governing colony, while the Tories hoped to retain power by limiting the reform impulse of certain elements in the local population.[86]

The Black Refugees used these tensions in white society to assert their own political interests. Generally, they voted based on local issues such as continuing land reform, better roads, and relations with the wider community. It is also possible that the significant presence of white Baptists in the Tory party encouraged black Baptists to support the Tories. Although the leaders of black political involvement usually held positions of importance in the community, through either the church or social organizations, they advocated improvements that would help the entire community, such as better roads to and through the rural settlements. Also, the Refugees generally supported the party that promised to continue, nurture, and support their connection with Great Britain. In contrast to the United States, loyalty did not hinge on which party opposed slavery, as both the Tories and the Reformers, claiming to be good British subjects, spoke out against the Peculiar Institution.

Even before the Preston Refugees could vote, they participated in political events, because citizenship meant more than the exercise of the franchise. For example, during the election of 1840, the Preston Refugees paraded through Halifax and, though unable to exercise the franchise, "took complete possession of the passage for the entree and exit of the voters," meaning that they campaigned boisterously in front of the polling place.[87] The occupation of public space previously reserved for whites illustrated the willingness of the Refugees to push the local population to recognize their presence as part of the body politic. Several weeks later community leader Septimus Clark held a Christmas dinner banquet that offered black support for the Tories, as they promised to uphold the existing constitution and maintain the British connection.[88]

Many Refugees tied the Tories to the British Crown, while the Reformers were partly perceived as wanting to undermine the constitution and cooperate with the United States. But other community members favored the opposition party. For example, in 1841 a meeting of the "colored re-formers" gathered at Preston for political and social discussions. The chair of this meeting, Samson Carter, declared that the "loyalty" of the Black Refugees who lived among the "rocks at Preston" was strong. The meeting also included toasts to Victoria, to her husband, Prince Albert, to Lieu-tenant Governor Falkland, to the "Reformers of Nova Scotia," and to local political figures.[89] These public displays of black political interest chal-lenged many prevailing assumptions among local whites about the ability of the Refugees to grasp the basic tenets of local and imperial politics. Publicly demonstrating an understanding of political issues allowed the Refugees to claim civic rights, which had been systematically denied them in previous decades.

At this same time of increasing political involvement, the Refugees con-tinued to participate in public parades and festivals in honor of British royalty. In 1841 the Refugees celebrated the birth of the future Prince of Wales. This celebration began with ringing church bells and artillery, while the city council distributed food to Halifax's poor. The day contin-ued with a procession through the town to Government House, where speeches were given extolling Britain and the Queen. The day concluded with various dinners, dance parties, and fireworks. The patriotic town was filled with British flags and monuments to British military victories.[90] The Black Refugees, represented by the African Friendly Society, participated in the procession along with other local societies and gave an address that extolled British liberty, described themselves as "loyal" subjects, and of-fered thanks for the gift of an "enlightened" government.[91]

Two years later, during provincial elections, Reformer Joseph Howe gave speeches at Preston and pressed the Refugees to vote for his party. Many Refugees at Preston favored Howe because as a member of the coalition government he had played an important role in changing their tickets of location to freehold grants. At the "New Year's African Jubilee," the Afri-can Constitution Society had toasted Joseph Howe, Lieutenant Governor Falkland, the army, the navy, and Prince Albert. More important, the so-ciety tied itself closely to Britain by also toasting, "The Queen—God Bless Her—May she reign in the hearts of a free loyal and happy people." More-over, it also memorialized Wilberforce, "[t]he friend and benefactor of the African race, who by his Philanthropy has conferred the blessing of eman-cipation upon the slave, who no longer writhes under the taskmaster."[92]

In publicly reiterating their loyalty to the Crown and famous Britons, the Refugees were drawing a strict line between their lives in Nova Scotia and their former existence in the United States. It is worth asking whether they entertained this public face of loyalty out of genuine feelings of connection to Britain or simply as a mechanism to achieve political inclusion and citizenship in Nova Scotia. Feelings of loyalty or connection to Britain were not limited to blacks in the British Empire. Indeed, radical abolitionist David Walker discussed the escape of black Americans to the "hospitable shores of Canada" and noted that they were among "the English, our real friends and benefactors."[93] Certainly, black people knew that Britain had held and traded slaves in the recent past, but the public proclamations and writings of some black people simply extolled more recent examples of supposed British liberty. Does this mean that the Refugees entertained an uncritical attitude toward Great Britain? In all likelihood the Refugees' public relationship with the Crown represented a pragmatic attempt to gain rights and respect for their community within the framework of the British Empire, even if this meant ignoring or discussing only privately some of Britain's history with slavery. Yet the Refugees' actions and attitudes could have resulted from genuine feelings of patriotism. The British had ended slavery before the Americans, and the Refugees owed their escape from slavery in part to the British. Whatever the case may have been, the Refugees continued to highlight their connection with the Crown throughout the 1840s.

By 1846 the Reformers and the Tories were hoping to attract Black Refugee votes. Despite the Refugees' poverty and marginal status in society, the battle between the Tories and the Reformers for control over Nova Scotia resulted in both parties fighting for every vote that might tip an election in their favor. In the eyes of many Refugees, the Tories had not worked hard enough to improve the Refugees' land situation, and as a result the Tories lost some black support in the election of 1843. But the Refugees remained tied to the Tories because Richard Preston, among others, viewed the Reformers as political opportunists who might sever the connection between Nova Scotia and the Crown. This view had little substance in that Nova Scotia Reformers did not harbor a hope for annexation to the United States, but the Tories continually hammered away at this image in order to frighten some blacks into backing the Tory candidates. Although Reformer Joseph Howe had maintained close contact with blacks at Preston and Hammonds Plains and had attempted to improve their standing in the colony, the Refugees still engaged in several public displays of loyalty to and support of the Tory party. They were present, for example, at the farewell for Howe's archrival Lord Falkland, the lieutenant governor of Nova Scotia.

This was a significant event in provincial politics. Although a Tory, Falkland had supported some changes to local government, including inviting some of the Reformers to serve on the colony's Executive Council; but Falkland had resisted Howe's attempts to institute responsible government, which would have meant that elected officials as opposed to appointees would govern Nova Scotia. Eventually, in 1846, Howe insulted Falkland by publicly threatening to have him flogged. The governor, angered by this comment and finding his position untenable, resigned and left Nova Scotia in the summer. At his farewell, the Charitable African Society (CAS) gave an address dominated by proclamations of loyalty but also claims to being part of Nova Scotia's political culture.

We the Members, numbering about three hundred males, of the Charitable African Society of Halifax, Nova Scotia . . . thank Your Excellency for your constant kindness and attention to the coloured People since the Queen sent you to be our Governor. But finding that your Excellency has determined to leave Nova Scotia on Monday next, we shall be unable to do all that we wished. We, therefore, in this manner, take the liberty of stating to your Excellency, that we are true, loyal and grateful subjects of Her Royal Majesty, that we love the Constitution under which we live, that we wish to be good subjects, and to treat our Governors and Rulers with respect. Many of us are poor and unlearned, and we cannot for our parts understand what the gentleman [*sic*] have been quarreling about for three or four years past, in a country where all are free and enjoy equal rights. Your Excellency knows that no coloured man ever showed disrespect to Your Excellency since you came to Nova Scotia. We are all sorry that Your Excellency is going to leave us. We hope our beloved Queen will send us another Governor like Lord Falkland. We also respectfully beg leave to express our humble and grateful thanks for Your Excellency's constant kindness and attention to the people of colour. Your noble Lady has also been kind to many of us. We are at a loss what words to use in thanking Her Ladyship. We hope Her Ladyship and Your Excellency will have a safe and pleasant voyage . . . Passed unanimously at a full meeting of the Society, and signed on their behalf, by their order, at Halifax, 31st July 1846.[94]

The Charitable African Society's presence at Lord Falkland's farewell was important for several reasons. First, the Refugees continued their claim to participate in events of importance to the wider community, but in a publicly deferential way, which played quite well with many elements of the white population. Second, in their own voice, the black community underlined their claim to the rights of British subjects. In doing this, they continued to contest the meaning of Britishness in Nova Scotia. Third, by giving this address, black activists had strategically placed themselves between the two feuding parties eager to offer the Refugees various inducements for political support. Finally, the Refugees knew that the political conflict opened up avenues for community assertion.

The fight between the Reformers and the Tories over the question of self-government divided Nova Scotia's population, including the Black Refugees. The choice between the two parties was particularly difficult for the local black community because each party had made a strong case for the black vote. Richard Preston had long supported the entrenched Tory elite because of his Anglophilia. Also, former Tory lieutenant governors Falkland and Colin Campbell had attempted to improve relations between the government and the Refugees by advocating a few land reforms. On the other hand, Reformer Joseph Howe had always maintained a close relationship with the Refugees by attending several soirees and other community events. Activist and well-respected community member Septimus Clark disagreed with his associate Richard Preston and held a dinner in support of the Reform cause in early 1846. These two important figures in the black community thus overtly disagreed over which party the community should support.[95] But Howe had weakened his own position by asserting in the Assembly that some black person might be employed by an angry Nova Scotian to whip Falkland for his continuing opposition to responsible government.[96] This comment had unintended consequences for Howe. Several black people found it offensive to connect free British subjects, especially those who had been slaves, with any proposed whipping of the Queen's representative. Indeed, at a meeting of the Tories in Preston one local man noted "the indignity" uttered by Howe and declared it to be offensive to his "color."[97]

In early May 1847, on the eve of the general election that would put the Reformers in government, the community of Preston became a battleground between supporters of the Tories and the Reformers. The Reformers had organized a public meeting for their constituents, but the Tories planned to destroy any momentum this rally might engender by organizing their own rally, complete with flags, liquor, food, and gaudy horse coaches.[98] The Reformers began their rally early in the day, and Howe enjoyed the support of a "staunch and enthusiastic" crowd. Local black farmers criticized the governing Tories and also made a claim to the British connection, which the Liberals promised to maintain. The black Reformers noted that they "value too highly our rights as British Subjects, and particularly the Elective franchise, to barter away our independence, believing that those who would buy a Constituency would sell a Country."

Joseph Howe also addressed the crowd and reminded them of his role in making them freehold farmers rather than keeping the Refugees as "tenants of the Crown."[99]

At the opposing rally several Tory candidates promised better roads and the upholding of the constitution. More important, Richard Preston and Septimus Clark now both supported the Tories. Clark claimed to have been so offended by Howe's whipping comment that he had decided to withdraw his support from the Reformers.[100] As Nomination Day approached for the election of 1847, both parties held rallies at Hammonds Plains, where violence almost broke out as black Tories attempted to remove a banner held by the Reformers and emblazoned with the words "Victoria and British Liberty."[101] Not surprisingly, given the rising tensions, several days later a riot erupted in Halifax between black Tories and white supporters of the Reformers.

Historian David Sutherland has accurately described the racial violence that enveloped Halifax on Nomination Day in 1847 as a conflict between the local Irish and black populations.[102] Increasing numbers of indigent Irish immigrants had been migrating into Nova Scotia, and they competed with blacks for menial labor during the 1840s. These new settlers wanted to be incorporated into local society.[103] One way to accomplish this was through political involvement. In 1847 Nova Scotia had a property qualification for voting that barred most urban laborers, especially recent Irish immigrants, from exercising the franchise. In contrast, landholders from Preston and Hammonds Plains could vote. But events such as Nomination Day involved much more than simply voting. Opposing political parties encouraged their supporters to gather at the County Court House to listen to nomination speeches and cheer on individual candidates. Thus, large groups of possibly drunken partisan political supporters were put together in a relatively small area. As the day progressed, black supporters of the Tories came to blows with white Reformers; members of both groups started to push one another and a "melee" ensued. Participants attacked each other with fists, sticks, and clubs. Several papers reported on the event but offered differing accounts. For example, the *Standard* claimed that the black Tories had more of a right to attend the event than "the fellows who insulted them."[104] In contrast, one newspaper argued that the Tories had brought blacks to Halifax to "terrify" whites and that the Refugees had behaved in an "overbearingly insolent" manner.[105]

It is unclear which party landed the first blows, but the row was an attempt to assert white citizenship, while denying it to local blacks.[106] One letter to a local newspaper, from "IRISH CATHOLIC," wondered how anyone would "imagine that a handful of Blacks from Hammonds Plains could terrify the Irishmen of Halifax?" The letter went on to blame the Tories and suggested that if the blacks ever "paraded again through the streets of Halifax," their white Tory leaders should "apply some burnt cork to their dirty faces."[107]

The Refugees, however, refused to be deterred by the events of 1847 and continued to maintain an important presence at public events. For example, at the celebrations in 1849 for the one-hundred-year anniversary of Halifax's founding, the African Society participated along with other groups, including the Charitable Irish Society.[108] Three years later at the funeral for Lieutenant Governor Harvey, the African Abolition Society participated in the procession, which was conducted with "decorum."[109] In 1860, during the visit of the Prince of Wales, "a strong company of Negroes" participated in the procession for Victoria's son.[110] And not surprisingly, they declared "God Bless Queen Victoria, the Liberator of the Slave."[111] In the wake of the racial tensions of 1847, the black community continued to declare its loyalty to the Queen and British institutions, while placing Britain at the forefront of the community's emerging identity.

Abolitionism

The Refugees also engaged in a struggle for abolition, which included other aspects of their identity and community values such as the importance of their memory of the United States and Africa. The African Abolition Society was the most active and important organization created by the Black Refugees. It sponsored several public lectures against slavery during the 1840s and 1850s, while offering help to a small number of Fugitives from the United States. The AAS organized Emancipation Day celebrations in honor of the anniversary of the abolition of slavery in the British West Indies. The Black Refugees did not celebrate their own emancipation from slavery but rather focused on the liberation of their brethren in another part of the Black Atlantic. The Refugees' focus on slavery in the United States further illustrated their commitment to an international abolitionist movement. The Refugees' antislavery organization had American and Black Atlantic foundations; these former American slaves in Nova Scotia continued to engage with ideas and problems beyond the borders of British North America. The African Abolition Society complicated and contested the border by engaging with the United States and memorializing Africa during its public processions. In doing this, the AAS threaded together several aspects of the Refugees' emerging identity, which included memories of slavery, continuing engagement with the United States, expressions of loyalty to Great Britain, and their idea of Africa.

Abolitionism held an important place in the Black Refugee community. The African Abolition Society, run almost exclusively by former slaves, did not allow whites to join the society's executive. The AAS did encourage white people to attend its public lectures and some meetings, but it did not allow them to participate in any decisions regarding the internal policies or practices of the society. The Refugees did not want to lose autonomy by allowing local whites to influence the AAS.

This type of tension also could be found within the American antislavery movement. Some black abolitionists, such as Frederick Douglass, expressed frustration with the paternalistic and racist attitudes of some white abolitionists. Although many African Americans recognized the significance of the American Anti-Slavery Society and the importance of forging contacts with white abolitionists, by the early 1840s some black leaders had turned to the Black National Convention meetings in an effort to assert some autonomy from the influence of whites. Yet such major antislavery organizations as the American and Foreign Anti-Slavery Society encouraged interracial contact and the development of a biracial abolitionism. The paternalism that marked the attitudes of many white abolitionists contributed to the schism between William Lloyd Garrison and Frederick Douglass. The much larger antislavery movement in the United States also divided over several issues including whether abolitionists should be politically involved, women's rights, the Constitution, and the merits of nonviolent resistance.[112] In Nova Scotia, AAS members were more unified than their brethren in the United States, supported black political involvement, and on a few occasions spoke about their preparedness to fight the Yankees if necessary. For example, one black woman told a newspaper about her poverty in Nova Scotia but reported her willingness to "fight" the Americans because "we [the Refugees] will never be slaves again."[113]

In the winter of 1846, at an "African" soiree, Richard Preston "prayed . . . long and loud for the happiness of the African race, morally, politically, socially, and spiritually." Part of this happiness included a resolution that black people in the Halifax region should annually observe a day of emancipation.[114] Preston was not satisfied with his own freedom and always felt connected with those he had left behind in bondage. "Our young men . . . are brutalized in intellect, and their manly energies are chilled by the frosts of slavery; sometimes they are called to witness the agonies of the mothers who bore them, writhing under the lash."[115] Given these views, it is not clear why the Refugees waited until 1846 to establish the AAS. Perhaps the founding of this society can be understood as part of the Refugees' wider attempts at social and political inclusion during the 1840s.

The African Abolition Society held a variety of lectures and events, in which the participants discussed slavery, brought in speakers, and engaged with their former homeland by debating American laws. The Refugees had not simply escaped from slavery in the United States and become removed from the experience of friends and relatives left behind in Maryland, Virginia, Georgia, and other areas. In August 1846, for example, the Refugees held two meetings to advocate the abolition of slavery. At the first gathering, the AAS stated that its twin objectives were the suppression of slavery and the relief of fugitive slaves in Nova Scotia. A local newspaper commented that "several who were once slaves, took part in the business of the evening." Moreover, "the members, not selfishly satisfied with their own freedom . . . wish to see others similarly privileged."[116] Several weeks later the AAS held another meeting and resolved "[t]hat the operations of this society shall continue until the entire abolition of slavery has been secured."[117] In these meetings the Refugees developed another aspect of their consciousness, one that focused on the freedom of their brethren in the United States. Although slavery was a distant memory for most Refugees by the mid-1840s, it still remained an important part of their identity and community development as they retained psychosocial and political ties to black southerners. The goals of the AAS were respected by many sectors of the local white population because the society represented not only a challenge to the United States but also a tangible example of liberty in British North America. Thus when drunken vandals disturbed a meeting of the African Abolition Society, the *Novascotian* declared it "a matter of regret that there should exist a disposition on the part of some of the white population to annoy and persecute a society having so worthy an object as the deliverance from slavery of their brethren."[118]

During the late 1840s and the early 1850s, the AAS made several pragmatic attempts to put its antislavery ideals into action. The Refugees wanted to use Nova Scotia's location as a port to facilitate the escape of slaves from various locations throughout the United States and the Caribbean. In 1848 the African Abolition Society petitioned the government, claiming that an unscrupulous ship's captain had left a black immigrant, a seaman who had recently arrived in Nova Scotia, in a Georgia prison. They demanded that the fate of this black seaman be fully investigated. The government took action and pursued the captain, who claimed that the seaman was a native of Nassau and had supposedly requested a discharge, which the captain granted.[119] Perhaps this unfortunate man had fallen victim to Georgia's version of the Negro Seamen Act. In 1829 the state government passed an act whereby "vessels coming into ports of the state with free Negroes on board, either as employees or as passengers, be subjected to quarantine for forty days." If a free black seaman broke this law and spoke with any black Georgians, he could be imprisoned. According to historian Philip Hamer, Savannah had a "less oppressive" version of this law because a ship "could be released from quarantine if its free Negroes were placed in prison and bond given to pay their expenses and take them away."[120] Sometimes, black seamen from the North were captured by southern officials and sold into slavery. The imprisonment of this black Nova Scotian seaman in Georgia was part of a broader pattern, as historian Jeffrey Bolster points out, to "cut off the means of livelihood for seamen of color and their dependents in the North."[121] One year later, the AAS held a meeting to provide food, shelter, and any other necessaries of life for a recently escaped slave from Cuba.[122] In 1850 the AAS promised to help "two SLAVES, who have lately made their escape from slavery."[123] During the same year, the celebrated William and Ellen Craft escaped from the United States and briefly stayed in Halifax.[124]

Unfortunately, the Crafts' experience in Nova Scotia turned out to be less than pleasant. Running from slaveholders, the Crafts made it to Nova Scotia in 1850. Despite arriving in Her Majesty's domain, William and Ellen Craft realized that they were still surrounded by "low Yankee prejudice."[125] Indeed, in search of lodging, the Crafts finally found a small "dirty hole" of an inn.

> I sent my wife in with the other passengers, to engage a bed for herself and husband. I stopped outside in the rain till the coach came up. If I had gone in and asked for a bed they would have been quite full. But as they thought my wife was white, she had no difficulty in securing apartments, into which the luggage was afterwards carried. The landlady, observing that I took an interest in the baggage, became somewhat uneasy, and went into my wife's room, and said to her 'Do you know the dark man downstairs?' 'Yes, he is my husband.' 'Oh! I mean the black man—the nigger?' 'I quite understand you; he is my husband.' 'My God!' exclaimed the woman as she flounced out and banged to the door.[126]

After the Crafts had stayed one night, the "mistress" of the hotel informed them that they needed to seek accommodations elsewhere but also mentioned that "I have no prejudice myself; I think a good deal of the coloured people, and have always been their friend; but if you stop here we shall lose all our customers." The Crafts were grateful to know that this woman "was such a staunch friend to the coloured people."[127] Faced with the "vulgar prejudice of the town," the Crafts were given the addresses of "some respectable coloured families" and eventually stayed with the Reverend Cannady and his wife before heading to England.[128]

Several months later, Halifax's African Abolition Society called for a meeting to "present before the public, about fourteen persons, together with men, women, and children, who have recently escaped from oppression, to a place of safety and liberty."[129] The society called on Nova Scotians to attend the gathering and provide the Fugitives with financial support. In addition to aiding American Fugitives in Nova Scotia, the African Abolition Society maintained connections with black abolitionists in Canada West. For example, after Richard Preston had been separated from his family for nearly thirty years, the society asked for donations as he was about to "proceed to Canada, to see his daughter, who has recently made her escape from Virginia, the state of Slavery."[130] These practical attempts, though small in number, represented the Refugees' continuing connections with the United States.

Another way that members of the African Abolition Society maintained intellectual and emotional connections with their former homeland was through public lectures. Unlike the vast majority of American Fugitives in Canada West, the Refugees had been in Nova Scotia for three decades by the late 1840s and the early 1850s. Yet they remained interested in the state of African American life in the southern United States. Public lectures allowed the Refugees to express their understanding of American slavery and slave laws. Moreover, these lectures connected the Refugees with events and issues of importance throughout the Black Atlantic. Generally, local speakers gave addresses about the evils of slavery, but occasionally lecturers also came from the United States and Britain. During the summer of 1850, the AAS sponsored a lecture about the origins of the African and Indian races. The speaker, a clergyman from the United States, also spoke about American slavery. In their advertisement for this event, the Refugees made an interesting commentary on the state of American politics. The society declared that "the rail roads [that lead] to Emancipation, can not rest on clay foundation [referring to Henry Clay and the 1850 compromise], and the road that [James K. Polk] erects leads us to Slavery and to Texas—come and help us roll it along."[131] Several months later, at another meeting, one speaker declared his preparedness to travel to the United States and give the Americans "musket balls for breakfast, cannon balls for dinner, and bomb-shells for tea."[132]

The 1850 enactment of the Fugitive Slave Law did not escape the attention of the AAS, and it immediately called a meeting to discuss the "'Fugitive Slave Bill' recently passed by the Congress of the United States."[133] In 1853 former slave Moses Roper gave a speech about his own well-known experience with the Peculiar Institution and also discussed the religious condition of slaves and their masters.[134] The African Abolition Society's willingness to engage with topics of importance for Afro-America underlines the transnational foundations of the Refugees' community and identity. These expatriate African Americans did not erase or forget their own history. The British element of the Refugees' community and identity was strong, but also significant were the community's memories of slavery, interest in United States politics, and relationships with African Americans inside the borders of the United States.

The African Abolition Society also held annual Emancipation Day parades between 1846 and 1867.[135] These parades were an essential expression of the community's self-consciousness and an acknowledgment of various aspects of its overlapping identity as celebrations connected the Black Refugees with people of African descent in the Caribbean, United States, Africa, and Canada West. Emancipation Day usually consisted of a procession through Halifax followed by speeches from former slaves and government dignitaries. These were followed by picnics and other festivities into the evening. In 1847, for example, the AAS marched through the city and held banners extolling freedom and British liberty, while a military band provided music. Several speakers celebrated the end of slavery and gave "loyal" addresses at Government House to the crowd of well-wishers.[136] Three years later the Emancipation Day event had gained popularity among white and black people in Nova Scotia.

In celebrating freedom, the Refugees not only engaged with slavery in the United States but also connected themselves to black people throughout the British Empire. For example, in an advertisement for the 1850 celebration, the AAS promised to "celebrate the 1st of August, in which our brethren was set at liberty in the British West India Islands, by walking in procession together from the African School House to the African Baptist Chapel, in Cornwallis street, where a sermon will be delivered; and from thence to Bell Mount where the society will occupy themselves by speeches."[137] During the celebrations, the AAS made several toasts that expressed the Refugees' consciousness. The toasts saluted several British figures including the Queen, Prince Albert, and local government officials. Most significantly, the first toast memorialized "AFRICA, the land of our Forefathers."[138]

The African Abolition Society continued to hold celebrations during the early 1850s, which were well attended. In 1855 the African Abolition Society held another celebration and parade for Emancipation. The toasts given during this parade illustrate several aspects of the Refugees' overlapping and complex identity. First, the participants gave a standing toast to Africa, but it is interesting that the society's members had imbibed notions that the so-called Dark Continent needed to be Christianized. "Africa—the land of our Fathers—May the spirit of true religion be exercised among her sons and daughters, until they all become civilised throughout their vast country." The participants also declared their hope that "the Allied armies in the Crimea . . . [would] subdue their [Russian] enemy." In addition to their support for British military expeditions, the AAS membership toasted the "health of the Abolition Society in Canada, Bermuda, and all the West India Islands, who assemble in honor of this day."[139] Clearly, the society entertained ideas of an international and pan-African abolitionism. The members connected their own history and experience with slavery to the histories of escaped and emancipated people of African descent throughout the British Empire. The African Abolitionist Society's toasts and public processions blended understandings of slavery, emancipation, Africa, and America into a festival of memory based on the foundation of freedom in British North America. Through its many activities the AAS played an important role in the transition of various former slaves into a coherent and definitive community that forged a space in the social and political milieu of Nova Scotia.

The fate of the African Abolition Society is not clear. It remained active during the early years of the Civil War but was not as visible after 1865 as it had been during the 1840s and 1850s. The conclusion of the American Civil War renewed fears among some sectors of the white population that African Americans might migrate to Nova Scotia. As a result, one of the post–Civil War Emancipation Day events resulted in an outbreak of racial violence. In 1867 local blacks planned to hold a procession through Halifax and a picnic. They hoped to conclude the evening with a soiree at the Mason Hall. But this day was cut short when a "mob, who seemed perfectly lawless," attacked the marchers. Violence continued until the city police organized a posse to stop the vigilantes.[140]

Contrary to the spirit of this violent act, meant to strip the local black community of its dignity by interrupting a long-standing and respected public festival, and despite economic hardship, racial prejudice, and civic discrimination, the Refugees and their descendants created, developed, and maintained a cohesive society. The Black Refugees also maintained and developed a community in Nova Scotia that had many similarities with black communities in New England. The key difference lay in the Refugees' position in British North America. They used this position to claim the rights of British subjects, while blurring the border with the United States in an attempt to retain social and political ties with black Americans. As historian Jane Rhodes and other scholars have noted, the contested relationship between the articulation of blackness and Britishness troubled several black communities throughout the British world. The Refugees rejected the notion that to be British one had to be white. They refused to be "disavowed or discounted" by the majority population. The Refugees did not slip into a state of invisibility but rather challenged certain doctrines that attempted to make blackness and Britishness mutually exclusive categories.[141] The Refugees and their descendants engaged in a constant struggle to claim the rights of citizenship in Nova Scotia, while supporting black freedom struggles in the United States and elsewhere.

Epilogue

DURING THE 1860S three significant themes emerged from the black communities in Nova Scotia. First, unlike the experience of the 1830s and 1840s, people of color became more isolated from the mainstream of society. It is true that they continued to participate in certain public celebrations such as the visit of the Prince of Wales in 1860, but the general trend seemed to be isolation from the mainstream of Nova Scotia's society. For example, the rural settlement of Hammonds Plains had a population of less than 200 in 1838, but by 1861 it had increased to 770. Preston also saw its population increase, from 496 to 641 between 1851 and 1861. The increases in rural population were tied to increasingly isolationist sentiments that removed the black population from the colonial mainstream. These isolationist sentiments may have been tied to agricultural improvements and farming innovations at the two settlements. Additionally, although the Refugees did not simply retreat to their rural homesteads immediately after the outbreak of racial violence in 1847, lingering feelings of discord and racial snubs and insults at nearly every corner in Halifax (as experienced by William and Ellen Craft) may have encouraged the Refugees to seek their future away from the white mainstream.

The Refugees also attracted much less government attention, and the number of their petitions to the government dropped during the 1860s as compared with the 1840s. Petitioning had been a form of political inclusion and protest, but it waned during the early 1860s perhaps as a result of increasing racial hostility, difficult economic circumstances, and government neglect. Of course, black people might simply have turned inward in an effort to redirect energies from local politics to church matters and other community issues. This inward or internal focus would change during the battle with the school system in the 1880s, and local blacks again would return to engaging with issues of importance to the wider community, but local white society's rejection of the possibility of integrated schools resulted in black community leaders turning "increasingly to the promotion of separatism as a crucible for encouraging race pride and racial unity in turn-of-the-century Halifax."[1]

The second theme was the development of internal fragmentation within the African Baptist Association after the death of Richard Preston in 1861. James Thomas, a white man, replaced Preston as the head of the African Baptist Association. Black preachers such as Benson Smithers and eventually George Neale objected to him, and the ABA eventually excluded both men for their rejection of Thomas's leadership. Smithers and the First Preston church left the ABA and did not return until after Thomas's death in 1879. The increasing isolation from Nova Scotia's mainstream and the internal factionalism of the 1860s were in stark contrast to the push for community development and political integration of the 1840s and 1850s.

The third important theme of post-1860 black life in Nova Scotia was the migration of several community members to New England. As the original Refugees had children and grandchildren, some of these younger people engaged in a redefinition of the border by migrating to New England. The first-generation Refugees usually defined the border in sharp terms between the slaveholding United States and free British North America, including Nova Scotia. Yet many of their children and grandchildren never experienced slavery firsthand. With the conclusion of the American Civil War in 1865, some migrated to Massachusetts and in the process demonstrated the changing meaning of the border for the Refugees' descendants.

According to the 1880 United States census, several black families living in Massachusetts had roots in Nova Scotia. Some of these people's parents were Refugees. Born in Nova Scotia in 1828, William Allen migrated to Boston and worked as a laborer. His parents had been born in Virginia. A child of black Georgians who migrated to Nova Scotia, Lillie Allen had settled in Boston by 1880 and was married to William Allen. Jane Butler and Mary Cooper were born in Nova Scotia in 1824 and 1826 respectively. Butler eventually moved to Lynn, Massachusetts, and was "keeping house," while Cooper migrated to West Roxbury and worked as a servant. Both of these women's parents had been born in Virginia. Abraham Boyd found work as a servant in Boston. Interestingly, he claimed that his parents had been born in Africa before settling in Nova Scotia.[2] In 1892 the *Acadian Recorder* recounted the story of the recently deceased Margaret Grandison. A former resident of Halifax, she had been "about the last of those brought over from Baltimore by the British during the War of 1812." She died in

Cambridge, Massachusetts, at her daughter's home.[3] Another family of African Nova Scotians, Mary and John Taylor, also moved to Cambridge. According to eminent historian David Levering Lewis, these were "strong working-class" people who rented out a room to a young, aspiring African American student at Harvard University, William Edward Burghardt Du Bois, in the late nineteenth century.[4]

The lack of opportunities faced by the Black Refugees continued for their children and grandchildren, and this partly explains their migration to the United States. For many in the black community, it was a bitter pill to swallow that racial discrimination was impeding the employment of the Refugees' descendants. In 1895 the secretary of the African Baptist Association described the continuing problems of employment in Nova Scotia and the successful careers that some had found abroad.

> The United States with her faults, which are many, has done much for the elevation of the [C]oloured race. She has given to the race Professors in Colleges, Senators, Engineers, Doctors, Lawyers, Mechanics of every description. Sad and sorry are we to say that is more than we can boast of here in Nova Scotia. Our young men as soon as they receive a common school education must flee away to the United States [to] seek employment, as did W. H. Gol[a]r, a young Haligonian, who is now a Professor of Ancient Languages in Livingstone College, [Salisbury], N.C. [He would later become president of the college.] Very few ever receive a trade from the large employers, even in the factories, on account of race prejudices, which is a terrible barrier, and an direct insult to Almighty God . . . when young mechanics have arrived in our city [Halifax] from the West Indies, they could not obtain a situation, simply on account of color. [They] had to accept something very menial, and subsequently [they] had to leave [our city to] go to the United States to prosecute their mechanical skill.[5]

The migration of black people from Nova Scotia to New England and other parts of the United States in the late nineteenth century, especially after the Civil War and the end of slavery, highlights the important question of the possibilities of an African Canadian identity. The late historian Robin Winks argued in 1969 that there "is, in fact, no *Canadian* Negro, for the Negroes of Nova Scotia and those of British Columbia have never been brought together in common cause."[6] Winks believed that this problem was the result of a lack of national leadership, plus a lack of national newspapers, and because black Canadians did not necessarily share a common history as did their American cousins. These obstacles presented a multiplicity of difficulties for the development of an African Canadian identity.

Canadians generally had more difficulty than their American neighbors in establishing a national consciousness, for various reasons including a longer colonial history and the identification of many English-Canadians, especially important elements of the political elite and the intelligentsia, with Britain as opposed to Canada. This problem can also be found among black people in Nova Scotia, who also identified with Britain despite their location after Confederation in the new nation of Canada. In the United States, in contrast, despite pervasive racism, de jure and de facto, African Americans developed a national identity along with regional variations before and after the Civil War. In Nova Scotia, black people created a regional identity, but not quite a national one, in the late nineteenth century.

African Nova Scotian migration to New England in the late nineteenth century underlines not only the limitations of the post-Confederation economy but also the difficulties that black people had in establishing an African Canadian identity. Despite the challenge of creating (and perhaps developing) a national consciousness, perhaps the migration of some black people from Nova Scotia to New England shows an emerging international identity that tied together African Nova Scotians and Afro–New Englanders. Is it possible that further explorations of identity in the Great Lakes region or the western states and provinces might also highlight the international and regional aspects of black Canadian consciousness? But was this consciousness a one-way street? In other words, did African Canadian connections with the United States represent an international or diasporic aspect of the black Canadian experience that is much less nationalist than the identity of their American brethren? The migration of black Nova Scotians to New England or black Ontarians to Michigan does not necessarily inhibit or deny the development of an African Canadian consciousness. Instead, it adds a layer of complexity to African Canadian identity, which might be an interaction of international, national, regional, local, and racial aspects; and not necessarily in that order. The study of African Nova Scotian identity and African Canadian identity is such an unbelievably complex task that it awaits serious and sustained investigation, which can build on the work of George Elliot Clarke, Afua Cooper, Jane Rhodes, and Nora Faires.[7] Hopefully, this study of the Black Refugees is a small step toward understanding one of the regional aspects of African Canadian identity, which can be used in conjunction with newer and better studies in order to understand the question of African Canadian identity.

This study is dedicated to developing a comparative conversation among students and scholars of the African American experience in New England and those interested in the African Canadian experience in the Maritime Provinces. As discussed in the chapters above, there were significant similarities between the Black Refugees in Nova Scotia and their counterparts in various parts of New England, including work patterns, the importance of the black church, social organizations, abolitionism, and the fight to be recognized as citizens of their respective regions. Yet it might be the differences between the two regions that open up questions for serious study.

The black population of antebellum New England was partly composed of people who descended from northern slaves. In contrast, the majority of the black population in Nova Scotia and New Brunswick during the mid–nineteenth century descended from southern slaves. It is quite possible that small-scale household slavery in New England produced much different cultural dynamics than the more substantial plantation slavery in the Chesapeake and Georgia, which was infused with new Africans during the eighteenth and early nineteenth centuries. For example, did these different backgrounds result in more African diasporic traits—language, memorials, folktales, or music—among the black population in Nova Scotia as opposed to their counterparts in New England?

There are two other points of comparison between the two regions worthy of brief comment. First, the Black Refugees left their homes in various southern states to settle in Nova Scotia. In contrast, blacks in nineteenth-century New England lived as free people, for the most part, in communities where they had been enslaved in the eighteenth century. In some cases, this resulted in patron-client relationships between former slave owners and their former slaves, as was the case with Moses Brown of Rhode Island.[8] This type of social arrangement was rare in Nova Scotia, especially in the case of the Refugees, for obvious reasons. However, it might have been much more common among the former slaves of Loyalists. Indeed, as there were still slaves in Nova Scotia during the early nineteenth century, gradual emancipation might have resulted in the formation of alliances between former slaves and their owners. How the relationships between former slaves and their owners played out in early nineteenth-century Nova Scotia is an important point of comparison with the New England experience.

The second point of comparison revolves around the crucial question of political affiliation and disagreement. In New England, those African Americans who could exercise the franchise during the antebellum period generally voted against the Democratic Party because of its support for antiblack measures in the North and support of slavery in the South. In Nova Scotia, neither major party supported slavery, at least publicly. As a result, the voting patterns of blacks in Nova Scotia revolved around different issues than those of their counterparts in New England. Interestingly, black people in both regions forged alliances with different segments of the white elite in order to advance various political causes. This might also mark another important point of contrast between the two regions.

Perhaps the most appropriate way this study can end is with a point of convergence or confluence between African Americans, soon-to-be African Canadians, and their use of Britain in public celebrations. In 1863, as war raged throughout the United States, black people in New Brunswick consisting of some Black Refugees and their descendants, along with a visitor from Boston, joined together to celebrate Emancipation Day. A local newspaper recorded the festivities.

> A portion of the coloured people of this city celebrated the anniversary of the Emancipation of the West India slaves by holding a meeting in Mr. Smith's building on Monday evening. Mr. Watson was in the chair, and several speeches were made. Mr. Westel's speech was very effective and a young colored man named Francis, said to be from Boston, spoke eloquently and well. They all glorified British institutions and the British flag, and expressed earnest wishes for the success of the North in the present war and the total abolition of Slavery. Mr. Patterson sung a song on Emancipation to the air of "Old Dan Tucker," which afforded much amusement . . . Some four or five hundred persons were present.[9]

Notes

PREFACE (pp. xi–xiii)

1. Paul Gilroy, *The Black Atlantic: Modernity and Double Consciousness* (Cambridge, Massachusetts: Harvard University Press, 1993), 16.

INTRODUCTION (pp. 1–6)

1. Some sources, such as the 1861 African Baptist Association Minutes, indicate that Preston escaped from slavery: "In 1816 he was found clear gone and safely landed in Halifax, Nova Scotia." In contrast, historian Frank S. Boyd Jr. argues that Preston purchased his freedom.

2. *Novascotian* (Halifax), 24 August 1846; *British Colonist* (Halifax), 31 October 1850; *British Colonist* (Halifax), 18 March 1851; *British Colonist* (Halifax), 29 March 1853; Peter McKerrow, *A Brief History of the Coloured Baptists of Nova Scotia, 1783–1895,* ed. Frank S. Boyd Jr. (1895; reprint, Halifax: Afro Nova Scotian Enterprises, 1976), 11–17; Frank S. Boyd Jr., "Richard Preston," in *Dictionary of Canadian Biography,* ed. Frances G. Halpenny and Jean Hamelin (Toronto: University of Toronto Press, 1985), 8:968–70; Savannah E. Williams, "The Role of the African United Baptist Association in the Development of Indigenous Afro-Canadians in Nova Scotia," in *Repent and Believe: The Baptist Experience in Maritime Canada,* ed. Barry Moody (Hantsport, Nova Scotia: Lancelot Press, 1980); Pearleen Oliver, *A Brief History of the Coloured Baptists of Nova Scotia, 1782–1953* (Halifax: African United Baptist Association, 1953).

3. Oliver, *Brief History;* Pearleen Oliver, *A Root and a Name* (Halifax: self-published, 1977).

4. Previous historical accounts mention Preston but do not use his story to explore the themes of identity, community formation, migration, and borders.

Instead, the few pieces of scholarship about the Black Refugees have focused on racism, private and public philanthropy, or black struggle. Although these approaches have resulted in substantial insights about government relief, discrimination, and white benevolence, the history of Black Refugee life and its changes over time has not been examined in detail. Here the focus is on the community itself, its members and leaders, its problems, conditions, and development. C. B. Fergusson, *A Documentary Study of the Establishment of the Negroes in Nova Scotia between the War of 1812 and the Winning of Responsible Government* (Halifax: Public Archives of Nova Scotia, 1948); Robin W. Winks, *The Blacks in Canada: A History* (New Haven, Connecticut: Yale University Press, 1971), 114–41; James W. St. G. Walker, "The Establishment of a Free Black Community in Nova Scotia, 1783–1840," in *The African Diaspora: Interpretive Essays*, ed. Martin L. Kilson and Robert I. Rotberg (Cambridge, Massachusetts: Harvard University Press, 1976), 205–36; John Grant, *The Immigration and Settlement of the Black Refugees of the War of 1812 in Nova Scotia and New Brunswick* (Dartmouth: Black Cultural Centre for Nova Scotia, 1990). Bryan Rommel-Ruiz will offer a new interpretation of black life in Nova Scotia and Rhode Island in his *Between African and Colored: Slavery and Freedom in Rhode Island and Nova Scotia, 1750–1850* (Philadelphia: University of Pennsylvania Press, under contract). John McNish Weiss offers an important study in his *On Stony Ground: American Origins of the Black Refugees of the War of 1812 Settled in Nova Scotia and New Brunswick* (London: McNish & Weiss, 2006). Robin D. G. Kelley, "'But a Local Phase of a World Problem': Black History's Global Vision, 1883–1950," *Journal of American History* 86 (December 1999): 1045–77; Earl Lewis, "To Turn as on a Pivot: Writing African Americans into a History of Overlapping Diasporas," *American Historical Review* 100 (June 1995): 765–87; Darlene Clark Hine and Jacqueline McLeod, eds., *Crossing Boundaries: Comparative History of Black People in Diaspora* (1999; reprint, Bloomington & Indianapolis: Indiana University Press, 2001); Joyce E. Chaplin, "Expansion and Exceptionalism in Early American History," *Journal of American History* 89 (March 2003): 1431–55.

5. There are also many similarities between the Refugees and the free black communities outside New England. The rich historiography includes, but is certainly not limited to, Leon Litwack, *North of Slavery: The Negro in the Free States, 1790–1860* (Chicago: University of Chicago Press, 1961); Ira Berlin, *Slaves Without Masters: The Free Negro in the Antebellum South* (New York: Pantheon, 1974); Leonard P. Curry, *The Free Black in Urban America, 1800–1850: The Shadow of the Dream* (Chicago: University of Chicago Press, 1981); Gary B. Nash, *Forging Freedom: The Formation of Philadelphia's Black Community, 1720–1840* (Cambridge, Massachusetts: Harvard University Press, 1988); Harry Reed, *Platform for Change: The Foundations of the Northern Free Black Community, 1775–1865* (East Lansing: Michigan State University Press, 1994); Graham Russell Hodges, *Slavery and Freedom in the Rural North: African Americans in Monmouth County, New Jersey, 1665–1865* (Lanham, Maryland: Rowman & Little-

field Publishers, 1997); James Oliver Horton and Lois E. Horton, *In Hope of Liberty: Culture, Community, and Protest Among Northern Free Blacks, 1700–1860* (New York: Oxford University Press, 1997); Graham Russell Hodges, *Root and Branch: African Americans in New York and East Jersey, 1613–1863* (Chapel Hill: University of North Carolina Press, 1999); Patrick Rael, *Black Identity and Black Protest in the Antebellum North* (Chapel Hill: University of North Carolina Press, 2002); for a critical view of free black historiography, see Wilson J. Moses, "Black Communities in Antebellum America: Buttressing Held Views," *Reviews in American History* 25 (1997): 557–63.

6. Clayton E. Cramer, *Black Demographic Data, 1790–1860: A Sourcebook* (Westport, Connecticut: Greenwood Press, 1997), 99–104; Journal of the House of Assembly, 1852. In 1850 the following number of African Americans lived in the New England states respectively: 1,356 in Maine; 520 in New Hampshire; 718 in Vermont; 9,064 in Massachusetts; 3,670 in Rhode Island; and 7,693 in Connecticut. The number of black people in New Brunswick and Prince Edward Island remained relatively small.

7. James Oliver Horton and Lois E. Horton, *Black Bostonians: Family Life and Community Struggle in the Antebellum North* (1979; reprint, New York: Holmes & Meier, 1999); George A. Levesque, *Black Boston: African American Life and Culture in Urban America, 1750–1860* (New York: Garland, 1994); Robert J. Cottrol, *The Afro-Yankees: Providence's Black Community in the Antebellum Era* (Westport, Connecticut: Greenwood Press, 1982); William D. Piersen, *Black Yankees: The Development of an Afro-American Subculture in Eighteenth-Century New England* (Amherst: University of Massachusetts Press, 1988); Robert J. Cottrol, *From African to Yankee: Narratives of Slavery and Freedom in Antebellum New England* (Armonk, New York: M. E. Sharpe, 1998); Robert Warner, *New Haven Negroes: A Social History* (1940; reprint, New York: Arno Press, 1969); Lorenzo Greene, *The Negro in Colonial New England* (1942; reprint, New York: Atheneum, 1968); E. A Guyette, "Black Lives and White Racism in Vermont, 1760–1870" (master's thesis, University of Vermont, 1992); Mark J. Sammons and Valerie Cunningham, *Black Portsmouth: Three Centuries of African-American Heritage* (Durham: University of New Hampshire Press, 2004); Randolph Stakeman, "The Black Population of Maine, 1764–1900," *New England Journal of Black Studies* 8 (1989): 17–35. Most recent, but focusing on the period after the Civil War, is Maureen Elgersman Lee, *Black Bangor: African Americans in a Maine Community, 1880–1950* (Durham: University of New Hampshire Press, 2005).

8. Journal of the House of Assembly, 1852; Nova Scotia Census, 1851, RG 12, Nova Scotia Archives and Records Management, Halifax, Nova Scotia (hereafter NSARM); Horton and Horton, *Black Bostonians*, 2; Curry, *Free Black*, 244–45; Cottrol, *Afro-Yankees*, 114. In using the term "Halifax region" I am including Halifax, Dartmouth, Preston, Hammonds Plains, Beech Hill, and other small enclaves around the town of Halifax.

9. Claude A. Clegg, *The Price of Liberty: African Americans and the Making of Liberia* (Chapel Hill: University of North Carolina Press, 2004); Leon D. Pamphile, *Haitians and African Americans: A Heritage of Tragedy and Hope* (Gainesville: University Press of Florida, 2001); Alfred N. Hunt, *Haiti's Influence on Antebellum America: Slumbering Volcano in the Caribbean* (Baton Rouge: Louisiana State University Press, 1988); William H. Pease and Jane H. Pease, *Black Utopia: Negro Communal Experiments in America* (1963; reprint, Madison: State Historical Society of Wisconsin, 1972); Allen P. Stouffer, *The Light of Nature and the Law of God: Antislavery in Ontario, 1833–1877* (Montreal and Kingston: McGill-Queen's University Press, 1992); Michael Wayne, "The Black Population of Canada West on the Eve of the American Civil War: A Reassessment Based on the Manuscript Census of 1861," *Histoire Sociale/Social History* 28 (November 1995): 465–85; Jane Rhodes, *Mary Ann Shadd Cary: The Black Press and Protest in the Nineteenth Century* (Bloomington: Indiana University Press, 1998); Sharon A. Roger Hepburn, "Crossing the Border from Slavery to Freedom: The Building of a Community at Buxton, Upper Canada," *American Nineteenth Century History* 3 (Summer 2002): 25–68; James W. St. G. Walker, *The Black Loyalists: The Search for a Promised Land in Nova Scotia and Sierra Leone, 1783–1870* (London: Longman and Dalhousie University Press, 1976).

10. Elizabeth Rauh Bethel, *The Roots of African-American Identity: Memory and History in Free Antebellum Communities* (New York: St. Martin's Press, 1997), 141.

11. Ibid., 142.

12. Felicia R. Lee, "Black Migration, Both Slave and Free," *New York Times* (New York), 2 February 2005. In February 2005 the Schomburg Center for Research in Black Culture highlighted the importance of migration to understanding the history of African Americans in the exhibit In Motion: The African American Migration Experience. Scholars have long engaged the connection of migration and the black experience prior to the Civil War; John Hope Franklin and Loren Schweninger, *Runaway Slaves: Rebels on the Plantation* (New York: Oxford University Press, 1999); Floyd J. Miller, *The Search for a Black Nationality: Black Emigration and Colonization, 1787–1863* (Urbana: University of Illinois Press, 1975); Michael Tadman, *Speculators and Slaves: Masters, Traders, and Slaves in the Old South* (Madison: University of Wisconsin Press, 1989); Walter Johnson, *Soul by Soul: Life Inside the Antebellum Slave Market* (Cambridge, Massachusetts: Harvard University Press, 1999).

13. Jeremy Adelman and Stephen Aron, "From Borderlands to Borders: Empires, Nation-States, and the Peoples in Between in North American History," *American Historical Review* 104 (June 1999): 814–41; also see responses in *American Historical Review* 104 (October 1999): 1221–40.

14. W. J. Eccles, *The Canadian Frontier, 1534–1760* (1969; reprint, Albuquerque: University of New Mexico Press, 1983); J. M. S. Careless, *Frontier and Metropolis: Regions, Cities, and Identities in Canada before 1914* (Toronto: Uni-

versity of Toronto Press, 1989); Francis M. Carroll, *A Good and Wise Measure: The Search for the Canadian-American Boundary, 1783–1842* (Toronto: University of Toronto Press, 2001).

15. Margaret Conrad, ed., *They Planted Well: New England Planters in Maritime Canada* (Fredericton: Acadiensis Press, 1988); Margaret Conrad, ed., *Making Adjustments: Change and Continuity in Planter Nova Scotia, 1759–1800* (Fredericton: Acadiensis Press, 1991); Margaret Conrad and Barry Moody, eds., *Planter Links: Community and Culture in Colonial Nova Scotia* (Fredericton: Acadiensis Press, 2001); Stephen J. Hornsby and John G. Reid, eds., *New England and the Maritime Provinces: Connections and Comparisons* (Montreal and Kingston: McGill-Queen's University Press, 2005); Elizabeth Mancke, *The Fault Lines of Empire: Political Differentiation in Massachusetts and Nova Scotia, ca. 1760–1830* (New York: Routledge, 2005).

16. Afua Cooper, "The Fluid Frontier: Blacks and the Detroit River Region—a Focus on Henry Bibb," *Canadian Review of American Studies* 30 (2000): 129–49; Nora Faires, "Leaving the 'Land of the Second Chance': Migration from Ontario to the Great Lakes States in the Nineteenth and Early Twentieth Centuries," in *Permeable Border: The Great Lakes Basin as Transnational Region, 1650–1990*, ed. John J. Bukowczyk et al. (Pittsburgh: University of Pittsburgh Press, 2005).

17. Nora Faires, "Going Across the River: Black Canadians and Detroit Before the Great Migration," *Citizenship Studies* 10 (February 2006): 118.

18. Adelman and Aron, "From Borderlands to Borders," 814–41.

19. *Acadian Recorder* (Halifax), 4 July 1818.

CHAPTER 1: SLAVERY AND FREEDOM IN NOVA SCOTIA (pp. 9–24)

1. On the problems of referring to the land occupied variously by the Mi'kmaq, Acadians, Scottish, and eventually British, see John G. Reid, "The Nova Scotia Historian: A Creature of Paradox?" *Journal of the Royal Nova Scotia Historical Society* 5 (2002): 106–11.

2. Ralph Pastore, "The Sixteenth Century: Aboriginal Peoples and European Contact," in *The Atlantic Region to Confederation: A History*, ed. Phillip A. Buckner and John G. Reid (Toronto: University of Toronto Press, 1994), 22–39; John G. Reid, "1686–1720: Imperial Intrusions," in *The Atlantic Region to Confederation: A History*, ed. Phillip A. Buckner and John G. Reid (Toronto: University of Toronto Press, 1994), 78–103; Naomi E. S. Griffiths, *Contexts of Acadian History, 1686–1784* (Montreal and Kingston: McGill-Queen's University Press, 1992); Margaret Conrad, ed., *Making Adjustments: Change and Continuity in Planter Nova Scotia, 1759–1800* (Fredericton: Acadiensis Press, 1991); Margaret Conrad and Barry Moody, eds., *Planter Links: Community and Culture in Colonial Nova Scotia* (Fredericton: Acadiensis Press, 2001); Neil MacKinnon, *This Unfriendly*

Soil: The Loyalist Experience in Nova Scotia, 1783–1791 (Montreal and Kingston: McGill-Queen's University Press, 1986); George A. Rawlyk and Gordon T. Stewart, *A People Highly Favoured of God: The Nova Scotia Yankees and the American Revolution* (Toronto: Macmillan, 1972); David A. Sutherland, "1810–1820: War and Peace," in *The Atlantic Region to Confederation: A History*, ed. Phillip A. Buckner and John G. Reid (Toronto: University of Toronto Press, 1994), 234–260.

3. Kenneth Donovan, "Slaves and Their Owners in Ile Royale, 1713–1760," *Acadiensis* 25 (Autumn 1995): 3–32; Kenneth Donovan, " A Nominal List of Slaves and Their Owners in Ile Royale, 1713–1760," *Nova Scotia Historical Review* 16 (1996): 151–62; James W. St. G. Walker, *The Black Loyalists: The Search for a Promised Land in Nova Scotia and Sierra Leone, 1783–1870* (London: Longman and Dalhousie University Press, 1976).

4. Scholars such as Barry Cahill question the terminology and interpretation underlying the story and history of the Black Loyalists. Cahill argues that the Black Loyalists should be referred to as freed blacks. He notes that there were Loyalists who happened to be black as opposed to Black Loyalists. Barry Cahill, "The Black Loyalist Myth in Atlantic Canada," *Acadiensis* 29 (Autumn 1999): 76–87; also see Cassandra Pybus, "Jefferson's Faulty Math: The Question of Slave Defections in the American Revolution," *William and Mary Quarterly* 62 (April 2005): 243–64.

5. Nova Scotia adopted a form of gradual emancipation in the early 1790s.

6. John G. Reid, *Six Crucial Decades: Times of Change in the History of the Maritimes* (Halifax: Nimbus, 1987), 3–26; N. E. S. Griffiths, "1600–1650: Fish, Fur, and Folk," in *The Atlantic Region to Confederation: A History*, ed. Phillip A. Buckner and John G. Reid (Toronto: University of Toronto Press, 1994), 40–60.

7. John Johnston, "Research Note: Mathieu Da Costa along the Coasts of Nova Scotia: Some Possibilities," *Journal of the Royal Nova Scotia Historical Society* 4 (2001): 152–64.

8. Ibid.

9. Ira Berlin, *Many Thousands Gone: The First Two Centuries of Slavery in North America* (Cambridge, Massachusetts: Harvard University Press, 1998), 17.

10. Robin W. Winks, *The Blacks in Canada: A History* (New Haven, Connecticut: Yale University Press, 1971); C. B. Fergusson, *A Documentary Study of the Establishment of the Negroes in Nova Scotia between the War of 1812 and the Winning of Responsible Government* (Halifax: Public Archives of Nova Scotia, 1948).

11. Donovan, "Nominal List," 151–62; Donovan, "Slaves and Their Owners," 3–32; Kenneth Donovan, "Slaves in Ile Royale," *French Colonial History* 5 (2004): 25–42.

12. "Code Noir (The Black Code)," <http://chmn.gmu.edu/revolution/d/335> March 2004.

13. Donovan, "Slaves and Their Owners," 5.

14. Donovan, "Slaves in Ile Royale," 31.

15. Ibid., 29.

16. Donovan, "Nominal List," 151–62; Donovan, "Slaves and Their Owners," 4–9; Donovan, "Slaves in Ile Royale," 25–42; on the slave trade generally, see Herbert S. Klein, *The Atlantic Slave Trade* (Cambridge: Cambridge University Press, 1999); David Eltis, *The Rise of African Slavery in the Americas* (Cambridge: Cambridge University Press, 2000); Robert L. Stein, *The French Slave Trade in the Eighteenth Century: An Old Regime Business* (Madison: University of Wisconsin Press, 1979).

17. Donovan, "Slaves and Their Owners," 6; on slaveholding patterns in New England, see Ira Berlin, *Many Thousands Gone: The First Two Centuries of Slavery in North America* (Cambridge, Massachusetts: Harvard University Press, 1998), 177–94; Edgar J. McManus, *Black Bondage in the North* (Syracuse, New York: Syracuse University Press, 1973); William D. Piersen, *Black Yankees: The Development of an Afro-American Subculture in Eighteenth-Century New England* (Amherst: University of Massachusetts Press, 1988).

18. Donovan, "Slaves in Ile Royale," 31.

19. Stephen E. Patterson, "1744–1763: Colonial Wars and Aboriginal Peoples," in *The Atlantic Region to Confederation: A History,* ed. Phillip A. Buckner and John G. Reid (Toronto: University of Toronto Press, 1994), 125–55; Reid, *Crucial,* 29–51; Griffiths, *Acadian History,* 62–94.

20. Barry Cahill, "Colchester Men: The Pro-Slavery Presbyterian Witness of the Reverends Daniel Cock of Truro and David Smith of Londonderry," in *Planter Links: Community and Culture in Colonial Nova Scotia,* ed. Margaret Conrad and Barry Moody (Fredericton: Acadiensis Press, 2001), 133–44.

21. Generally on the planters, see Margaret Conrad, ed., *They Planted Well: New England Planters in Maritime Canada* (Fredericton: Acadiensis Press, 1988); Conrad, ed., *Making Adjustments;* Conrad and Moody, eds., *Planter Links.*

22. Letter from Governor Cornwallis about Captain Bloss and his slaves, 22 September 1750, RG 1, vol. 35, doc. 25, Nova Scotia Archives and Records Management, Halifax, Nova Scotia (hereafter NSARM).

23. James S. MacDonald, "Life and Administration of Governor Charles Lawrence, 1749–1760," *Collections of the Nova Scotia Historical Society* 12 (1905): 23; also see page 24. I would like to thank Ken Donovan for this reference.

24. *Gazette* (Halifax), 30 May 1752.

25. T. W. Smith, "The Slave in Canada," *Collections of the Nova Scotia Historical Society* 10 (1899): 10.

26. Ibid., 10.

27. Ibid., 9.

28. Malachy Salter to Mrs. Salter, 2 September 1759, MG 100, vol. 217, doc. 27f, NSARM.

29. Smith, "Slave," 10–16.

30. 1767 Nova Scotia Census, RG 12, NSARM.

31. Cahill, "Colchester Men," 134.

32. Bryan Rommel-Ruiz, *Between African and Colored: Slavery and Freedom in Rhode Island and Nova Scotia, 1750–1850* (Philadelphia: University of Pennsylvania Press, under contract).

33. Smith, "Slave," 9.

34. W. Jeffrey Bolster, *Black Jacks: African American Seaman in the Age of Sail* (Cambridge, Massachusetts: Harvard University Press, 1997); Peter Linebaugh and Marcus Rediker, *The Many-Headed Hydra: Sailors, Slaves, Commoners, and the Hidden History of the Revolutionary Atlantic* (Boston: Beacon, 2000).

35. *Gazette* (Halifax), 28 May 1776.

36. *Gazette* (Halifax), 19 January 1779.

37. Jeffrey Brace, *The Blind African Slave, or Memoirs of Boyrereau Brinch, Nicknamed Jeffrey Brace, as told to Benjamin F. Prentiss, Esq.* ed. Kari J. Winter (Madison: University of Wisconsin Press, 2004), 62–63.

38. James W. St. G. Walker, "The Establishment of a Free Black Community in Nova Scotia, 1783–1840," in *The African Diaspora: Interpretive Essays*, ed. Martin L. Kilson and Robert I. Rotberg (Cambridge, Massachusetts: Harvard University Press, 1976), 208.

39. Ibid.

40. Sylvia Frey, *Water from the Rock: Black Resistance in a Revolutionary Age* (Princeton, New Jersey: Princeton University Press, 1991); Ellen Gibson Wilson, *The Loyal Blacks* (New York: Capricorn Books, 1976); Graham Russell Hodges, ed., *The Black Loyalist Directory: African Americans in Exile after the American Revolution* (New York: Garland, 1996); Michael McDonnell, "Other Loyalists: A Reconsideration of the Black Loyalist Experience in the American Revolutionary Era," *Southern Historian* 16 (Spring 1995): 5–25. Cassandra Pybus offers an important revision of the numbers of slave fugitives; see "Jefferson's Faulty Math," 243–64. The classic interpretation is Benjamin Quarles, *The Negro in the Age of the American Revolution* (Chapel Hill: University of North Carolina Press, 1961). The most recent and revisionist treatment is Cassandra Pybus, *Epic Journeys of Freedom: Runaway Slaves of the American Revolution and Their Global Quest for Liberty* (Boston: Beacon Press, 2006).

41. Book of Negroes, RG 1, vol. 423, NSARM.

42. Walker, *Black Loyalists;* Walker, "Establishment," 205–27; Ira Berlin and Ronald Hoffman, eds., *Slavery and Freedom in the Age of the American Revolution* (Charlottesville: University Press of Virginia, 1983). According to the "Return of the disbanded troops and Loyalists settling in the Province of Nova Scotia, mustered in the summer 1784," Lieutenant Colonel Robert Morse listed 1,232 slaves who also found their way to Nova Scotia courtesy of the slaveholding Loyalists who remained determined to continue the institution in the northern reaches of the British Empire. In fact, this number is artificially low because it does not include slaves brought to Shelburne, where many Loyalist slave owners also settled.

43. Walker, "Establishment," 208.

44. Ann G. Condon, "1783–1800: Loyalist Arrival, Acadian Return, Imperial Reform," in *The Atlantic Region to Confederation: A History,* ed. Phillip A. Buckner and John G. Reid (Toronto: University of Toronto Press, 1994), 184–209; MacKinnon, *Unfriendly Soil;* Winks, *Blacks,* 24–60.

45. Muster of Blacks at Birchtown, 3 and 4 July 1784, RG 1, vol. 19, doc. 37, NSARM; Negroes at Annapolis County, 28 May to 30 June 1784, RG 1, vol. 376, docs. 73–77, NSARM; Blacks at Digby, March 1785, RG 1, vol. 19, doc. 38, NSARM.

46. Walker, "Establishment," 212–13.

47. *Methodist Magazine* (London), 1798.

48. John Clarkson, *Clarkson's Mission to America, 1791–1792,* ed. C. B. Fergusson (Halifax: Public Archives of Nova Scotia, 1971), 46.

49. Walker, "Establishment," 209–10.

50. For the debate over the importance of slavery in Nova Scotia, see Cahill, "Black Loyalist Myth," 76–87; James W. St. G. Walker, "Myth, History, and Revisionism: The Black Loyalists Revisited," *Acadiensis* 29 (Autumn 1999): 88–105.

51. Smith, "Slave," 23; also see Ruth Holmes Whitehead, ed., *The Shelburne Black Loyalists: A Short Biography of All Blacks Emigrating to Shelburne County, Nova Scotia, after the American Revolution, 1783* (Halifax: Nova Scotia Museum, 2000).

52. Barry Cahill, "Habeas Corpus and Slavery in Nova Scotia: *R v. Hecht Ex Parte Rachel, 1798," University of New Brunswick Law Journal* 44 (1995): 193.

53. Smith, "Slave," 49–71.

54. Ibid., 51–52.

55. Wentworth's Instructions for the Jamaican Maroons, 29 June 1797, RG 1, vol. 419, doc. 19, NSARM.

56. Report on Maroons, 15 January 1800, RG 1, vol. 52, pp. 377–79, NSARM.

57. Mavis Campbell, ed., *Nova Scotia and the Fighting Maroons: A Documentary History* (Williamsburg, Virginia: Department of Anthropology, College of William and Mary, 1990); Lennox Picart, "The Trelawny Maroons and Sir John Wentworth: The Struggle to Maintain Their Culture," *Collections of the Royal Nova Scotia Historical Society* 44 (1996): 165–87; Allister Hines, "Deportees in Nova Scotia: The Jamaican Maroons, 1796–1800," in *Working Slavery, Pricing Freedom: Perspectives from the Caribbean, Africa and the African Diaspora,* ed. Verene Shepherd (New York: Palgrave, 2002), 206–22; John Grant, *The Maroons in Nova Scotia* (Halifax: Formac, 2002).

58. John Grant, *The Immigration and Settlement of the Black Refugees of the War of 1812 in Nova Scotia and New Brunswick* (Dartmouth: Black Cultural Centre for Nova Scotia, 1990), 103.

59. Walker, "Establishment," 205–37.

60. Winks, *Blacks,* 114–41.

61. House of Assembly, 1 April 1815, RG 1, vol. 305, doc. 3, NSARM.

62. Chamberlain to Morris, 11 November 1815, RG 1, vol. 419, doc. 41, NSARM.
63. Mary Jane Katzmann (Mrs. William Lawson), *History of the Townships of Dartmouth, Preston and Lawrencetown* (Halifax: Morton, 1893), 187–88.

CHAPTER 2: TWO DISTINCT CULTURES OF SLAVERY (pp. 25–40)

1. Some important treatments of slavery in the Lowcountry and Chesapeake include Philip D. Morgan, *Slave Counterpoint: Black Culture in the Eighteenth-Century Chesapeake and Lowcountry* (Chapel Hill: University of North Carolina Press, 1998); Ira Berlin, *Many Thousands Gone: The First Two Centuries of Slavery in North America* (Cambridge, Massachusetts: Harvard University Press, 1998); Judith A. Carney, *The African Origins of Rice Cultivation in the Americas* (Cambridge, Massachusetts: Harvard University Press, 2001); Betty Wood, *Gender, Race, and Rank in a Revolutionary Age: The Georgia Lowcountry, 1750–1820* (Athens: University of Georgia Press, 2000); Lorena S. Walsh, *From Calabar to Carter's Grove: The History of a Virginia Slave Community* (Charlottesville: University Press of Virginia, 1997); William Dusinberre, *Them Dark Days: Slavery in the American Rice Swamps* (New York: Oxford University Press, 1996); Allan Kulikoff, *Tobacco and Slaves: The Development of Southern Cultures in the Chesapeake, 1680–1800* (Chapel Hill: University of North Carolina Press, 1986); Lorena S. Walsh, "Work & Resistance in the New Republic: The Case of the Chesapeake, 1770–1820," in *From Chattel Slaves to Wage Slaves: The Dynamics of Labour Bargaining in the Americas,* ed. Mary Turner (Bloomington: Indiana University Press, 1995), 105–12; Betty Wood, "'Never on a Sunday?': Slavery and the Sabbath in Lowcountry Georgia, 1750–1830," in *From Chattel Slaves to Wage Slaves: The Dynamics of Labour Bargaining in the Americas,* ed. Mary Turner (Bloomington: Indiana University Press, 1995), 79–94; Lorena S. Walsh, "Slave Life, Slave Society, and Tobacco Production in the Tidewater Chesapeake, 1620–1820," in *Cultivation and Culture: Labor and the Shaping of Slave Life in the Americas,* ed. Ira Berlin and Philip D. Morgan (Charlottesville: University Press of Virginia, 1993); James Sidbury, *Ploughshares into Swords: Race, Rebellion, and Identity in Gabriel's Virginia, 1730–1810* (Cambridge: Cambridge University Press, 1997); Julia Floyd Smith, *Slavery and Rice Culture in Low Country Georgia, 1750–1860* (Knoxville: University of Tennessee Press, 1985); Peter Wood, *Black Majority: Negroes in Colonial South Carolina from 1670 through the Stono Rebellion* (New York: Norton, 1974); Ira Berlin and Ronald Hoffman, eds., *Slavery and Freedom in the Age of the American Revolution* (Charlottesville: University Press of Virginia, 1983); Sarah S. Hughes, "Slaves for Hire: The Allocation of Black Labor in Elizabeth City County, Virginia, 1782 to 1810," *William and Mary Quarterly* 35 (April 1978): 260–86; Lorena S. Walsh, "Rural African Americans in the Constitutional Era in Maryland, 1776–1810," *Maryland Historical Magazine* 84 (Winter 1989): 338–39; Joyce E. Chaplin, "Tidal Rice Cultivation and the Prob-

lem of Slavery in South Carolina and Georgia, 1760–1815," *William and Mary Quarterly* 49 (January 1992): 29–61; Lois Green Carr and Lorena S. Walsh, "Economic Diversification and Labor Organization in the Chesapeake, 1650–1820," in *Work and Labor in Early America*, ed. Stephen Innes (Chapel Hill: University of North Carolina Press, 1988).

2. Roswell King Jr., "On the Management of the Butler Estate," *Southern Agriculturist* 1 (December 1828): 523–29; Basil Hall, *Travels in North America in the Years 1827 and 1828* (Philadelphia: Carney, Lea, & Carey, 1829), 2:229–30; Philip D. Morgan, "Task and Gang Systems: The Organization of Labor on New World Plantations," in *Work and Labor in Early America*, ed. Stephen Innes (Chapel Hill: University of North Carolina Press, 1988), 189–221; Philip D. Morgan, "Work and Culture: The Task System and the World of Lowcountry Blacks, 1700–1880," *William and Mary Quarterly* 39 (October 1982): 563–99.

3. Smith, *Rice Culture*, 46.

4. Ibid., 45–63; Hall, *Travels*, 2:213–14; Morgan, *Slave Counterpoint*, 147–59.

5. Hall, *Travels*, 2:230.

6. Ibid., 2:229–32; Morgan, "Work and Culture," 107.

7. Berlin, *Thousands*, 265–70.

8. Lorena S. Walsh, "Plantation Management in the Chesapeake, 1620–1820," *Journal of Economic History* 49 (June 1989): 401–6; Walsh, "Tobacco," 197–98; Walsh and Carr, "Labor Organization," 175–76.

9. Walsh, "Work & Resistance," 107, also see 106–9; Walsh, "Plantation Management," 405–6.

10. Walsh and Carr, "Labor Organization," 179.

11. Ibid., 183, also see 176–83; Walsh, "Rural," 327; Berlin, *Thousands*, 270–71; Carole Shammas, "Black Women's Work and the Evolution of Plantation Society in Virginia," *Labor History* 26 (Winter 1985): 5–28.

12. Berlin, *Thousands*, 274–77; Walsh, "Plantation Management," 401; Walsh, "Work & Resistance," 110–11.

13. Hughes, "Slaves for Hire," 260–86; Jonathan D. Martin, *Divided Mastery: Slave Hiring in the American South* (Cambridge, Massachusetts: Harvard University Press, 2004); Morgan, *Slave Counterpoint*, 515–16; Walsh, "Plantation Management," 405; John Hope Franklin and Loren Schweninger, *Runaway Slaves: Rebels on the Plantation* (New York: Oxford University Press, 1999), 4–6, 32–37.

14. Peter McKerrow, *A Brief History of the Coloured Baptists in Nova Scotia, 1783–1895*, ed. Frank S. Boyd Jr. (1895; reprint, Halifax: Afro Nova Scotian Enterprises, 1976), 11.

15. Sylviane Diouf, *Servants of Allah: African Muslims Enslaved in the Americas* (New York: New York University Press, 1998).

16. John Weiss to Harvey Amani Whitfield, 9 March 2004, personal correspondence.

17. The question of Muslims in Nova Scotia after the War of 1812 deserves scholarly attention.

18. On the continuation of African cultures in the United States, see Michael A. Gomez, *Exchanging Our Country Marks: The Transformation of African Identities in the Colonial and Antebellum South* (Chapel Hill: University of North Carolina Press, 1998).

19. Ira Berlin, "Time, Space, and the Evolution of Afro-American Society on British Mainland North America," *American Historical Review* 85 (February 1980), 54; Albert J. Raboteau, *Slave Religion: The "Invisible Institution" in the Antebellum South* (New York: Oxford University Press, 1978); Morgan, *Slave Counterpoint*, 420–37; Sidbury, *Ploughshares*, 35–38; Mechal Sobel, *The World They Made Together: Black and White Values in Eighteenth-Century Virginia* (Princeton, New Jersey: Princeton University Press, 1987); Mechal Sobel, *Trabelin' On: The Slave Journey to an Afro-Baptist Faith* (Westport, Connecticut: Greenwood Press, 1979); Eddie S. Glaude, *Exodus! Religion, Race, and Nation in Early Nineteenth-Century Black America* (Chicago: University of Chicago Press, 2000); Berlin, *Thousands*, 272–73; Roswell King to Pierce Butler, 30 March 1804, Butler Plantation Papers (hereafter BPP), University of Toronto, Toronto, Ontario; Dusinberre, *Dark Days*, 259. On African naming patterns in the Sea Islands, see A List of Negroes in possession of the British Forces in the State of Georgia, under the command of Rear Admiral Cockburn with the period of their being taken, and the period of their removal from Cumberland Island, or the Waters adjacent to the same, Misc., War of 1812 Blacks, MG 15, Nova Scotia Archives and Records Management, Halifax, Nova Scotia (hereafter NSARM); Georgia Writers' Project, *Drums and Shadows: Survival Studies among the Georgia Coastal Negroes* (1940; reprint, Westport, Connecticut: Greenwood Press, 1973); Malcolm Bell, *Major Butler's Legacy: Five Generations of a Slaveholding Family* (Athens: University of Georgia Press, 1987), 126–54; Lydia Parrish, *Slave Songs of the Georgia Sea Islands* (1942; reprint, Athens: University of Georgia Press, 1992); Sterling Stuckey, *Slave Culture: Nationalist Theory and the Foundations of Black America* (New York: Oxford University Press, 1987); Margaret Washington Creel, *"A Peculiar People": Slave Religion and Community-Culture among the Gullahs* (New York: New York University Press, 1988); Lorenzo Turner, *Africanisms in the Gullah Dialect* (1949; reprint, Ann Arbor: University of Michigan Press, 1973).

20. In 1810 there were 33,927 free blacks in Maryland and 30,570 free blacks in Virginia. There were also 13,136 free blacks living in Delaware at the same time. Clayton E. Cramer, *Black Demographic Data, 1790–1860: A Sourcebook* (Westport, Connecticut: Greenwood Press, 1997), 122–25.

21. Julius Scott, "The Common Wind: Currents of Afro-American Communication in the Era of the Haitian Revolution" (Ph.D. dissertation, Duke University, 1986).

22. Berlin, *Thousands*, 274–77; Sidbury, *Ploughshares*, 48–49, 140; Walsh, "Tobacco," 188–89; James W. St. G. Walker, "The Black Loyalists in Nova Scotia and Sierra Leone" (Ph.D. dissertation, Dalhousie University, 1973), 1–26.

23. Fanny Kemble, *Journal of a Residence on a Georgia Plantation in 1838–1839* (New York: Harper & Brothers Publishers, 1863), 140.

24. Morgan, "Work and Culture," 140.

25. The majority of free blacks resided in Maryland.

26. Bathurst to Ross, 1814, "Out letters of the War Office, North America, 1814," Public Record Office, War Office 6, Secretary of State/Out-Letters, Vol. 2, Library of Congress, Washington, D.C.

27. For other interpretations of the role of African Americans, the War of 1812, and slavery, see Matthew Mason, "The Battle of the Slaveholding Liberators: Great Britain, the United States, and Slavery in the Early Nineteenth Century," *William and Mary Quarterly* 59 (July 2002): 665–96; Christopher T. George, "Mirage of Freedom: African Americans in the War of 1812," *Maryland Historical Magazine* 91 (Winter 1996): 427–50. John McNish Weiss published a very detailed examination of British policy in regard to the Refugees; see *On Stony Ground: American Origins of the Black Refugees of the War of 1812 Settled in Nova Scotia and New Brunswick* (London: McNish & Weiss, 2006).

28. African Americans absconded before Cochrane's proclamation; see *National Intelligencer* (Washington), 1 May 1813; Shipping Log, HMS *Junon*, September 1813, RG 1, vol. 420, doc. 1, NSARM.

29. John Grant, "Black Immigrants into Nova Scotia, 1776–1815," *Journal of Negro History* 58 (July 1973): 253–70; Frank Cassell, "Slaves of the Chesapeake Bay Area and the War of 1812," *Journal of Negro History* 57 (April 1972): 144–55; W. A. Spray, "The Settlement of the Black Refugees in New Brunswick, 1815–1836," *Acadiensis* 6 (Spring 1977): 64–79; J. C. A. Stagg, *Mr. Madison's War: Politics, Diplomacy, and Warfare in the Early American Republic, 1783–1830* (Princeton, New Jersey: Princeton University Press, 1983); *Documents Furnished by the British Government Under The Third Article of the Convention of St. Petersburg, And Bayly's List of Slaves And Of Public And Private Property Remaining On Tangier Island And On Board H.B.M. Ships of War, After The Ratification Of The Treaty Of Ghent* (Washington, D.C.: Gales & Seaton, 1827), 63; Bell, *Butler's Legacy,* 172; King to Butler, 18 March 1815, BPP. Pierce Butler and John Hamilton lost over one hundred and over two hundred slaves respectively, while their neighbor John Couper also lost slaves; Mary Bullard, *Black Liberation on Cumberland Island in 1815* (South Dartmouth, Mass.: M. R. Bullard, 1983), 63–65.

30. In using the term "British military policy," I want to recognize that the British government, the Admiralty, various field commanders, and other officers entertained very different ideas about how the war should be run. I am also thankful for John McNish Weiss's suggestions about British involvement in the War of 1812.

31. Barrie to Warren, 14 November 1813, in Grant, "Black Immigrants," 264.

32. Bathurst to Ross, 1814, "Out letters of the War Office, North America, 1814," Public Record Office, War Office 6, Secretary of State/Out-Letters, Vol. 2.

33. Cited in Walter Lord, *The Dawn's Early Light* (New York: W. W. Norton, 1972), 44.

34. Cochrane to Sherbrooke, 5 October 1814, RG 1, vol. 111, pp. 97–98, NSARM.

35. Adams to Monroe, 5 September 1814, *Diplomatic Correspondence of the United States: Canadian Relations, 1784–1860 Volume I, 1784–1820, Documents 1–661*, ed. William R. Manning (Washington, D.C.: Carnegie Endowment for International Peace, 1940) 1:652.

36. Cockburn to Cochrane, 29 April 1814, Container 10, Papers of Sir George Cockburn, 1788–1847, Archival Manuscript Material, Library of Congress, Washington, D.C.

37. Bathurst to Adams, 24 October 1815, *American State Papers: Class I, Foreign Relations* (Buffalo: William S. Hein, 1998), 4:119.

38. *Enquirer* (Richmond), 8 October 1813. Slave owners who lost slaves in this manner could apply for compensation.

39. King to Butler, 18 March 1815, BPP; *Documents Furnished by the British Government*, 63; Bullard, *Liberation*, 63–65.

40. *American State Papers*, 118–25. Slaveholders in the United States greatly resented that the British did not return as many slaves as they thought themselves entitled to from the Treaty of Ghent.

41. Mason, "Battle," 665–96.

42. John Weiss, "Black American Resistance to Slavery in the War of 1812: The Corps of Colonial Marines" (paper presented at the British Association for American Studies, Norwich, England, 1998).

43. Cockburn to Cochrane, 9 May 1814, Papers of Vice Admiral Sir Alexander Forrester Inglis Cochrane, 1813–15, Florida State University Libraries, Tallahassee, Florida.

44. George, "Mirage of Freedom," 427–50. If the War of 1812 constituted a "mirage of freedom" for some African Americans, those who achieved liberty used British military strategy to their own advantage.

45. Cited in Cassell, "Chesapeake," 152. The Colonial Marines consisted of six companies as of 1816, when they were disbanded; see John McNish Weiss, *The Merikens: Free Black Settlers in Trinidad, 1815–1816* (London: McNish & Weiss, 2002), 24.

46. Weiss, *The Merikens*, 24–47.

47. *Niles Weekly Register* (Baltimore), 22 May 1813.

48. Cockburn to Cochrane, 25 June 1814, Cochrane Papers.

49. Cockburn to Cochrane, 24 July 1814, Cochrane Papers.

50. *Niles Weekly Register* (Baltimore), 30 September 1815; Bullard, *Liberation*, 62–80.

51. King to Butler, 18 March 1815, BPP.

52. King to Butler, 26 February 1815, BPP.

53. Cassell, "Chesapeake," 155; Bell, *Butler's Legacy*, 170–91; Bullard, *Libera-*

tion, 62–80; Charles Ball, *Slavery in the United States: A Narrative of the Life and Adventures of Charles Ball, a Black Man* (1837; reprint, New York: Negro Universities Press, 1969), 472; *Niles Weekly Register* (Baltimore), 30 September 1815.

54. Ball, *Slavery*, 472.

55. G. R. Gleig, *A Narrative of the Campaigns of the British Army at Washington and New Orleans under Generals Ross, Pakenham, and Lambert, in the years 1814 and 1815* (London: J. Murray, 1821), 144; for the Refugees' emphasis on freedom and land, see Cassell, "Chesapeake," 152.

56. William Moorsom, *Letters from Nova Scotia: Comprising Sketches of a Young Country* (London: H. Colburn & R. Bentley, 1830), 126.

57. *Morning Chronicle* (Halifax), 7 October 1889.

58. Ibid.

59. Ibid.

60. On gender and age breakdown of the Refugees, see *Documents Furnished by the British Government*, 67–106. Earlier escapees to Halifax can be found in shipping records: HMS *Rifleman*, September 1813, RG 1, vol. 420, doc. 1, NSARM; HMS *Marlborough*, September 1813, RG 1, vol. 420, doc. 2, NSARM; HMS *Junon*, September 1813, RG 1, vol. 420, doc. 4, NSARM; HMS *Mariner*, September 1813, RG 1, vol. 420, doc. 5, NSARM; HMS *Diomede*, September 1813, RG 1, vol. 420, doc. 7, RG 1, NSARM; HMS *Diadem*, September 1813, RG 1, vol. 420, doc. 8, NSARM; Claims for Slaves in Virginia, Misc., Blacks War of 1812, MG 15, NSARM; Thomas Newell and Thomas Spalding, A list of negroes in possession of the British forces in the state of Georgia (16 March 1815), Misc., Blacks War of 1812, MG 15, NSARM; *Documents Furnished by the British Government*, 60–66, 103.

61. On family structure from the Chesapeake, see Return of black people at Halifax arrived from the Chesapeake, [1815], RG 1, vol. 305, doc. 7, NSARM (in this document the total of 336 people does not include 39 women who came without family, so the actual total is 375); on counties of origin and numbers of escaped slaves per owner, see Claims for Slaves in Virginia, Misc., Blacks War of 1812, MG 15, NSARM; *Documents Furnished by the British Government*, 104–7; Claims for Slaves in Virginia, Misc., Blacks War of 1812, MG 15, NSARM.

62. *Documents Furnished by the British Government*, 75, 78, 88.

63. King to Butler, 14 February 1815, BPP.

64. *Documents Furnished by the British Government*, 68–70. It should be noted that some Butlers on this list were not from Georgia but rather from the Chesapeake. Yet the majority of Butlers originated from the Sea Islands.

65. Claims for Slaves in Virginia, Misc., Blacks War of 1812, MG 15, NSARM.

66. HMS *Rifleman*, September 1813, RG 1, vol. 420, doc. 1, NSARM; HMS *Marlborough*, September 1813, RG 1, vol. 420, doc. 2, NSARM; HMS *Junon*, September 1813, RG 1, vol. 420, doc. 4, NSARM; HMS *Mariner*, September 1813, RG 1, vol. 420, doc. 5, NSARM; HMS *Diomede*, September 1813, RG 1, vol. 420, doc. 7, NSARM; HMS *Diadem*, September 1813, RG 1, vol. 420, doc. 8, NSARM. The

breakdown of occupations: farmer, laborer, sawyer, shoemaker, servant, washer-woman, wheelwright, fisherman, hostler, blacksmith, and carpenter.

67. On slaves and market trading, see Betty Wood, "'Never on a Sunday?'"; Robert Olwell, "'Loose, Idle, and Disorderly': Slave Women in the Eighteenth-Century Charleston Marketplace," in *More Than Chattel: Black Women and Slavery in the Americas,* ed. David Gasper and Darlene Clark Hine (Bloomington: Indiana University Press, 1996), 97–110; Morgan, *Slave Counterpoint,* 372–73.

68. *Documents Furnished by the British Government,* 76 and 90.

69. Names, Age, Description and present State of the Blacks, Melville Island, 6 May 1816, RG 1, vol. 421, doc. 1, NSARM; Names, Age, Diseases + present State of the Patients, Black Hospital, Melville Island, 9 May 1816, RG 1, vol. 421, doc. 2, NSARM.

70. Black Refugees desirous of settling upon lands at Preston, 1815, RG 1, vol. 419, doc. 93, NSARM.

71. Eric Foner, *Nothing But Freedom: Emancipation and Its Legacy* (Baton Rouge: Louisiana State University Press, 1983).

CHAPTER 3: SETTLEMENT AND STRUGGLE (pp. 43–62)

1. On the debate over colonization see James Oliver Horton and Lois E. Horton, *In Hope of Liberty: Culture, Community, and Protest Among Northern Free Blacks, 1700–1860* (New York: Oxford University Press, 1997), 177–202.

2. Leon D. Pamphile, *Haitians and African Americans: A Heritage of Tragedy and Hope* (Gainesville: University Press of Florida, 2001); Claude A. Clegg, *The Price of Liberty: African Americans and the Making of Liberia* (Chapel Hill: University of North Carolina Press, 2004); Jane Rhodes, *Mary Ann Shadd Cary: The Black Press and Protest in the Nineteenth Century* (Bloomington: Indiana University Press, 1998); Robin W. Winks, *The Blacks in Canada: A History* (New Haven, Connecticut: Yale University Press, 1971); Jane H. Pease and William H. Pease, *Black Utopia: Negro Communal Experiments in America* (1963; reprint, Madison: State Historical Society of Wisconsin, 1972); Floyd J. Miller, *The Search for a Black Nationality: Black Emigration and Colonization, 1787–1863* (Urbana: University of Illinois Press, 1975).

3. Pamphile, *Haitians and African Americans,* 40.

4. Horton and Horton, *In Hope of Liberty,* 195, also 192–96; Christopher Dixon, "Nineteenth Century African American Emigrationism: The Failure of the Haitian Alternative," *Western Journal of Black Studies* 18 (1994): 77–88.

5. James Fairhead et al., eds., *African-American Exploration in West Africa: Four Nineteenth-Century Diaries* (Bloomington: Indiana University Press, 2003), 9–30; P. J. Staudenraus, *The African Colonization Movement, 1816–1865* (New York: Columbia University Press, 1961).

6. Calvin Yale, *A Sermon, Delivered before the Vermont Colonization Society*

at Montpelier, October 17, 1827 (Montpelier, Vermont: E. P. Walton, 1827), 3, Special Collections, University of Vermont Libraries.

7. Clegg, *Price of Liberty,* 6.

8. Howard Holman Bell, *A Survey of the Negro Convention Movement, 1830–1861* (New York: Arno Press, 1969), 10–37.

9. Upper Canada consisted of what is today the southern portion of the province of Ontario. In 1791 the province of Quebec was divided into Upper and Lower Canada so that English-speaking Protestant Loyalists could retain British civil laws.

10. Pease and Pease, *Black Utopia,* 46–108; Winks, *Blacks,* 142–232; Rhodes, *Mary Ann Shadd Cary;* Samuel Ringgold Ward, *Autobiography of a Fugitive Negro: His Anti-Slavery Labours in the United States, Canada, & England* (1855; reprint, New York: Arno Press, 1968).

11. Cited in Pease and Pease, *Black Utopia,* 12.

12. The number of African Americans who returned to the United States has been disputed; see Michael Wayne, "The Black Population of Canada West on the Eve of the American Civil War: A Reassessment Based on the Manuscript Census of 1861," *Histoire Sociale/Social History* 28 (November 1995): 465–85.

13. *Acadian Recorder* (Halifax), 23 December 1815.

14. House of Assembly, 1 April 1815, RG 1, vol. 305, doc. 3, Nova Scotia Archives and Records Management, Halifax, Nova Scotia (hereafter NSARM).

15. *Statutes of Nova Scotia,* 1834, chap. 68, NSARM.

16. *Free Press* (Halifax), 30 March 1824.

17. Barry Cahill, "Habeas Corpus and Slavery in Nova Scotia: *R v. Hecht Ex Parte Rachel, 1798,*" *University of New Brunswick Law Journal* 44 (1995): 179–209.

18. Joanne Pope Melish, *Disowning Slavery: Gradual Emancipation and "Race" in New England, 1780–1860* (Ithaca, New York: Cornell University Press, 1998), 119.

19. Dalhousie to Bathurst, 29 December 1816, RG 1, vol. 112, pp. 6–9, NSARM.

20. *Acadian Recorder* (Halifax), 21 February 1824.

21. Thomas Chandler Haliburton, *An Historical and Statistical Account of Nova-Scotia* (Halifax: J. Howe, 1829), 292.

22. Melish, *Disowning Slavery,* 192.

23. Pease and Pease, *Black Utopia,* 11.

24. Ibid., 105.

25. J. Murray Beck, *The Politics of Nova Scotia: I, 1710–1896* (Tantallon, Nova Scotia: Four East Publications, 1985); H. T. Dickinson, *Liberty and Property: Political Ideology in Eighteenth-Century Britain* (New York: Holmes and Meier, 1977).

26. David A. Sutherland, "1810–1820: War and Peace," in *The Atlantic Region to Confederation: A History,* ed. Philip A. Buckner and John G. Reid (Toronto: University of Toronto Press, 1994).

27. Castlereagh to Prevost, 10 April 1808, RG 1, vol. 420, doc. 9, NSARM.

28. Sherbrooke to the House of Assembly, 24 February 1815, RG 1, vol. 288, doc. 101, NSARM.

29. Ibid.

30. Coleman to Sabatier, 23 March 1815, RG 5 A, vol. 21, doc. 84, NSARM.

31. Clegg, *Price of Liberty*, 80.

32. Names, Ages, Diseases, + present State of the Patients, Black Hospital, Melville Island, 9 May 1816, RG 1, vol. 421, doc. 2, NSARM.

33. Fairbank's letter, 8 March 1815, RG 1, vol. 305, doc. 22, NSARM.

34. Coleman to Sabatier, 6 February 1815, RG 1, vol. 305, doc. 5, NSARM.

35. Bathurst to Sherbrooke, 13 June 1815, RG 1, vol. 63, doc. 12, NSARM.

36. Morris to Sherbrooke, 6 September 1815, RG 1, vol. 420, doc. 76, NSARM.

37. Rusty Bittermann, "The Hierarchy of the Soil: Land and Labour in a 19th Century Cape Breton Community," *Acadiensis* 18 (Autumn 1988): 33–55; J. S. Martell, *Immigration to and Emigration from Nova Scotia, 1815–1838* (Halifax: Public Archives of Nova Scotia, 1942); J. S. Martell, "Military Settlements in Nova Scotia after the War of 1812," *Nova Scotia Historical Society Collections* 24 (1938): 75–108.

38. Dalhousie to Bathurst, 14 August 1817, RG 1, vol. 112, pp. 32–35, NSARM.

39. C. Peter Ripley, ed., *The Black Abolitionist Papers: Volume II, Canada, 1830–1865* (Chapel Hill: University of North Carolina Press, 1986), 15.

40. In order to encourage immigrants, the government offered most new white settlers free grants of land until 1827. Crown land policies were changed in 1827, and settlers who had financial resources could purchase land, while poorer settlers could rent land for a yearly price. In 1831 Crown lands could only be sold.

41. Memorial of John Chamberlain, Alexander Lyle, Alexander Farquharson, Frederick Major and Allan McDonald . . . Reside in the neighbourhood of the people of colour settled in Preston, 8 June 1838, RG 1, vol. 422, doc. 49, NSARM.

42. Coleman to Sabatier, 23 March 1815, RG 5 A, vol. 21, doc. 84, NSARM.

43. Chamberlain to Morris, 11 November 1815, RG 1, vol. 419, doc. 41, NSARM.

44. Joseph Bouchette, *The British Dominions in North America* (London: H. Colburn and R. Bentley, 1831), 2:16.

45. *Acadian Recorder* (Halifax), 21 February 1824; *Morning Post* (Halifax), 29 October 1841.

46. Memorial of John Chamberlain, Alexander Lyle, Alexander Farquharson, Frederick Major and Allan McDonald . . . Reside in the neighbourhood of the people of colour settled in Preston, 8 June 1838, RG 1, vol. 422, doc. 49, NSARM.

47. Report of the Inspection of Preston Lots, August 1818, RG 1, vol. 419, doc. 90, NSARM.

48. Petition of the Colored People at Preston, 1841, RG 20 C, vol. 31, doc. 124, NSARM.

49. *Halifax Monthly Magazine* (Halifax), January 1852, 27.

50. Clegg, *Price of Liberty*, 80.

51. *Free Press* (Halifax), 22 July 1817.

52. Bathurst to Sherbrooke, 10 November 1815, RG 1, vol. 63, doc. 121, NSARM.

53. Winks, *Blacks*, 121; Martell, *Immigration*, 7–33.

54. Memorial of John Chamberlain, Alexander Lyle, Alexander Farquharson, Frederick Major, and Allan MacDonald . . . Reside in the neighbourhood of the people of colour settled in Preston, 8 June 1838, RG 1, vol. 422, doc. 49, NSARM.

55. Petition of the Colored People at Preston, 1841, RG 20 C, vol. 31, doc. 124, NSARM.

56. Report of the Lands cleared by the People of Colour in the settlement of Preston, 9 May 1816, RG 1, vol. 421, doc. 3, NSARM; License of occupation at Hammond's Plains, RG 1, vol. 419, doc. 119, NSARM.

57. License of occupation at Hammond's Plains, RG 1, vol. 419, doc. 119, NSARM.

58. Return of the Black American Refugees residing at Hammonds Plains, RG 1, vol. 422, doc. 19, NSARM.

59. Report of the Lands cleared by the People of Colour in the settlement of Preston, 9 May 1816, RG 1, vol. 421, doc. 3, NSARM; Report of the Inspection of Preston Lots, August 1818, RG 1, vol. 419, doc. 90, NSARM.

60. Herbert Gutman, *The Black Family in Slavery and Freedom, 1750–1925* (New York: Pantheon Books, 1976); a revisionist account is Wilma A. Dunaway, *The African-American Family in Slavery and Emancipation* (Cambridge: Cambridge University Press, 2003).

61. Report of the Lands cleared by the People of Colour in the settlement of Preston, 9 May 1816, RG 1, vol. 421, doc. 3, NSARM.

62. Morris to Haliburton, 11 December 1817, RG 1, vol. 419, doc. 102, NSARM; Dalhousie to Bathurst, 14 August 1817, RG 1, vol. 112, pp. 32–35, NSARM.

63. Report of the Lands cleared by the People of Colour in the settlement of Preston, 9 May 1816, RG 1, vol. 421, doc. 3, RG 1, NSARM; Scott to Kempt, 19 March 1821, RG 1, vol. 422, doc. 28, NSARM.

64. Head to Morris, 1816, RG 1, vol. 419, doc. 47, NSARM; Report of Charles Morris, RG 1, vol. 421, doc. 22, NSARM.

65. Report on Preston [not dated, 1817?], RG 1, vol. 419, doc. 81, NSARM.

66. Report of the Inspection of Preston Lots, August 1818, RG 1, vol. 419, doc. 90, NSARM.

67. Scott to Kempt, 19 March 1821, RG 1, vol. 422, doc. 28, NSARM.

68. Report of Charles Morris, RG 1, vol. 421, doc. 22, NSARM.

69. Report on Preston [not dated, 1817?], RG 1, vol. 419, doc. 81, NSARM.

70. Report on Hammonds Plains, 15 January 1827, RG 1, vol. 422, doc. 35, NSARM.

71. We the undersigned Inhabitants of Halifax humbly beg leave to call the

attention of Your Honorable House to the deplorable state of the Black Settlers at Hammonds Plains and Preston, 12 March 1825, RG 1, vol. 80, doc. 35, NSARM.

72. Coleman to Sabatier, 23 March 1815, RG 5 A, vol. 21, doc. 84, NSARM.

73. American Slaves in the eighteenth-century Chesapeake and Lowcountry endured diets that included maize, occasional meat and water. In the Chesapeake, maize and animal rations were more readily available than in the Lowcountry. Slaves also added to their diets through hunting, fishing, and growing vegetables. It is very possible that the Refugees suffered intestinal problems after arriving in Nova Scotia, especially if they experienced serious changes in their diets. Philip D. Morgan, *Slave Counterpoint: Black Culture in the Eighteenth-Century Chesapeake and Lowcountry* (Chapel Hill: University of North Carolina Press, 1998), 134–43.

74. Carter to Baxter, 16 January 1827, RG 1, vol. 422, doc. 37, NSARM.

75. C. B. Fergusson, *A Documentary Study of the Establishment of the Negroes in Nova Scotia between the War of 1812 and the Winning of Responsible Government* (Halifax: Public Archives of Nova Scotia, 1948), 45.

76. Black Refugees of Nova Scotia, letter, 28 July 1834, Reports of the Associates of the Late Dr. Bray, NSARM.

77. Baxter to Kempt, 15 January 1827, RG 1, vol. 422, doc. 35, NSARM.

78. Thomas Desbrisay and Edward Lowe, 9 March 1837, Journal of the House of Assembly, 1837, NSARM.

79. Report of the People off [*sic*] Colour at and about Preston, PANS-Box Halifax County Land Grants 1787–1835, doc. 169, NSARM; Return of the Black American Refugees residing at Hammonds Plains, RG 1, vol. 422, doc. 19, NSARM. This document lists the male or female head of household along with a category for women; it also lists several categories for females and males under or over the ages of seven or fourteen. The category for women, usually next to the male head of household, could be the wife.

80. Report of the Lands cleared by the People of Colour in the settlement of Preston, 9 May 1816, RG 1, vol. 421, doc. 3, NSARM.

81. Return of the Black American Refugees residing at Hammonds Plains, RG 1, vol. 422, doc. 19, NSARM.

82. On the importance of black extended households in free states, see Horton and Horton, *In Hope of Liberty*, 77–100.

83. Bathurst to Sherbrooke, 10 November 1815, RG 1, vol. 63, doc. 21, NSARM.

84. Dalhousie to Bathurst, 16 May 1817, RG 1, vol. 112, pp. 23–26, NSARM.

85. John McNish Weiss, *Free Black Settlers in Trinidad, 1815–1816* (London: McNish and Weiss, 1995).

86. Return of the Black American Refugees residing at Hammonds Plains, RG 1, vol. 422, doc. 19, NSARM; Those who wish to go to Trinidad, RG 1, vol. 422, doc. 20, NSARM.

87. Kempt to Harrison, 20 January 1821, RG 1, vol. 113, doc. 35, NSARM.

88. Those who wish to go to Trinidad, RG 1, vol. 422, doc. 20, NSARM. Once in Trinidad, these Refugees did quite well.

89. John Hough, *A Sermon, Delivered before the Vermont Colonization Society at Montpeleir [sic], October 18, 1826* (Montpelier, Vermont: E. P. Walton, 1826), 10–11, Special Collections, University of Vermont Libraries; also see Melish, *Disowning Slavery*, 194–97.

90. Ibid., 8.

91. *Free Press* (Halifax), 2 September 1817.

92. David Walker, *Appeal to the Coloured Citizens of the World* (1829; reprint, New York: Hill & Wang, 1995), 55.

93. Kempt to Horton, 4 May 1825, Colonial Office 217/144, NSARM.

CHAPTER 4: WORKING FOLKS (pp. 63–83)

1. James Oliver Horton and Lois E. Horton, *In Hope of Liberty: Culture, Community, and Protest Among Northern Free Blacks, 1700–1860* (New York: Oxford University press, 1997), 110.

2. Robert L. Hall and Michael M. Harvey, eds., *Making a Living: The Work Experience of African-Americans in New England, Selected Readings* (Boston: New England Foundation for the Humanities, 1995), 132.

3. James Oliver Horton and Lois E. Horton, *Black Bostonians: Family Life and Community Struggle in the Antebellum North* (1979; reprint, New York: Holmes & Meier, 1999), 9 & 148.

4. Horton and Horton, *Black Bostonians*, 10.

5. Ibid., 8–10.

6. Robert J. Cottrol, *The Afro-Yankees: Providence's Black Community in the Antebellum Era* (Westport, Connecticut: Greenwood Press, 1982), 113–43.

7. Ibid., 119–20, 134 (for the percentage of unskilled workers).

8. Ibid., 129–30.

9. Mark J. Sammons and Valerie Cunningham, *Black Portsmouth: Three Centuries of African-American Heritage* (Durham: University of New Hampshire Press, 2004), 80.

10. Ibid., 113.

11. C. Peter Ripley, ed., *Black Abolitionist Papers: Volume II, Canada, 1830–1865* (Chapel Hill: University of North Carolina Press), 16–17.

12. Scott to Kempt, 19 March 1821, RG 1, vol. 422, doc. 28, Nova Scotia Archives and Records Management, Halifax, Nova Scotia (hereafter NSARM).

13. Joseph Howe, *Western and Eastern Rambles: Travel Sketches of Nova Scotia*, ed. M. G. Parks (1828; reprint, Toronto: University of Toronto Press, 1973), 55.

14. T. H. Breen and Stephen Innes, *"Myne Owne Ground": Race and Freedom on Virginia's Eastern Shore, 1640–1676* (New York: Oxford University Press, 1980); Eric Foner, *Reconstruction: America's Unfinished Revolution, 1863–1877*

(New York: Harper & Row, 1988); Nancy Ladd Muller, "W. E. B. Du Bois and the House of the Black Burghardts: Land, Family and African Americans in New England," (Ph.D. dissertation, University of Massachusetts, 2001).

15. Stephen Vincent, *Southern Seed, Northern Soil: African-American Farm Communities in the Midwest, 1765–1900* (Bloomington: Indiana University Press, 1999), xv–xvi.

16. Petition of Jacob Allen, 1822, RG 20 A, NSARM.

17. Petition of Elizabeth Grant, 1823, RG 20 A, NSARM.

18. Lowe to James, 7 June 1836, Journal of the House of Assembly, 1837, NSARM.

19. Vincent, *Southern Seed,* xiii.

20. Petition of Charles Arnold, 1820, RG 20 A, NSARM.

21. Petition of Levin Winder, 1821, RG 20 A, NSARM.

22. Report of Lands cleared by the People of Colour in the settlement of Preston, 9 May 1816, RG 1, vol. 421, doc. 3, NSARM.

23. Petition of Richard Smothers, 1819, RG 20 A, NSARM.

24. Petition of Septimus Clark, 1819, RG 20 A, NSARM. According to C. B. Fergusson, Clark was later offered 100 acres by the lieutenant governor, but in 1842 was granted land in Preston; C. B. Fergusson, *A Documentary Study of the Establishment of Negroes in Nova Scotia between the War of 1812 and the Winning of Responsible Government* (Halifax: Public Archives of Nova Scotia, 1948), 45.

25. Petition of Suther Blair, 1820, RG 20 A, NSARM.

26. Petition of Gabriel Hall, 1824, RG 20 A, NSARM.

27. Petition of David Page, 1825, RG 20 A, NSARM.

28. HMS *Diadem,* September 1813, RG 1, vol. 420, doc. 8, NSARM.

29. Petition of Bray Cooper, 1820, RG 20 A, NSARM.

30. Report of Lands cleared by the People of Colour in the settlement of Preston, 9 May 1816, RG 1, vol. 421, doc. 3, NSARM.

31. Petition of Basil Crowd, 1823, RG 20 A, NSARM.

32. Report of Lands cleared by the People of Colour in the settlement of Preston, 9 May 1816, RG 1, vol. 421, doc. 3, NSARM; Petition of Solomon Crawley, 1823, RG 20 A, NSARM.

33. In Council, 11 March 1841, Box-Crown Lands-Peninsula of Halifax-1840–1845, RG 20 C, vol. 31, doc. 124, NSARM.

34. Petition of Henry Lee, Sr., Henry Lee Jr., Winslow Sparkes, William Bunday, 1820, RG 20 A, NSARM.

35. Naith Johnson and James Downing, 1822, RG 20 A, NSARM.

36. Fergusson, *Documentary,* 51–52.

37. Hammonds Plains Land Grant, 1834, RG 1, NSARM.

38. Petition of William Deer [as spelled in Petition], Naith or Nace Leach, Henry Broad, and John Collins, 1824, RG 20 A, NSARM. These men probably did not receive this land. Indeed, William Deer was granted land at the original Preston settlement in 1842.

39. *Morning Chronicle* (Halifax), 7 June 1909; Frederic Cozzens, *Acadia, or a Month with the Blue Noses* (New York: Derby & Jackson, 1859), 43.

40. Cited in John Grant, *The Immigration and Settlement of the Black Refugees of the War of 1812 in Nova Scotia and New Brunswick* (Dartmouth: Black Cultural Centre for Nova Scotia, 1990), 106.

41. Halifax County Land Grants-1787–1835, RG 20 C, doc. 185, NSARM.

42. Ibid.

43. Report of the Inspection of Preston Lots, August 1818, RG 1, vol. 419, doc. 90, NSARM.

44. Land Grant for the People of Colour at Preston, May 1842, RG 20 C, NSARM.

45. Petition of William McLaughlin, 1836, RG 5 P, vol. 52, doc. 45, NSARM; Claims for Slaves in Virginia, Misc., Blacks War of 1812, MG 15, NSARM.

46. Betty Wood, "'Never on a Sunday?' Slavery and the Sabbath in Lowcountry Georgia, 1750–1830," in *From Chattel Slaves to Wage Slaves: The Dynamics of Labour Bargaining in the Americas,* ed. Mary Turner (Bloomington: Indiana University Press, 1995); Malcolm Bell, *Major Butler's Legacy: Five Generations of a Slaveholding Family* (Athens: University of Georgia Press, 1987), 134 and 151; Philip D. Morgan, *Slave Counterpoint: Black Culture in the Eighteenth-Century Chesapeake and Lowcountry* (Chapel Hill: University of North Carolina Press, 1998), 372–73.

47. *Morning Post* (Halifax), 29 October 1840; Mary Jane Katzmann (Mrs. William Lawson), *History of the Townships of Dartmouth, Preston and Lawrencetown* (Halifax: Morton, 1893), 46–48; Joan Payzant and Lewis J. Payzant, *Like a Weaver's Shuttle: A History of the Halifax-Dartmouth Ferries* (Halifax: Nimbus, 1979).

48. William Moorsom, *Letters from Nova Scotia: Comprising Sketches of a Young Country* (London: H. Colburn & R. Bentley, 1830), 126.

49. *Novascotian* (Halifax), 27 June 1832.

50. Campbell Hardy, *Sporting Adventures in the New World: or, Days and Nights of Moose-Hunting in the Pine Forests of Acadia* (London: Hurst and Blackett Publishers, 1855), 2: 22.

51. *Acadian Recorder* (Halifax), 21 February 1824.

52. Howe, *Rambles,* 55.

53. *British Colonist* (Halifax), 19 March 1850.

54. Elizabeth Frame, *Descriptive Sketches of Nova Scotia in Prose and Verse* (Halifax: A&W MacKinley, 1864), 3.

55. Morris to Sherbrooke, 6 September 1815, RG 1, vol. 420, doc. 76, NSARM.

56. *Novascotian* (Halifax), 27 June 1832.

57. *Halifax Monthly Magazine* (Halifax), January 1852, 27.

58. Nevertheless, Hammonds Plains farmers had petitioned the government several times for increased land since their initial settlement and eventually obtained title to the farms. Petition of Robin Cunard, 1821, RG 20 A, NSARM;

Petition of William Days, 1823, RG 20 A, NSARM; Petition of James Watson, 1827, RG 20 A, NSARM; Petition of Andrew Smith, 1829, RG 20 A, NSARM.

59. Halifax County Land Grants-1787–1835, RG 20 C, Commissioner of Crown Lands, doc. 185, NSARM.

60. Dylan Penningroth, *The Claims of Kinfolk: African American Property and Community in the Nineteenth-Century South* (Chapel Hill: University of North Carolina Press, 2003), 131–62.

61. Those that embrace the opportunity of going into the Country, 26 March 1837, RG 1, vol. 422, doc. 47, NSARM; Howe to George, 12 June 1837, RG 1, vol. 422, doc. 48, NSARM.

62. Campbell to Glenelg, 25 August 1837, RG 1, vol. 115, pp. 56–57, NSARM.

63. Ibid.

64. Glenelg to Campbell, 25 October 1837, RG 1, vol. 422, doc. 50, NSARM. Glenelg's official title was Secretary of State for War and the Colonies.

65. The Memorial of the People of Colour Settled in Preston, RG 1, vol. 422, doc. 46, NSARM.

66. Petition of the Colored People at Preston, 1841, RG 20 C, vol. 31, doc. 124, NSARM.

67. Land grant for the People of Colour at Preston, May 1842, RG 20 C, NSARM.

68. Advance for Colored People in Halifax County, 1847, RG 7, vol. 16, doc. 87, NSARM; Journal of the House of Assembly, 1848, NSARM; Journal of the House of Assembly, 1849, NSARM; Journal of the House of Assembly, 1850, NSARM; Government Relief for Negroes, 1854, RG 5 P, vol. 86, doc. 27, NSARM.

69. Preston Petition, 23 February 1847, RG 5 P, vol. 83, doc. 117, NSARM.

70. Petition of the People of Collor [*sic*] at Preston, c. 1846, RG 5 GP, vol. 7, doc. 22, NSARM.

71. Preston Petition, 23 February 1847, RG 5 P, vol. 83, doc. 117, NSARM.

72. Petition of James Barron, 29 February 1848, RG 5 P, vol. 84, doc. 54, NSARM.

73. Petition from Blacks at Preston, 14 February 1848, RG 5 GP, vol. 7, doc. 28, NSARM.

74. Preston Petition, 1849, RG 5 P, vol. 85, doc. 8, NSARM; Preston Petition, 1850, RG 5 P, vol. 85, doc. 21, NSARM; Preston Petition, 1852, RG 5 P, vol. 85, doc. 85, NSARM.

75. *Morning Post* (Halifax), 16 January 1841.

76. Petition on Behalf of the People of Colour in the Township and County of Halifax, 1847, RG 5 P, vol. 83, docs. 129–30, NSARM.

77. Ibid.

78. Ibid.

79. Report of Daniel Gallagher, 1849, RG 1, vol. 435, doc. 25, NSARM.

80. Nova Scotia Census, 1851, RG 12, NSARM.

81. The 1851 Nova Scotia census is not very accurate.

82. *Novascotian* (Halifax), 27 June 1832.

82. It must be noted that many black people in Halifax were Refugees, but other people of color could have been descendants of Black Loyalists, former slaves, or migrants from the Caribbean and elsewhere.

84. *British Colonist* (Halifax), 1 March 1856; Nova Scotia Census, 1838, RG 12, NSARM.

85. Moorsom, *Letters*, 131.

86. Nova Scotia Census, 1838, RG 12, NSARM.

87. Thomas Chandler Haliburton, *An Historical and Statistical Account of Nova-Scotia* (Halifax: J. Howe, 1829), 293.

88. E. T. Coke, *A Subaltern's Furlough* (London: Saunders and Otley, 1833), 415–16; also see *Acadian Recorder* (Halifax), 4 January 1817. In this edition of the newspaper the public was encouraged not to trust black servants, because a young girl had recently burned down the house of her wealthy white employer.

89. Petition of Reverend Willis, 8 February 1842, RG 5 P, vol. 73, doc. 95, NSARM.

90. *British Colonist* (Halifax), 19 July 1851.

91. His Majesty's Council to Dalhousie, 29 November 1816, RG 1, vol. 421, doc. 37, NSARM.

92. Desbrisay and Lowe, 9 March 1837, Journal of the House of Assembly, RG 1, No. 44, NSARM.

93. Report of Daniel Gallagher, 1849, RG 1, vol. 435, doc. 25, NSARM.

94. Fergusson, *Documentary,* 51 and 54.

95. Halifax County Land Grants-1787–1835, RG 20 C, doc. 185, NSARM. It is possible that some of these people died.

96. Report of the Inspection of Preston Lots, August 1818, RG 1, vol. 419, doc. 90, NSARM; Nova Scotia Census, 1827, RG 12, NSARM.

97. Report of the Inspection of Preston Lots, August 1818, RG 1, vol. 419, doc. 90, NSARM; Nova Scotia Census, 1838, RG 12, NSARM.

98. Nova Scotia Census, 1838, RG 12, NSARM.

99. Halifax County Land Grants-1787–1835, RG 20 C, doc. 185, NSARM; Nova Scotia Census, 1838, RG 12, NSARM.

100. Report of Lands cleared by the People of Colour in the settlement of Preston, 9 May 1816, RG 1, vol. 421, doc. 3, NSARM; Report of the Inspection of Preston Lots, August 1818, RG 1, vol. 419, doc. 90, NSARM; Nova Scotia Census, 1827, RG 12, NSARM; Nova Scotia Census, 1838, RG 12, NSARM.

101. Report of Lands cleared by the People of Colour in the settlement of Preston, 9 May 1816, RG 1, vol. 421, doc. 3, NSARM.

102. The Memorial of George Winder, 1829, RG 5 P, vol. 57, doc. 82, NSARM.

103. Report to Cogswell, 15 May 1816, RG 1, vol. 419, doc. 34, NSARM

104. Petition of Dean Atkins and William Wise, 1821, RG 20 A, NSARM.

105. Journal of the House of Assembly, 1847, NSARM.

106. Journal of the House of Assembly, 1843, NSARM.

107. *Morning Chronicle* (Halifax), 24 October 1844.

108. Death of a Black Man, March 1850, RG 7, vol. 23, doc. 76.

109. T. B. Akins, *History of Halifax City* (1895; reprint, Belleville, Ont.: Mika Publishing, 1973), 207.

110. *Morning Post* (Halifax), 7 May 1842.

111. Haliburton, *Historical*, 292.

112. Alan Cobley, "Black West Indian Seamen in the British Merchant Marine in the Midnineteenth Century," *History Workshop Journal* 58 (Autumn 2004): 266.

113. *Acadian Recorder* (Halifax), 29 August 1818.

114. Petition of Andrew Smith, 1829, RG 20 A, NSARM.

115. David W. States, "William Hall, V.C. of Horton Bluff, Nova Scotia, Nineteenth Century Naval Hero," *Collections of the Nova Scotia Historical Society* 44 (1996): 71–81.

116. Petition of Reverend Willis, 27 January 1840, RG 1, vol. 296, doc. 48, NSARM.

117. Judith Fingard, *The Dark Side of Life in Victorian Halifax* (Halifax: Pottersfield Press, 1989), 19.

118. W. Jeffrey Bolster, *Black Jacks: African American Seaman in the Age of Sail* (Cambridge, Massachusetts: Harvard University Press, 1997), 158–89.

CHAPTER 5: COMMUNITY AND IDENTITY (pp. 84–115)

1. *British North America: copies or extracts of correspondence relative to the affairs of British North America* (London: HMSO, 1839), 389.

2. Paul Du Gay and Stuart Hall, eds., *Questions of Cultural Identity* (London: Sage Publications, 1996); also see the critical essay of Rogers Brubaker and Frederick Cooper, "Beyond Identity," *Theory and Society* 29 (2000): 1–47.

3. Joseph Reidy, "'Negro Election Day' and Black Community Life in New England, 1750–1860," *Marxist Perspectives* 1 (Fall 1978): 102–17.

4. John Wood Sweet, *Bodies Politic: Negotiating Race in the American North, 1730–1830* (Baltimore: Johns Hopkins University Press, 2003), 353–409; Joanne Pope Melish, *Disowning Slavery: Gradual Emancipation and "Race" in New England, 1780–1860* (Ithaca, New York: Cornell University Press, 1998), 1–10; also see Bruce Dain, *A Hideous Monster of the Mind: American Race Theory in the Early Republic* (Cambridge, Massachusetts: Harvard University Press, 2002).

5. *Acadian Recorder* (Halifax), 15 September 1838.

6. *Morning Post* (Halifax), 27 May 1843.

7. *Morning Herald* (Halifax), 12 May 1843; *British Colonist* (Halifax), 28 December 1852.

8. *Morning Chronicle* (Halifax), 16 February 1844.

9. *Novascotian* (Halifax), 30 August 1847.

10. *Sun* (Halifax), 26 February 1851.

11. *Sun* (Halifax), 24 March 1845.

12. *Acadian Recorder* (Halifax), 22 March 1845.

13. *Acadian Recorder* (Halifax), 23 December 1815.

14. *Morning Herald* (Halifax), 8 September 1843.

15. *Acadian Recorder* (Halifax), 28 September 1833.

16. *British North American* (Halifax), 11 January 1854.

17. *Citizen* (Halifax) 22 July 1865.

18. George Elliot Clarke, "White Niggers, Black Slaves: Slavery, Race, and Class in T. C. Haliburton's *The Clockmaker*," *Nova Scotia Historical Review* 14 (1994): 13–40.

19. Samuel Ringgold Ward, *Autobiography of a Fugitive Negro: His Anti-Slavery Labours in the United States, Canada, & England* (1855; reprint, New York: Arno Press, 1968), 260–61.

20. Ibid., 261

21. Ibid., 266.

22. *Acadian Recorder* (Halifax), 30 December 1815; Coleman to Sabatier, 23 March 1815, RG 5 A, vol. 21, doc. 84, Nova Scotia Archives and Records Management, Halifax, Nova Scotia (hereafter NSARM).

23. *Novascotian* (Halifax), 27 June 1832.

24. S. F. Wise and Robert Craig Brown, *Canada Views the United States: Nineteenth-Century Political Attitudes* (Toronto: Macmillan, 1967), 46–73.

25. *Morning Chronicle* (Halifax), 12 December 1844.

26. *Sun* (Halifax), 9 January 1850; *Sun* (Halifax), 21 October 1850.

27. *Novascotian* (Halifax), 19 June 1854.

28. *British Colonist* (Halifax), 22 August 1854.

29. *Letter addressed to the Earl of Carnarvon by Mr. Joseph Howe, Mr. William Annand, and Mr. Hugh McDonald, stating their objections to the proposed scheme of union of the British North American provinces* (London: G.E. Eyre and W. Spottiswoode, 1867), 17.

30. *Morning Herald* (Halifax), 6 October 1841; *Morning Post* (Halifax), 2 July 1842.

31. *Morning Herald* (Halifax), 12 June 1843.

32. *Morning Chronicle* (Halifax), 17 December 1844.

33. *British Colonist* (Halifax), 20 March 1849.

34. The 1840s saw an ill-defined reform movement transformed into a disciplined political party. In other words, the key change came between 1843 and 1847 when leaders of the reform movement such as Joseph Howe rejected a coalition government in favor of a one-party administration. Thus, after 1848 the Reformers became the Liberal Party.

35. Dylan C. Penningroth, *The Claims of Kinfolk: African American Property and Community in the Nineteenth-Century South* (Chapel Hill: University of North Carolina Press, 2003), 188.

36. Halifax County, Court of Sessions: J.P.'s and Magistrates Papers, 1799–1879; Returns of Convictions, Trials, Suits, and Fines, RG 34–312, 1789–1866, NSARM.

37. Peter McKerrow, *A Brief History of the Coloured Baptists of Nova Scotia, 1783–1895*, ed. Frank S. Boyd Jr. (1895; reprint, Halifax: Afro Nova Scotian Enterprises, 1976), 10–11.

38. McKerrow, *Coloured Baptists,* 71.

39. James Oliver Horton and Lois E. Horton, *In Hope of Liberty: Culture, Community, and Protest Among Northern Free Blacks, 1700–1860* (New York: Oxford University Press, 1997), 125–54; James Oliver Horton and Lois E. Horton, *Black Bostonians: Family Life and Community Struggle in the Antebellum North* (1979; reprint, New York: Holmes & Meier, 1999), 41–55; Robert J. Cottrol, *The Afro-Yankees: Providence's Black Community in the Antebellum Era* (Westport, Connecticut: Greenwood Press, 1982), 41–66.

40. William Moorsom, *Letters from Nova Scotia: Comprising Sketches of a Young Country* (London: H. Colburn & R. Bentley, 1830), 129–30.

41. McKerrow, *Coloured Baptists,* 17.

42. Nisbett's Report, 31 December 1826, *Journal of the Society for the Propagation of the Gospel.*

43. McKerrow, *Coloured Baptists,* 10.

44. The Petition of the Undersigned coloured people, residing at Hammonds Plains, 18 August 1826, RG 1, vol. 422, doc. 33, NSARM.

45. Frank S. Boyd Jr., "Richard Preston," in *Dictionary of Canadian Biography,* ed. Frances G. Halpenny and Jean Hamelin (Toronto: University of Toronto Press, 1985), 8:968–70.

46. Ibid., 8:968.

47. The Humble Petition of the Undersigned Trustees for and on behalf of the Congregation of the Baptist African Chapel established at Halifax, 25 February 1833, RG 5 P, vol. 42, doc. 51, NSARM.

48. Ibid. It is unclear precisely what these "unpleasant" circumstances entailed.

49. McKerrow, *Coloured Baptists,* 8–13.

50. Ibid., 17.

51. As reprinted in *Novascotian* (Halifax), 27 June 1832.

52. McKerrow, *Coloured Baptists,* 15. Meredith Stanley is also listed in sources as Marada Stanley.

53. Ibid., 25–28.

54. McKerrow, *Coloured Baptists,* 27.

55. *Minutes of the Fifth Session of the African Baptist Association of Nova Scotia* (Halifax: Printed by W. Cunnabell, 1858), Library and Archives Canada, Ottawa, Ontario.

56. *Minutes of the Eighth Session of the African Baptist Association of Nova Scotia* (Halifax: Printed by W. Cunnabell, 1861), University of Victoria Libraries, Victoria, British Columbia.

57. *Minutes of the Eleventh Session of the African Baptist Association of Nova Scotia* (Halifax: Printed by W. Cunnabell, 1864), University of Victoria Libraries, Victoria, British Columbia.

58. *Minutes of the Eighth Session of the African Baptist Association of Nova Scotia.*

59. *Sun* (Halifax), 19 August 1846.

60. J. W. Hood, *One Hundred Years of the African Methodist Episcopal Zion Church* (New York: AME Zion Book Concern, 1895), 93.

61. Hood, *One Hundred Years,* 96.

62. *Belchers Farmer's Almanack,* 1848–1859.

63. Petition of Citizens of Color, 28 January 1847, RG 5 P, vol. 45, doc. 12, NSARM.

64. *Novascotian* (Halifax), 16 October 1848.

65. *British Colonist* (Halifax), 17 May 1849.

66. *British Colonist* (Halifax), 2 March 1850; *British Colonist* (Halifax), 13 July 1850.

67. *British Colonist* (Halifax), 20 March 1852.

68. *British North American* (Halifax) 15 July 1853.

69. *British Colonist* (Halifax), 24 April 1852.

70. *Belchers Farmer's Almanack,* 1850–1857; McKerrow, *Coloured Baptists,* 25–27.

71. Petition of the Colored People at Preston, 1841, RG 20 C, vol. 31, doc. 124, NSARM.

72. On contested public space, see Mary P. Ryan, *Civic Wars: Democracy and Public Life in the American City during the Nineteenth Century* (Berkeley: University of California Press, 1997); Bonnie Huskins, "From Haute Cuisine to Ox Roasts: Public Feasting and the Negotiation of Class in Mid-19th-Century Saint John and Halifax," *Labour/Le Travail* 37 (Spring 1996): 9–36.

73. *British Colonist* (Halifax), 4 September 1849; *British Colonist* (Halifax), 26 May 1849; *British Colonist* (Halifax), 27 June 1850.

74. The historiography includes Mitch Kachun, *Festivals of Freedom: Memory and Meaning in African American Emancipation Celebrations, 1808–1915* (Amherst: University of Massachusetts Press, 2003); Elizabeth Rauh Bethel, *The Roots of African-American Identity: Memory and History in Free Antebellum Communities* (New York: St. Martin's Press, 1997); Genevieve Fabre and Robert O'Meally, eds., *History and Memory in African-American Culture* (New York: Oxford University Press, 1994); William B. Gravely, "The Dialectic of Double-Consciousness in Black American Freedom Celebrations, 1808–1863," *Journal of Negro History* 67 (Winter 1982): 302–17.

75. See *Belchers Farmer's Almanack,* 1850, 1851, 1856; *Novascotian* (Halifax), 13 February 1849.

76. Patrick Rael, *Black Identity and Black Protest in the Antebellum North* (Chapel Hill: University of North Carolina Press, 2002), 102–17.

77. James Oliver Horton, *Free People of Color: Inside the African American Community* (Washington, D.C.: Smithsonian Institution Press, 1993), 158–60.

78. Petition of Citizens of Color, 28 January 1847, RG 5 P, vol. 45, doc. 12, NSARM.

79. The Humble Petition of the Undersigned Trustees for and on behalf of the Congregation of the Baptist African Chapel established at Halifax, 25 February 1833, RG 1, Commissioner of Public Records, NSARM.

80. David Sutherland, "Race Relations in Halifax, Nova Scotia, During the Mid-Victorian Quest for Reform," *Journal of the Canadian Historical Association* 7 (1996): 35–54.

81. *Novascotian* (Halifax), 5 July 1838; *Acadian Recorder* (Halifax), 2 July 1838.

82. *Novascotian* (Halifax), 10 May 1847.

83. Petition of the Colored People at Preston, 1841, RG 20 C, vol. 31, doc. 124, NSARM.

84. In the free states, black voting varied widely. The following table is taken from Horton and Horton, *In Hope of Liberty*, 169. The original source is Paul Finkelman, "Prelude to the Fourteenth Amendment: Black Legal Rights in the Antebellum North," *Rutgers Law Journal* 17 (Spring and Summer 1986): 415–82.

BLACK VOTING RIGHTS

	1830	1860
Maine	Yes	Yes
New Hampshire	Yes	Yes
Vermont	Yes	Yes
Massachusetts	Yes	Yes
Connecticut	No	No
Rhode Island	No	Yes
New York	Restricted	Restricted
New Jersey	No	No
Pennsylvania	Yes	No
Ohio	No	Restricted
Indiana	No	No
Illinois	No	No
Michigan	No	Restricted
Iowa	No	No
Wisconsin	No	No
Minnesota	No	No
California	No	No
Oregon	No	No

85. During the 1840s, to vote in Halifax municipal elections or provincial elections one had to be an adult (age twenty-one) male and hold real estate. In the 1850s, Nova Scotia became increasingly democratic, moving through a ratepayer franchise to manhood suffrage in the early 1860s. But Joseph Howe and other politicians retreated from universal manhood suffrage because of deep anti–Irish Roman Catholic sentiment in Nova Scotia.

86. On politics in Nova Scotia, see J. Murray Beck, *Politics of Nova Scotia: I, 1710–1896* (Tantallon, Nova Scotia: Four East Publications, 1985); J. Murray Beck, *Joseph Howe: Conservative Reformer, 1804–1848* (Montreal and Kingston: McGill-Queen's University Press, 1982); an essential discussion of Nova Scotia's political culture is Brian Cuthbertson, *Johnny Bluenose at the Polls: Epic Nova Scotian Election Battles, 1758–1848* (Halifax: Formac, 1994).

87. *Morning Post* (Halifax) 5 November 1840.

88. *Morning Herald* (Halifax), 30 December 1840.

89. *Acadian Recorder* (Halifax), 16 January 1841.

90. *Morning Post* (Halifax), 28 December 1841.

91. *Morning Herald* (Halifax), 31 December 1841.

92. *Novascotian* (Halifax), 9 January 1843.

93. David Walker, *Appeal to the Coloured Citizens of the World*, ed. Sean Wilentz (1829; reprint, New York: Hill and Wang, 1995), 49.

94. *Novascotian* (Halifax), 10 August 1846.

95. *Sun* (Halifax), 23 January 1846.

96. *Sun* (Halifax), 23 February 1846.

97. *Sun* (Halifax), 3 May 1847.

98. *Novascotian* (Halifax), 10 May 1847.

99. Ibid.

100. *Standard* (Halifax), 14 May 1847.

101. *Sun* (Halifax), 28 July 1847.

102. Sutherland, "Race Relations," 35–54.

103. Thomas Power, *The Irish in Atlantic Canada, 1780–1900* (Fredericton: New Ireland Press, 1991).

104. *Standard* (Halifax), 30 July 1847.

105. *Acadian Recorder* (Halifax), 31 July 1847.

106. David Roediger, *The Wages of Whiteness: Race and the Making of the American Working Class* (New York: Verso, 1991).

107. *Sun* (Halifax), 2 August 1847.

108. *Acadian Recorder* (Halifax), 9 June 1849.

109. *Morning Chronicle* (Halifax), 30 March 1852.

110. *British Colonist* (Halifax), 13 September 1860.

111. *British Colonist* (Halifax), 11 October 1860.

112. Horton and Horton, *In Hope of Liberty*, 203–68.

113. *Morning Chronicle* (Halifax), 9 July 1844.

114. *Sun* (Halifax), 26 January 1846.

115. McKerrow, *Coloured Baptists*, 22.

116. *Sun* (Halifax), 5 August 1846.

117. *Novascotian* (Halifax), 24 August 1846.

118. *Novascotian* (Halifax), 23 November 1846.

119. Petition of Charles Roan, President of the African Abolition Society, 23 February 1848, RG 5 Series GP 1, vol. 1, doc. 181, NSARM.

120. Philip M. Hamer, "Great Britain, the United States, and the Negro Seamen Acts, 1822–1848," *Journal of Southern History* 1 (February 1935): 12–13.

121. W. Jeffrey Bolster, *Black Jacks: African American Seaman in the Age of Sail* (Cambridge, Massachusetts: Harvard University Press, 1997), 200, also see 190–214.

122. *British Colonist* (Halifax), 22 December 1849.

123. *British Colonist* (Halifax), 26 September 1850.

124. *British Colonist* (Halifax), 28 November 1850.

125. William and Ellen Craft, *Running a Thousand Miles for Freedom* (1860; reprint, New York: Arno Press, 1969), 105.

126. Ibid.

127. Ibid., 106.

128. Ibid., 107. Reverend Kennedy (possibly also known as Reverend Cannady) served at the African Methodist Church in Halifax at midcentury.

129. *British Colonist* (Halifax), 18 March 1851.

130. *British Colonist* (Halifax), 12 June 1855.

131. *British Colonist* (Halifax), 25 June 1850.

132. *Novascotian* (Halifax), 21 October 1850.

133. *British Colonist* (Halifax), 7 November 1850.

134. *British Colonist* (Halifax), 29 March 1853.

135. Abolition Day celebrations continued after 1867, but later perhaps more as picnics as opposed to parades.

136. *Novascotian* (Halifax), 9 August 1847.

137. *British Colonist* (Halifax), 30 July 1850.

138. *British Colonist* (Halifax), 6 August 1850.

139. *British Colonist* (Halifax), 4 August 1855.

140. *Acadian Recorder* (Halifax), 5 August 1867.

141. Jane Rhodes, "The Contestation over National Identity: Nineteenth-Century Black Americans in Canada," *Canadian Review of American Studies* 30 (2000): 175–86.

EPILOGUE (pp. 116–21)

1. Judith Fingard, "Race and Respectability in Victorian Halifax," *Journal of Imperial and Commonwealth History* 20 (May 1992): 190; Robin Winks, "Negro School Segregation in Ontario and Nova Scotia," *Canadian Historical Review* 50 (June 1969): 164–91.

2. United States Census, 1880, Population Schedules of the Tenth Census of the United States, University of Massachusetts Libraries, Amherst, Massachusetts. Abraham Boyd's father would have arrived in Nova Scotia during his midtwenties. Thus, if his father was born in Africa, he would have been brought over to the Chesapeake as a very young child in the late 1780s or early 1790s.

However, it is also possible that his recorded age was simply wrong. Another possibility is that Abraham wanted to claim African parentage.

3. I must thank Judith Fingard for this reference: *Acadian Recorder* (Halifax), 6 January 1892.

4. David Levering Lewis, *W. E. B. Du Bois: Biography of a Race, 1868–1919* (New York: Henry Holt, 1993), 84.

5. Peter McKerrow, *A Brief History of the Coloured Baptists of Nova Scotia, 1783–1895*, ed. Frank S. Boyd, Jr. (1895; reprint, Halifax: Afro Nova Scotian Enterprises, 1976), 101.

6. Robin Winks, "The Canadian Negro: A Historical Assessment, Part II: The Problem of Identity," *Journal of Negro History* 54 (January 1969): 3.

7. George Elliot Clarke, "Must All Blackness Be American?: Locating Canada in Borden's 'Tightrope Time,' or Nationalizing Gilroy's *The Black Atlantic*," *Canadian Ethnic Studies* 28 (1996): 56–71. Afua Cooper, "The Fluid Frontier: Blacks and the Detroit River Region—a Focus on Henry Bibb," *Canadian Review of American Studies* 30 (2000): 129–49; Jane Rhodes, "The Contestation over National Identity: Nineteenth-Century Black Americans in Canada," *Canadian Review of American Studies* 30 (2000): 175–86; Nora Faires, "Leaving the 'Land of the Second Chance': Migration from Ontario to the Great Lakes States in the Nineteenth and Early Twentieth Centuries," in *Permeable Border: The Great Lakes Basin as Transnational Region, 1650–1990*, ed. John J. Bukowczyk et al. (Pittsburgh: University of Pittsburgh Press, 2005).

8. Joanne Pope Melish, *Disowning Slavery: Gradual Emancipation and "Race" in New England, 1780–1860* (Ithaca, New York: Cornell University Press, 1998), 240–41.

9. *Sun and Advertiser* (Halifax), 12 August 1863.

Bibliography

ARCHIVES AND COLLECTIONS

Amherst, Massachusetts University of Massachusetts–Amherst Libraries
Population Schedules of the Tenth Census of the United States, 1880

Burlington, Vermont Special Collections, University of Vermont Libraries
Vermont Colonization Society Sermons

Halifax, Nova Scotia Nova Scotia Archives and Records Management
Assembly Papers
Book of Negroes
Census and Poll Tax Rolls
Colonial Office Papers
Crown Lands
Dispatches from Secretary of State to Lieutenant Governor
Ethnic Groups: Blacks
Files of the House of Assembly
Governor's Petitions
Journal of His Majesty's Council in their legislative capacity
Journal of the House of Assembly
Journal of the Society for the Propagation of the Gospel
Land Papers
Legislative Files of the Council
Lieutenant Governor's Letter Books
Minutes of Council
Minutes of the Court of Quarter Sessions
Miscellaneous Documents
Negro and Maroon Settlements

Official Correspondence and Legislative Papers
Papers of the Provincial Secretary
School Petitions
Selections from the Files of the House of Assembly
Statutes of Nova Scotia

Ottawa, Ontario Library and Archives Canada
Minutes of the African Baptist Association

Tallahassee, Florida Florida State University Libraries
Papers of Vice Admiral Sir Alexander Forrester Inglis Cochrane

Toronto, Ontario University of Toronto Libraries
Butler Plantation Papers, the Papers of Pierce Butler (1744–1822)

Washington, D.C. Library of Congress
Papers of Sir George Cockburn
Public Record Office, War Office 6, Secretary of State/Out-Letters

Victoria, British Columbia University of Victoria Libraries
Minutes of the African Baptist Association

NEWSPAPERS

Acadian Recorder (Halifax)
British Colonist (Halifax)
British North American (Halifax)
Citizen (Halifax)
Enquirer (Richmond)
Free Press (Halifax)
Gazette (Halifax)
Halifax Monthly Magazine (Halifax)
Methodist Magazine (London)

Morning Chronicle (Halifax)
Morning Herald (Halifax)
Morning Post (Halifax)
National Intelligencer (Washington)
Niles Weekly Register (Baltimore)
Novascotian (Halifax)
Standard (Halifax)
Sun (Halifax)
Sun and Advertiser (Halifax)
Times (New York)

BOOKS

Akins, T. B. *History of Halifax City.* 1895. Reprint. Belleville, Ont.: Mika Publishing, 1973.
American State Papers: Class I, Foreign Relations. Volume 4. Buffalo: William S. Hein, 1998.

Ball, Charles. *Slavery in the United States: A Narrative of the Life and Adventures of Charles Ball, a Black Man.* 1837. Reprint. New York: Negro Universities Press, 1969.

Beck, J. Murray. *Joseph Howe: Conservative Reformer, 1804–1848.* Montreal and Kingston: McGill-Queen's University Press, 1982.

———. *The Politics of Nova Scotia: I, 1710–1896.* Tantallon, Nova Scotia: Four East Publications, 1985.

Belchers Farmer's Almanack, 1848–1862.

Bell, Howard Holman, ed. *Minutes of the Proceedings of the National Negro Conventions, 1830–1864.* New York: Arno Press, 1969.

———. *A Survey of the Negro Convention Movement, 1830–1861.* New York: Arno Press, 1969.

Bell, Malcolm. *Major Butler's Legacy: Five Generations of a Slaveholding Family.* Athens: University of Georgia Press, 1987.

Berlin, Ira. *Slaves Without Masters: The Free Negro in the Antebellum South.* New York: Pantheon, 1974.

———. *Many Thousands Gone: The First Two Centuries of Slavery in North America.* Cambridge, Massachusetts: Harvard University Press, 1998.

Berlin, Ira, and Ronald Hoffman, eds. *Slavery and Freedom in the Age of the American Revolution.* Charlottesville: University Press of Virginia, 1983.

Bethel, Elizabeth Rauh. *The Roots of African-American Identity: Memory and History in Free Antebellum Communities.* New York: St. Martin's Press, 1997.

Bird, Isabella. *The Englishwoman in America.* London: J. Murray, 1856.

Bolster, W. Jeffrey. *Black Jacks: African American Seaman in the Age of Sail.* Cambridge, Massachusetts: Harvard University Press, 1997.

Bouchette, Joseph. *The British Dominions in North America.* Volume 2. London: H. Colburn and R. Bentley, 1831.

Boyd, Frank S., Jr. "Richard Preston." In *Dictionary of Canadian Biography.* Edited by Frances G. Halpenny and Jean Hamelin. Volume 8. Toronto: University of Toronto Press, 1985.

Brace, Jeffrey. *The Blind African Slave, or Memoirs of Boyrereau Brinch, Nicknamed Jeffrey Brace, as told to Benjamin F. Prentiss.* Edited by Kari J. Winter. Madison: University of Wisconsin Press, 2004.

Breen, T. H., and Stephen Innes. *"Myne Owne Ground": Race and Freedom on Virginia's Eastern Shore, 1640–1676.* New York: Oxford University Press, 1980.

British North America: copies or extracts of correspondence relative to the affairs of British North America. London: HMSO, 1839.

Brown, Robert Craig, and S. F. Wise. *Canada Views the United States: Nineteenth-Century Political Attitudes.* Toronto: Macmillan, 1967.

Bullard, Mary. *Black Liberation on Cumberland Island in 1815.* South Dartmouth, Mass.: M. R. Bullard, 1983.

Cahill, Barry. "Colchester Men: The Pro-Slavery Presbyterian Witness of the Reverends Daniel Cock of Truro and David Smith of Londonderry." In

Planter Links: Community and Culture in Colonial Nova Scotia. Edited by Margaret Conrad and Barry Moody. Fredericton: Acadiensis Press, 2001.

Campbell, Mavis, ed. *Nova Scotia and the Fighting Maroons: A Documentary History*. Williamsburg, Virginia: Department of Anthropology, College of William and Mary, 1990.

Careless, J. M. S. *Frontier and Metropolis: Regions, Cities, and Identities in Canada before 1914*. Toronto: University of Toronto Press, 1989.

Carney, Judith A. *Black Rice: The African Origins of Rice Cultivation in the Americas*. Cambridge, Massachusetts: Harvard University Press, 2001.

Carr, Lois Green, and Lorena S. Walsh. "Economic Diversification and Labor Organization in the Chesapeake, 1650–1820." In *Work and Labor in Early America*. Edited by Stephen Innes. Chapel Hill: University of North Carolina Press, 1988.

Carroll, Francis M. *A Good and Wise Measure: The Search for the Canadian-American Boundary, 1783–1842*. Toronto: University of Toronto Press, 2001.

Clarkson, John. *Clarkson's Mission to America, 1791–1792*. Edited by C. B. Fergusson. Halifax: Public Archives of Nova Scotia, 1971.

Clegg, Claude A. *The Price of Liberty: African Americans and the Making of Liberia*. Chapel Hill: University of North Carolina Press, 2004.

Coke, E. T. *A Subaltern's Furlough*. London: Saunders and Otley, 1833.

Condon, Ann G. "1783–1800: Loyalist Arrival, Acadian Return, Imperial Reform." In *The Atlantic Region to Confederation: A History*. Edited by Phillip A. Buckner and John G. Reid. Toronto: University of Toronto Press, 1994.

Conrad, Margaret, ed. *They Planted Well: New England Planters in Maritime Canada*. Fredericton: Acadiensis Press, 1988.

———, ed. *Making Adjustments: Change and Continuity in Planter Nova Scotia, 1759–1800*. Fredericton: Acadiensis Press, 1991.

Conrad, Margaret, and Barry Moody, eds. *Planter Links: Community and Culture in Colonial Nova Scotia*. Fredericton: Acadiensis Press, 2001.

Cottrol, Robert J. *The Afro-Yankees: Providence's Black Community in the Antebellum Era*. Westport, Connecticut: Greenwood Press, 1982.

———. *From African to Yankee: Narratives of Slavery and Freedom in Antebellum New England*. Armonk, New York: M. E. Sharpe, 1998.

Cozzens, Frederic. *Acadia, or a Month with the Blue Noses*. New York: Derby & Jackson, 1859.

Cramer, Clayton E. *Black Demographic Data, 1790–1860: A Sourcebook*. Westport, Connecticut: Greenwood Press, 1997.

Creel, Margaret Washington. *"A Peculiar People": Slave Religion and Community-Culture among the Gullahs*. New York: New York University Press, 1988.

Curry, Leonard P. *The Free Black in Urban America, 1800–1850: The Shadow of the Dream*. Chicago: University of Chicago Press, 1981.

Cuthbertson, Brian. *Johnny Bluenose at the Polls: Epic Nova Scotian Election Battles, 1758–1848*. Halifax: Formac, 1994.

Dain, Bruce. *A Hideous Monster of the Mind: American Race Theory in the Early Republic*. Cambridge, Massachusetts: Harvard University Press, 2002.

Dickinson, H. T. *Liberty and Property: Political Ideology in Eighteenth-Century Britain.* New York: Holmes and Meier, 1977.

Diouf, Sylviane. *Servants of Allah: African Muslims Enslaved in the Americas.* New York: New York University Press, 1998.

Documents Furnished by the British Government Under The Third Article of the Convention of St. Petersburg, And Bayly's List of Slaves And Of Public And Private Property Remaining On Tangier Island And On Board H.B.M. Ships of War, After The Ratification Of The Treaty Of Ghent. Washington, D.C.: Gales and Seaton, 1827.

Dunaway, Wilma A. *The African-American Family in Slavery and Emancipation.* Cambridge: Cambridge University Press, 2003.

Dusinberre, William. *Them Dark Days: Slavery in the American Rice Swamps.* New York: Oxford University Press, 1996.

Eccles, W. J. *The Canadian Frontier, 1534–1760.* 1969. Reprint. Albuquerque: University of New Mexico Press, 1983.

Eltis, David. *The Rise of African Slavery in the Americas.* Cambridge: Cambridge University Press, 2000.

Evans, Dorothy. *Hammonds Plains: The First 100 Years.* Halifax: Bounty Print, 1993.

Fabre, Genevieve, and Robert O'Meally, eds. *History and Memory in African-American Culture.* New York: Oxford University Press, 1994.

Faires, Nora. "Leaving the 'Land of Second Chance': Migration from Ontario to the Great Lakes States in the Nineteenth and Early Twentieth Centuries." In *Permeable Border: The Great Lakes Basin as Transnational Region, 1650–1990.* Edited by John J. Bukowczyk et al. Pittsburgh: University of Pittsburgh Press, 2005.

Fairhead, James, et al., eds. *African-American Exploration in West Africa: Four Nineteenth-Century Diaries.* Bloomington: Indiana University Press, 2003.

Fergusson, C. B. *A Documentary Study of the Establishment of the Negroes in Nova Scotia between the War of 1812 and the Winning of Responsible Government.* Halifax: Public Archives of Nova Scotia, 1948.

Fingard, Judith. *The Dark Side of Life in Victorian Halifax.* Halifax: Pottersfield Press, 1989.

Foner, Eric. *Nothing But Freedom: Emancipation and Its Legacy.* Baton Rouge: Louisiana State University Press, 1983.

———. *Reconstruction: America's Unfinished Revolution, 1863–1877.* New York: Harper and Row, 1988.

Frame, Elizabeth. *Descriptive Sketches of Nova Scotia in Prose and Verse.* Halifax: A&W MacKinley, 1864.

Franklin, John Hope, and Loren Schweninger. *Runaway Slaves: Rebels on the Plantation.* New York: Oxford University Press, 1999.

Frey, Sylvia. *Water from the Rock: Black Resistance in a Revolutionary Age.* Princeton, New Jersey: Princeton University Press, 1991.

Gay, Paul Du, and Stuart Hall, eds. *Questions of Cultural Identity.* London: Sage Publications, 1996.

Georgia Writers' Project. *Drums and Shadows: Survival Studies among the Georgia Coastal Negroes.* 1940. Reprint. Westport, Connecticut: Greenwood Press, 1973.

Glaude, Eddie S. *Exodus! Religion, Race, and Nation in Early Nineteenth-Century Black America.* Chicago: University of Chicago Press, 2000.

Gleig, G. R. *A Narrative of the Campaigns of the British Army at Washington and New Orleans under Generals Ross, Pakenham, and Lambert, in the years 1814 and 1815.* London: J. Murray, 1821.

Gomez, Michael. *Exchanging Our Country Marks: The Transformation of African Identities in the Colonial and Antebellum South.* Chapel Hill: University of North Carolina Press, 1998.

Grant, John. *The Immigration and Settlement of the Black Refugees of the War of 1812 in Nova Scotia and New Brunswick.* Dartmouth: Black Cultural Centre for Nova Scotia, 1990.

———. *The Maroons in Nova Scotia.* Halifax: Formac, 2002.

Greene, Lorenzo J. *The Negro in Colonial New England.* 1942. Reprint. New York: Atheneum, 1968.

Griffiths, Naomi E. S. *Contexts of Acadian History, 1686–1784.* Montreal and Kingston: McGill-Queen's University Press, 1992.

———. "1600–1650: Fish, Fur, and Folk." In *The Atlantic Region to Confederation: A History.* Edited by Phillip A. Buckner and John G. Reid. Toronto: University of Toronto Press, 1994.

Gutman, Herbert. *The Black Family in Slavery and Freedom, 1750–1925.* New York: Pantheon Books, 1976.

Haliburton, Thomas Chandler. *An Historical and Statistical Account of Nova-Scotia.* Halifax: J. Howe, 1829.

Hall, Basil. *Travels in North America in the Years of 1827 and 1828.* Volume 2. Philadelphia: Carney, Lea, & Carey, 1829.

Hall, Robert L., and Michael M. Harvey, eds. *Making a Living: The Work Experience of African-Americans in New England, Selected Readings.* Boston: New England Foundation for the Humanities, 1995.

Hardy, Campbell. *Sporting Adventures in the New World; or Days and Nights of Moose-Hunting in the Pine Forests of Acadia.* Volume 2. London: Hurst and Blackett Publishers, 1855.

Hine, Darlene Clark, and Jacqueline McLeod, eds. *Crossing Boundaries: Comparative History of Black People in Diaspora.* 1999. Reprint. Bloomington & Indianapolis: Indiana University Press, 2001.

Hines, Allister. "Deportees in Nova Scotia: The Jamaican Maroons, 1796–1800." In *Working Slavery, Pricing Freedom: Perspectives from the Caribbean, Africa, and the African Diaspora.* Edited by Verene Shepherd. New York: Palgrave, 2002.

Hodges, Graham Russell, ed. *The Black Loyalist Directory: African Americans in Exile after the American Revolution.* New York: Garland, 1996.

————. *Slavery and Freedom in the Rural North: African Americans in Monmouth County, New Jersey, 1665–1865.* Madison, Wisconsin: Madison House, 1997.

————. *Root and Branch: African Americans in New York and East Jersey, 1613–1863.* Chapel Hill: University of North Carolina Press, 1999.

Hood, J. W. *One Hundred Years of the African Methodist Episcopal Zion Church.* New York: AME Zion Book Concern, 1895.

Hornsby, Stephen J., and John G. Reid, eds. *New England and the Maritime Provinces: Connections and Comparisons.* Montreal and Kingston: McGill-Queen's University Press, 2005.

Horton, James Oliver. *Free People of Color: Inside the African American Community.* Washington, D.C.: Smithsonian Institution Press, 1993.

Horton, James Oliver, and Lois E. Horton. *Black Bostonians: Family Life and Community Struggle in the Antebellum North.* 1979. Reprint. New York: Holmes & Meier, 1999.

————. *In Hope of Liberty: Culture, Community, and Protest Among Northern Free Blacks, 1700–1860.* New York: Oxford University Press, 1997.

Hough, John. *A Sermon, Delivered before the Vermont Colonization Society at Montpeleir [sic], October 18, 1826.* Montpelier, Vermont: E. P. Walton, 1826.

Howe, Joseph. *Western and Eastern Rambles: Travel Sketches of Nova Scotia.* Edited by M. G. Parks. 1828. Reprint. Toronto: University of Toronto Press, 1973.

Hunt, Alfred N. *Haiti's Influence on Antebellum America: Slumbering Volcano in the Caribbean.* Baton Rouge: Louisiana State University Press, 1988.

Johnson, Walter. *Soul by Soul: Life Inside the Antebellum Slave Market.* Cambridge, Massachusetts: Harvard University Press, 1999.

Kachun, Mitch. *Festivals of Freedom: Memory and Meaning in African American Emancipation Celebrations, 1808–1915.* Amherst: University of Massachusetts Press, 2003.

Katzmann, Mary Jane (Mrs. William Lawson). *History of the Townships of Dartmouth, Preston and Lawrencetown.* Halifax: Morton, 1893.

Kemble, Fanny. *Journal of a Residence on a Georgia Plantation in 1838–1839.* New York: Harper & Brothers Publishers, 1863.

Klein, Herbert S. *The Atlantic Slave Trade.* Cambridge: Cambridge University Press, 1999.

Kulikoff, Allan. *Tobacco and Slaves: The Development of Southern Cultures in the Chesapeake, 1680–1800.* Chapel Hill: University of North Carolina Press, 1986.

Lee, Maureen Elgersman. *Black Bangor: African Americans in a Maine Community, 1880–1950.* Durham: University of New Hampshire Press, 2005.

Letter addressed to the Earl of Carnarvon by Mr. Joseph Howe, Mr. William Annand, and Mr. Hugh McDonald, stating their objections to the proposed scheme of union of the British North American provinces. London: GE Eyre and W. Spottiswoode, 1867.

Levesque, George A. *Black Boston: African American Life and Culture in Urban America, 1750–1860*. New York: Garland, 1994.

Lewis, David Levering. *W. E. B. Du Bois: Biography of a Race, 1868–1919*. New York: Henry Holt, 1993.

Linebaugh, Peter, and Marcus Rediker. *The Many-Headed Hydra: Sailors, Slaves, Commoners, and the Hidden History of the Revolutionary Atlantic*. Boston: Beacon, 2000.

Lord, Walter. *The Dawn's Early Light*. New York: W. W. Norton, 1972.

MacKinnon, Neil. *This Unfriendly Soil: The Loyalist Experience in Nova Scotia, 1783–1791*. Montreal and Kingston: McGill-Queen's University Press, 1986.

Mancke, Elizabeth. *The Fault Lines of Empire: Political Differentiation in Massachusetts and Nova Scotia, ca. 1760–1830*. New York: Routledge, 2005.

Manning, William R., ed. *Diplomatic Correspondence of the United States: Canadian Relations, 1784–1860*, Volume 1. Washington D.C.: Carnegie Endowment for International Peace, 1940.

Martell, J. S. *Immigration to and Emigration from Nova Scotia, 1815–1838*. Halifax: Public Archives of Nova Scotia, 1942.

Martin, Jonathan D. *Divided Mastery: Slave Hiring in the American South*. Cambridge, Massachusetts: Harvard University Press, 2004.

McKerrow, Peter. *A Brief History of the Coloured Baptists of Nova Scotia, 1783–1895*. Edited by Frank S. Boyd Jr. 1895. Reprint. Halifax: Afro Nova Scotian Enterprises, 1976.

McManus, Edgar J. *Black Bondage in the North*. Syracuse, New York: Syracuse University Press, 1973.

Melish, Joanne Pope. *Disowning Slavery: Gradual Emancipation and "Race" in New England, 1780–1860*. Ithaca, New York: Cornell University Press, 1998.

Miller, Floyd J. *The Search for a Black Nationality: Black Emigration and Colonization, 1787–1863*. Urbana: University of Illinois Press, 1975.

Minutes of the Eighth Session of the African Baptist Association of Nova Scotia. (Halifax: Printed by W. Cunnabell, 1861), University of Victoria Libraries, Victoria, British Columbia.

Minutes of the Eleventh Session of the African Baptist Association of Nova Scotia. (Halifax: Printed by W. Cunnabell, 1864), University of Victoria Libraries, Victoria, British Columbia.

Minutes of the Fifth Session of the African Baptist Association of Nova Scotia. (Halifax: Printed by W. Cunnabell, 1858), Library and Archives Canada, Ottawa, Ontario.

Moorsom, William. *Letters from Nova Scotia: Comprising Sketches of a Young Country*. London: H. Colburn & R. Bentley, 1830.

Morgan, Philip D. "Task and Gang Systems: The Organization of Labor on New World Plantations." In *Work and Labor in Early America*. Edited by Stephen Innes. Chapel Hill: University of North Carolina Press, 1988.

———. *Slave Counterpoint: Black Culture in the Eighteenth-Century Chesapeake and Lowcountry*. Chapel Hill: University of North Carolina Press, 1998.

Nash, Gary B. *Forging Freedom: The Formation of Philadelphia's Black Community, 1720–1840.* Cambridge, Massachusetts: Harvard University Press, 1988.

Oliver, Pearleen. *A Brief History of the Coloured Baptists in Nova Scotia, 1782–1953.* Halifax: African United Baptist Association, 1953.

———. *A Root and a Name.* Halifax: self-published, 1977.

Olwell, Robert. "'Loose, Idle, and Disorderly': Slave Women in the Eighteenth-Century Charleston Marketplace." In *More Than Chattel: Black Women and Slavery in the Americas.* Edited by David Gasper and Darlene Clark Hine. Bloomington: Indiana University Press, 1996.

Pamphile, Leon D. *Haitians and African Americans: A Heritage of Tragedy and Hope.* Gainesville: University Press of Florida, 2001.

Parrish, Lydia. *Slave Songs of the Georgia Sea Islands.* 1942. Reprint. Athens: University of Georgia Press, 1992.

Pastore, Ralph. "The Sixteenth Century: Aboriginal Peoples and European Contact." In *The Atlantic Region to Confederation: A History.* Edited by Phillip A. Buckner and John G. Reid. Toronto: University of Toronto Press, 1994.

Patterson, Stephen E. "1744–1763: Colonial Wars and Aboriginal Peoples." In *The Atlantic Region to Confederation: A History.* Edited by Phillip A. Buckner and John G. Reid. Toronto: University of Toronto Press, 1994.

Payzant, Joan, and Lewis J. Payzant. *Like a Weaver's Shuttle: A History of the Halifax-Dartmouth Ferries.* Halifax: Nimbus, 1979.

Pease, Jane H., and William H. Pease. *Black Utopia: Negro Communal Experiments in America.* 1963. Reprint, Madison: State Historical Society of Wisconsin, 1972.

Penningroth, Dylan C. *The Claims of Kinfolk: African American Property and Community in the Nineteenth-Century South.* Chapel Hill: University of North Carolina Press, 2003.

Piersen, William D. *Black Yankees: The Development of an Afro-American Subculture in Eighteenth-Century New England.* Amherst: University of Massachusetts Press, 1988.

Power, Thomas. *The Irish in Atlantic Canada, 1780–1900.* Fredericton: New Ireland Press, 1991.

Pybus, Cassandra. *Epic Journeys of Freedom: Runaway Slaves of the American Revolution and Their Global Quest for Liberty.* Boston: Beacon Press, 2006.

Raboteau, Albert J. *Slave Religion: The "Invisible Institution" in the Antebellum South.* New York: Oxford University Press, 1978.

Rael, Patrick. *Black Identity and Black Protest in the Antebellum North.* Chapel Hill: University of North Carolina Press, 2002.

Rawlyk, George A., and Gordon T. Stewart. *A People Highly Favoured of God: The Nova Scotia Yankees and the American Revolution.* Toronto: Macmillan, 1972.

Reed, Harry. *Platform for Change: The Foundations of the Northern Free Black Community, 1775–1865.* East Lansing: Michigan State University Press, 1994.

Reid, John G. *Six Crucial Decades: Times of Change in the History of the Maritimes.* Halifax: Nimbus, 1987.

————. "1686–1720: Imperial Intrusions." In *The Atlantic Region to Confederation: A History.* Edited by Phillip A. Buckner and John G. Reid. Toronto: University of Toronto Press, 1994.

Rhodes, Jane. *Mary Ann Shadd Cary: The Black Press and Protest in the Nineteenth Century.* Bloomington: Indiana University Press, 1998.

Ripley, C. Peter, ed. *The Black Abolitionist Papers: Volume II, Canada, 1830–1865.* Chapel Hill: University of North Carolina Press, 1986.

Roediger, David. *The Wages of Whiteness: Race and the Making of the American Working Class.* New York: Verso, 1991.

Rommel-Ruiz, Bryan. *Between African and Colored: Slavery and Freedom in Rhode Island and Nova Scotia, 1750–1850.* Philadelphia: University of Pennsylvania Press, under contract.

Ryan, Mary P. *Civic Wars: Democracy and Public Life in the American City during the Nineteenth Century.* Berkeley: University of California Press, 1997.

Sammons, Mark J., and Valerie Cunningham. *Black Portsmouth: Three Centuries of African-American Heritage.* Durham: University of New Hampshire Press, 2004.

Schweninger, Loren. *Black Property Owners in the South, 1790–1915.* Urbana: University of Illinois Press, 1990.

Sidbury, James. *Ploughshares into Swords: Race, Rebellion, and Identity in Gabriel's Virginia, 1730–1810.* Cambridge: Cambridge University Press, 1997.

Smith, Julia Floyd. *Slavery and Rice Culture in Low Country Georgia, 1750–1860.* Knoxville: University of Tennessee Press, 1985.

Sobel, Mechal. *Trabelin' On: The Slave Journey to an Afro-Baptist Faith.* Westport, Connecticut: Greenwood Press, 1979.

————. *The World They Made Together: Black and White Values in Eighteenth-Century Virginia.* Princeton, New Jersey: Princeton University Press, 1987.

Stagg, J. C. A. *Mr. Madison's War: Politics, Diplomacy, and Warfare in the Early American Republic, 1783–1830.* Princeton, New Jersey: Princeton University Press, 1983.

Staudenraus, P. J. *The African Colonization Movement, 1816–1865.* New York: Columbia University Press, 1961.

Stein, Robert L. *The French Slave Trade in the Eighteenth Century: An Old Regime Business.* Madison: University of Wisconsin Press, 1979.

Stouffer, Allen P. *The Light of Nature and the Law of God: Antislavery in Ontario, 1833–1877.* Montreal and Kingston: McGill-Queen's University Press, 1992.

Stuckey, Sterling. *Slave Culture: Nationalist Theory and the Foundations of Black America.* New York: Oxford University Press, 1987.

Sutherland, David A. "1810–1820: War and Peace." In *The Atlantic Region to Confederation: A History.* Edited by Phillip A. Buckner and John G. Reid. Toronto: University of Toronto Press, 1994.

Sweet, John Wood. *Bodies Politic: Negotiating Race in the American North, 1730–1830.* Baltimore: Johns Hopkins University Press, 2003.

Tadman, Michael. *Speculators and Slaves: Masters, Traders, and Slaves in the Old South.* Madison: University of Wisconsin Press, 1989.

Turner, Lorenzo. *Africanisms in the Gullah Dialect.* 1949. Reprint. Ann Arbor: University of Michigan Press, 1973.

Vincent, Stephen. *Southern Seed, Northern Soil: African-American Farm Communities in the Midwest, 1765–1900.* Bloomington: Indiana University Press, 1999.

Walker, David. *Appeal to the Coloured Citizens of the World.* Edited by Sean Wilentz. 1829. Reprint. New York: Hill & Wang, 1995.

Walker, James W. St. G. *The Black Loyalists: The Search for a Promised Land in Nova Scotia and Sierra Leone, 1783–1870.* London: Longman and Dalhousie University Press, 1976.

———. "The Establishment of a Free Black Community in Nova Scotia, 1783–1840." In *The African Diaspora: Interpretive Essays.* Edited by Martin L. Kilson and Robert I. Rotberg. Cambridge, Massachusetts: Harvard University Press, 1976.

Walsh, Lorena S. "Slave Life, Slave Society, and Tobacco Production in the Tidewater Chesapeake, 1620–1820." In *Cultivation and Culture: Labor and the Shaping of Slave Life in the Americas.* Edited by Ira Berlin and Philip D. Morgan. Charlottesville: University Press of Virginia, 1993.

———. "Work & Resistance in the New Republic: The Case of the Chesapeake, 1770–1820." In *From Chattel Slaves to Wage Slaves: The Dynamics of Labour Bargaining in the Americas.* Edited by Mary Turner. Bloomington: Indiana University Press, 1995.

———. *From Calabar to Carter's Grove: The History of a Virginia Slave Community.* Charlottesville: University Press of Virginia, 1997.

Ward, Samuel Ringgold. *Autobiography of a Fugitive Negro: His Anti-Slavery Labours in the United States, Canada, & England.* 1855. Reprint. New York: Arno Press, 1968.

Warner, Robert. *New Haven Negroes: A Social History.* 1940. Reprint. New York: Arno Press, 1969.

Weiss, John McNish. *Free Black American Settlers in Trinidad, 1815–1816.* London: McNish & Weiss, 1995.

———. *The Merikens: Free Black American Settlers in Trinidad, 1815–1816.* London: McNish & Weiss, 2002.

———. *On Stony Ground: Origins of the Black Refugees of the War of 1812 Settled in Nova Scotia and New Brunswick.* London: McNish & Weiss, 2006.

Whitehead, Ruth Holmes, ed. *The Shelburne Black Loyalists: A Short Biography of All Blacks Emigrating to Shelburne County, Nova Scotia, after the American Revolution, 1783.* Halifax: Nova Scotia Museum, 2000.

Williams, Savannah E. "The Role of the African United Baptist Association in the Development of Indigenous Afro-Canadians in Nova Scotia." In *Repent and Believe: The Baptist Experience in Maritime Canada.* Edited by Barry Moody. Hantsport, Nova Scotia: Lancelot Press, 1980.

Wilson, Ellen Gibson. *The Loyal Blacks.* New York: Capricorn Books, 1976.

Winks, Robin W. *The Blacks in Canada: A History.* New Haven, Connecticut: Yale University Press, 1971.

Wood, Betty. "'Never on a Sunday?': Slavery and the Sabbath in Lowcountry Georgia, 1750–1830." In *From Chattel Slaves to Wage Slaves: The Dynamics of Labour Bargaining in the Americas.* Bloomington: Indiana University Press, 1995.

———. *Women's Work, Men's Work: The Informal Slave Economies of Lowcountry Georgia.* Athens: University of Georgia Press, 1995.

———. *Gender, Race, and Rank in a Revolutionary Age: The Georgia Lowcountry, 1750–1820.* Athens: University of Georgia Press, 2000.

Wood, Peter. *Black Majority: Negroes in Colonial South Carolina from 1670 through the Stono Rebellion.* New York: Norton, 1974.

Yale, Calvin. *A Sermon Delivered before the Vermont Colonization Society at Montpelier, October 17, 1827.* Montpelier, Vermont: E. P. Walton, 1827.

ARTICLES

Adelman, Jeremy, and Stephen Aron. "From Borderlands to Borders: Empires, Nation-States, and the Peoples in Between in North American History." *American Historical Review* 104 (June 1999): 814–41.

Berlin, Ira. "Time, Space and the Evolution of Afro-American Slavery on British Mainland North America." *American Historical Review* 85 (February 1980): 44–78.

Bittermann, Rusty. "The Hierarchy of the Soil: Land and Labour in a 19th-Century Cape Breton Community." *Acadiensis* 18 (Autumn 1988): 33–55.

Brubaker, Rogers, and Frederick Cooper. "Beyond Identity." *Theory and Society* 29 (2000): 1–47.

Cahill, Barry. "Habeas Corpus and Slavery in Nova Scotia: R v. Hecht Ex Parte Rachel, 1798." *University of New Brunswick Law Journal* 44 (1995): 179–209.

———. "The Black Loyalist Myth in Atlantic Canada." *Acadiensis* 29 (Autumn 1999): 76–87.

Cassell, Frank. "Slaves of the Chesapeake Bay Area and the War of 1812." *Journal of Negro History* 57 (April 1972): 144–55.

Chaplin, Joyce E. "Tidal Rice Cultivation and the Problem of Slavery in South Carolina and Georgia, 1760–1815." *William and Mary Quarterly* 49 (January 1992): 29–61.

———. "Expansion and Exceptionalism in Early American History." *Journal of American History* 89 (March 2003): 1431–55.

Clarke, George Elliot. "White Niggers, Black Slaves: Slavery, Race, and Class in T. C. Haliburton's *The Clockmaker*." *Nova Scotia Historical Review* 14 (1994): 13–40.

———. "Must All Blackness Be American?: Locating Canada in Borden's

'Tightrope Time,' or Nationalizing Gilroy's *The Black Atlantic.*" *Canadian Ethnic Studies* 28 (1996): 56–71.

Cobley, Alan. "Black West Indian Seamen in the British Merchant Marine in the Midnineteenth Century." *History Workshop Journal* 58 (Autumn 2004): 259–74.

Cooper, Afua. "The Fluid Frontier: Blacks and the Detroit River Region—a Focus on Henry Bibb." *Canadian Review of American Studies* 30 (2000): 129–49.

Dixon, Christopher. "Nineteenth Century African American Emigrationism: The Failure of the Haitian Alternative." *Western Journal of Black Studies* 18 (1994): 77–88.

Donovan, Kenneth. "Slaves and Their Owners in Ile Royale, 1713–1760." *Acadiensis* 25 (Autumn 1995): 3–32.

———. "A Nominal List of Slaves and Their Owners in Ile Royale." *Nova Scotia Historical Review* 16 (1996): 151–62.

———. "Slaves in Ile Royale." *French Colonial History* 5 (2004): 25–42.

Faires, Nora. "Going Across the River: Black Canadians and Detroit Before the Great Migration." *Citizenship Studies* 10 (February 2006): 117–34.

Fingard, Judith. "Race and Respectability in Victorian Halifax." *Journal of Imperial and Commonwealth History* 20 (May 1992): 169–95.

Finkelman, Paul. "Prelude to the Fourteenth Amendment: Black Legal Rights in the Antebellum North." *Rutgers Law Journal* 17 (Spring and Summer 1986): 415–82.

George, Christopher T. "Mirage of Freedom: African Americans in the War of 1812." *Maryland Historical Magazine* 91 (Winter 1996): 427–50.

Grant, John. "Black Immigrants into Nova Scotia, 1776–1815." *Journal of Negro History* 58 (July 1973): 253–70.

Gravely, William B. "The Dialectic of Double-Consciousness in Black American Freedom Celebrations, 1808–1863." *Journal of Negro History* 67 (Winter 1982): 302–17.

Hamer, Philip M. "Great Britain, the United States, and the Negro Seamen Acts, 1822–1848." *Journal of Southern History* 1 (February 1935): 3–28.

Hepburn, Sharon A. Roger. "Crossing the Border from Slavery to Freedom: The Building of a Community at Buxton, Upper Canada." *American Nineteenth Century History* 3 (Summer 2002): 25–68.

Hughes, Sarah S. "Slaves for Hire: The Allocation of Black Labor in Elizabeth City County, Virginia, 1782–1810." *William and Mary Quarterly* 35 (April 1978): 260–86.

Huskins, Bonnie. "From Haute Cuisine to Ox Roasts: Public Feasting and the Negotiation of Class in Mid-19th-Century Saint John and Halifax." *Labour/Le Travail* 37 (Spring 1996): 9–36.

Johnston, John. "Research Note: Mathieu Da Costa along the Coasts of Nova Scotia: Some Possibilities." *Journal of the Royal Nova Scotia Historical Society* 4 (2001): 152–64.

Kelley, Robin D. G. "'But a Local Phase of a Global Problem': Black History's

Global Vision, 1883–1950." *Journal of American History* 86 (December 1999): 1045–77.

King, Roswell, Jr. "On the Management of the Butler Estate." *Southern Agriculturist* 1 (December 1828): 523–29.

Lewis, Earl. "To Turn as on a Pivot: Writing African Americans into a History of Overlapping Diasporas." *American Historical Review* 100 (June 1995): 765–87.

MacDonald, James S. "Life and Administration of Governor Charles Lawrence, 1749–1760." *Collections of the Nova Scotia Historical Society* 12 (1905): 19–50.

Martell, J. S. "Military Settlements in Nova Scotia after the War of 1812." *Nova Scotia Historical Society Collections* 24 (1938): 75–108.

Mason, Matthew. "The Battle of the Slaveholding Liberators: Great Britain, the United States, and Slavery in the Early Nineteenth Century." *William and Mary Quarterly* 59 (July 2002): 665–96.

McDonnell, Michael. "Other Loyalists: A Reconsideration of the Black Loyalist Experience in the American Revolutionary Era." *Southern Historian* 16 (Spring 1995): 5–25.

Morgan, Philip D. "Work and Culture: The Task System and the World of Lowcountry Blacks, 1700–1880." *William and Mary Quarterly* 39 (October 1982): 563–99.

Moses, Wilson J. "Black Communities in Antebellum America: Buttressing Held Views." *Reviews in American History* 25 (1997): 557–63.

Picart, Lennox. "The Trelawny Maroons and Sir John Wentworth: The Struggle to Maintain Their Culture." *Collections of the Royal Nova Scotia Historical Society* 44 (1996): 165–87.

Pybus, Cassandra. "Jefferson's Faulty Math: The Question of Slave Defections in the American Revolution." *William and Mary Quarterly* 62 (April 2005): 243–64.

Reid, John G. "The Nova Scotia Historian: A Creature of Paradox?" *Journal of the Royal Nova Scotia Historical Society* 5 (2002): 106–21.

Reidy, Joseph. "'Negro Election Day' and Black Community Life in New England, 1750–1860." *Marxist Perspectives* 1 (Fall 1978): 102–17.

Rhodes, Jane. "The Contestation over National Identity: Nineteenth-Century Black Americans in Canada." *Canadian Review of American Studies* 30 (2000): 175–86.

Shammas, Carole. "Black Women's Work and the Evolution of Plantation Society in Virginia." *Labor History* 26 (Winter 1985): 5–28.

Smith, T. W. "The Slave in Canada." *Collections of the Nova Scotia Historical Society* 10 (1899): 1–161.

Spray, W. A. "The Settlement of the Black Refugees in New Brunswick, 1815–1836." *Acadiensis* 6 (Spring 1977): 64–79.

Stakeman, Randolph. "The Black Population of Maine, 1764–1900." *New England Journal of Black Studies* 8 (1989): 17–35.

States, David W. "William Hall, V.C. of Horton Bluff, Nova Scotia, Nineteenth Century Naval Hero." *Collections of the Nova Scotia Historical Society* 44 (1996): 71–81.

Sutherland, David. "Race Relations in Halifax, Nova Scotia, During the Mid-Victorian Quest for Reform." *Journal of the Canadian Historical Association* 7 (1996): 35–54.

Walker, James W. St. G. "Myth, History, and Revisionism: The Black Loyalists Revisited." *Acadiensis* 29 (Autumn 1999): 88–105.

Walsh, Lorena S. "Plantation Management in the Chesapeake, 1620–1820." *Journal of Economic History* 49 (June 1989): 393–406.

———. "Rural African Americans in the Constitutional Era in Maryland, 1776–1810." *Maryland Historical Magazine* 84 (Winter 1989): 327–41.

Wayne, Michael. "The Black Population of Canada West on the Eve of the American Civil War: A Reassessment Based on the Manuscript Census of 1861." *Histoire Sociale/Social History* 28 (November 1995): 465–85.

Whitfield, Harvey Amani. "'We Can Do As We Like Here': An Analysis of Self-Assertion and Agency among Black Refugees in Halifax, Nova Scotia, 1813–1821." *Acadiensis* 32 (Autumn 2002): 29–49.

———. "The Development of Black Refugee Identity in Nova Scotia, 1813–1850." *Left History: An Interdisciplinary Journal of Historical Inquiry and Debate* 10 (Fall 2005): 9–31.

Winks, Robin. "The Canadian Negro: A Historical Assessment, Part II: The Problem of Identity." *Journal of Negro History* 54 (January 1969): 1–18.

———. "Negro School Segregation in Ontario and Nova Scotia." *Canadian Historical Review* 50 (June 1969): 164–91.

THESES, DISSERTATIONS, AND UNPUBLISHED PAPERS

Guyette, E. A. "Black Lives and White Racism in Vermont, 1760–1870." Master's thesis, University of Vermont, 1992.

Muller, Nancy Ladd. "W. E. B. Du Bois and the House of the Black Burghardts: Land, Family and African Americans in New England." Ph.D. dissertation, University of Massachusetts, 2001.

Scott, Julius. "The Common Wind: Currents of Afro-American Communication in the Era of the Haitian Revolution." Ph.D. dissertation, Duke University, 1986.

Walker, James W. St. G. "The Black Loyalists in Nova Scotia and Sierra Leone." Ph.D. dissertation, Dalhousie University, 1973.

Weiss, John McNish. "Black American Resistance to Slavery in the War of 1812: The Corps of Colonial Marines." Paper presented at the British Association for American Studies, Norwich, England, 1998.

Index